Global TV

Global TV

*Exporting Television and
Culture in the World Market*

Denise D. Bielby and
C. Lee Harrington

NEW YORK UNIVERSITY PRESS

New York and London

NEW YORK UNIVERSITY PRESS
New York and London
www.nyupress.org

Library of Congress Cataloging-in-Publication Data
Bielby, Denise D.
Global TV : exporting television and culture in the world market /
Denise D. Bielby and C. Lee Harrington.
p.   cm.
Includes bibliographical references and index.
ISBN-13: 978-0-8147-9941-3 (cl : alk. paper)
ISBN-10: 0-8147-9941-8 (cl : alk. paper)
ISBN-13: 978-0-8147-9942-0 (pb : alk. paper)
ISBN-10: 0-8147-9942-6 (pb : alk. paper)
1. Television broadcasting—Social aspects. 2. Television programs—
Marketing.   I. Harrington, C. Lee, 1964– II. Title.
PN1992.6.G57 2008
302.23'45—dc22   2008010218

New York University Press books are printed on acid-free paper,
and their binding materials are chosen for strength and durability.

Manufactured in the United States of America

c 10 9 8 7 6 5 4 3 2 1
p 10 9 8 7 6 5 4 3 2 1

Contents

Figures and Tables

Acknowledgments

We thank the University of California, Santa Barbara, and Miami University, Oxford, Ohio, for financial support for this project. The Academic Senate and the Institute for Social, Behavioral, and Economic Research at the University of California, Santa Barbara, provided Faculty Research Grants that assisted in data collection and research travel, and the College of Letters and Science of the University of California, Santa Barbara, granted a sabbatical for additional work on this project. Excellent research assistance was provided by Molly Moloney, and Marie Vierra's expertise in graphic design assisted in final preparation of the illustrations for the book. Miami University provided additional research travel support for our fieldwork, and Andrea Parks offered skillful clerical assistance. We especially thank Dick Block of Dick Block Communications, Inc., and of the NATPE Educational Foundation, who generously and graciously assisted us in our study. Ilene Kalish, executive editor at NYU Press, offered her unswerving support and guidance throughout this project, and we appreciate as well the insightful feedback provided by anonymous reviewers on early chapters.

Portions of this project were presented at the International Communication Association, the Society for Cinema and Media Studies, the American Sociological Association, the Popular Culture Association, and the Console-ing Passions Television Conference. Additional presentations were delivered at the Program for the Study of Arts and Culture at Erasmus University, Rotterdam, The Netherlands; the Conference on Media Ownership organized by the Center for Film, Television, and New Media at the University of California, Santa Barbara; the Conference on Economic Representations sponsored by the Center for Ideas and Society at the University of California, Riverside; the Culture and Society Workshop in the Department of Sociology at Northwestern University; and the Department of Sociology Colloquium Series, University of California,

Davis. Portions of this manuscript previously appeared in *Global Culture*, *Poetics*, *American Behavioral Scientist*, and *Media Ownership*, and we thank their publishers and editors for permission to use material from these works.

Preface

One of the most recognizable features of the global television industry occurs to scholars and nonscholars alike while traveling abroad and stumbling upon American programs airing in other countries or learning through news reports of a series' popularity in other parts of the globe. *America's Next Top Model* is currently airing in its original U.S. version in more than one hundred countries, including Iceland, Nigeria, and the United Arab Emirates. The soap opera *The Bold and the Beautiful* enjoys similar global success, and *Dallas*, the prime-time serial of the 1980s, was a widespread hit throughout Europe and parts of the Middle East, although it was a failure in Japan. Such information often triggers worthy concerns about the global dominance of U.S. products in television trade flows, but to penetrate the issues raised by U.S. presence in global television markets requires a much more fine-grained understanding of the organization and cultural logics of international markets than can be gleaned from such crude evidence of program flows alone. Studying the television industry in comparative perspective is enormously complicated. Industry trade publications regularly feature lists of the top ten American shows in selected countries, and while such lists reveal what has been sold to particular locales, they do not tell us how those shows rank relative to imports from other countries or to local fare. Moreover, focusing on where a series ends up obscures the important insights that are gained by learning how television programs are modified for export and import. In short, while there is much to be learned from exploring why specific programs are marketed, adopted, or rejected by distributors, sticking to the level of trade flows hinders fuller understanding of the way the industry works.

Studying this industry is difficult, in large part, because it is constantly transforming. This change is led, just as it has been since television's launching, by a seemingly endless array of technological developments intended to enhance its production, distribution, and access. As we wrote this preface, for example, the long-envisioned convergence in the United States of established television distribution technologies with broadband access and content delivery via mobile distribution platforms and devices moved closer to reality. But in spite of the imminent convergence of these technologies, in the United States at least, network program availability on the Web remains spotty, only about 2 percent of U.S. cell phone users watch mobile video, and finding programs for viewing there takes effort, in large measure because of the firm grasp retained by the networks and studios on their properties as sources of revenue. Elsewhere, possibilities for convergence take on complicated forms specific to those locales. For example, even though Rupert Murdoch's Star TV satellite won the right in 2001 to broadcast within China, its viewing reach is prescribed, and access to the internet within that country is firmly regulated. Despite the promise of convergence's endless viewing possibilities—which some viewers have likened to falling down a rabbit hole—established media consultants who monitor audiences' practices find even as new technologies take off that taste for these options is largely limited to the tech-savvy and that most audiences steadfastly prefer watching traditional television screens in a comfortable setting. It would appear that widespread audience acceptance of a technology that will completely transform the way programming is accessed still appears to be a ways off. Perhaps the facts that television functions first and foremost as entertainment and that its consumers expect it to be a comfortable, engaging, and effortless experience are the industry's bigger hurdles.

Despite impediments to widespread acceptance of new technologies, change within all aspects of the industry is, nevertheless, a given. One need only read the industry trade publications to see just how rapidly the business of the industry transforms. Network deals and hits come and go, seemingly firm program decisions change at the last minute, successful executives are fired or quit and land at rival companies, corporate mergers or partnerships take place and then dissolve, and emerging markets that are on the verge of exploding suddenly contract. Such is the turbulent nature of business in this culture industry, both domestically and internationally, and that turbulence is consequential to its scholarly examination. Time-bound snapshots may not fully capture the current state of affairs. The abundance of information yielded by its constant change means that analysis of its architecture—its organizations, markets, and institutions— must necessarily omit a great deal of rich detail in order to be focused and succinct. Understanding the significance of incremental industry change, especially that occurring in other global regions, can be a challenge, and while it may go undetected by some, others taking a longer view may see the same shifts as evidence of significant maturation of the local scene. But how is such transformation best described and analyzed?

As an outgrowth of our prior work on the domestic fans of U.S. soap operas and our realization of just how popular these shows can be abroad, we became intrigued with the nature and quality of the global market for television—of all programming, not just soap operas and their Latin American counterpart, telenovelas. To gain perspective on television import/export, we directed our attention to the syndication market where such programming is traded. We quickly became aware of just how overlooked this important segment of the industry was by media sociologists. A limited amount of scholarly work existed, which we discuss in the introduction, but even in that work, from our viewpoint as sociologists of culture and media, we could not help but notice the curious lack of attention to the contribution—indeed the pivotal role—of culture per se to understanding the complexities of the industry's organizational structure and dynamics, particularly when it crosses borders. British cultural sociologist Keith Negus's[1] admonitions about such omissions reinforced our instincts to attend to such matters. In his writings about the structure of the music industry, Negus argued for the importance of a concerted refocusing in analyses of cultural industries away from the dominant view of *how industry produces culture* to one that attends to *how culture produces an industry*. His particular interest in culture's impact goes beyond registering how production takes place within a corporate environment; instead, he argued for attending to how "production takes place in relation to broader cultural formations and practices that may not be directly within the control or understanding of the company."[2] Negus's study of record companies found that as these entities sought to understand and intervene in local markets, corporate strategies and organizational practices were themselves shaped by the surrounding culture, largely through company decision makers' efforts to make sense of their corporate environment.

Organizational sociologists writing about other cultural industries have voiced calls increasingly similar to Negus's, although their focus has tended to remain on explaining organizational forms as economic indicators of an industry's or field's institutional logic. When these works find that the effect of these logics yields a change in the field, culture tends to remain in the background, an outcome rather than a precursor. Patricia Thornton's[3] insightful study of the higher education publishing industry, for example, found that the industry's shift over the last five decades from an institutional and managerial environment that focused on the production of *books* to one that foregrounded *markets* for its releases represented a cultural shift in the institutional logic of the industry. In a related vein, Tim Dowd's[4] thoroughgoing examination of the American music industry increasingly attends to the explicit influence of sociocultural factors such as race and gender on its *logics of production*. Compared to Thornton's, his work acknowledges the direct relevance of cultural influence upon organizational strategies, although his primary focus remains on accounting for these production logics' mediating effect on more classical *economic* issues of competition and concentration in shaping the content and structure of music markets and products. In short, examining the connections between culture as it is lived and experienced by industry participants as they go about their decision making regarding cultural production remains open to study.

Some years ago, noted anthropologist Mary Douglas[5] launched the important quest to penetrate "how institutions think." As we see in the discussion above, organizational sociologists studying institutional logics at the social structural level (the cultural determinants of organizational decisions) and production logics (the social contexts and historical contingencies that shape markets) have been attempting to introduce cultural analysis into traditional analyses of firms and industries. Studying institutional and production logics in this way is very important, but to better understand the mechanisms by which they operate, it is essential to consider the flip side—to bring evidence of organizational, institutional, or economic issues into cultural explanations. We believe we can productively move such an agenda forward by attending to the concrete operations and cultural logics of the global television market itself by engaging the effects of culture—its forms and practices—more directly and doing so at a middle-range or meso-level of conceptualization and analysis. This calls for analysis of television's marketplace, its cyclicality, its participants, and the fluidity of its products. The latter is especially important to us because in our view, sociological analysis of the television industry all too often loses sight of its commodity—the programs themselves. We are interested in seeing the sociological study of culture industries move toward more explicit engagement of the way the properties of its cultural products matter to the industry. Industry coverage of the hurdles facing media convergence, discussed above, underscores our perspective. Convergence's "dazzling potential" receives great coverage by the press, but according to industry journalists Steve Brennan and Mimi Turner, the importance of programs—"content" in industry vernacular—and access to them, remains key. "The bottom line for mobile-content purveyors is that they still badly need the 'old order' of studios—or more precisely, the vast array of content under studio ownership. And the studios still look to TV broadcasters, their traditional customers, for the bulk of their revenue and to launch and build franchise programming."[6]

We wanted our sociological approach to reflect the wide range of interdisciplinary knowledge that comprises study of the global television market, because confining its treatment to a particular disciplinary approach or perspective delimited our goal of opening its culture world. Consequently, we devised three sections to capture and reflect its range and complexity. The first section of our book, which consists of the introduction and chapters 1 and 2, covers the history and organization of the syndication market and its relevance to intellectual debates that have dominated the field for some time. In this section we address the way the market in this end of the industry affects the way business is transacted. The second section (chapters 3 and 4) delves into the cultural properties of television programs in order to examine the contribution of the industry's commodities to the global market. We do so by focusing attention on the complications its cultural products bring to the operation of this industry. The third section (chapters 5 and 6) presents the discursive organizing features that link the multiple sites of the global marketplace, and we consider how insight into the marketplace from a culture-world vantage point furthers understanding of the industry's institutional and production logics. We conclude by considering how a culture-world perspective can make a contribution to intellectual debates about media hegemony in the global economy.

Introduction

I Love Lucy is said to be on the air somewhere in the world 24 hours a day.   —quote from article in the *Los Angeles Times*[1]

Bonanza is watched by audiences all over the world. We've never been off the air in 42 years.   —series creator David Dortort[2]

This book is an examination of a lesser-known aspect of the entertainment medium of television: the international market for television programming. Others before us have focused upon the domestic television industry's history, its founders and innovators, and its organizational form when the broadcast networks ruled the airwaves. Still others have written about how its logic as a dominant corporate enterprise shapes, consciously or unconsciously, the social values embedded within its programming, and how specific populations, such as women and racial and ethnic groups, deconstruct those values as an integral part of their viewing habits and practices.[3] Television remains a ubiquitous presence in American daily life;[4] however, this earlier research was written about the domestic U.S. television market in an era when the three major networks —ABC, CBS, and NBC—were dominating viewing options. Global concerns were not in focus.

Beginning in the early 1990s, the U.S. cable industry expanded and other networks—Fox, WB, UPN—launched (the latter two having merged in 2006 into the CW network), bringing new and ever-increasing options that have seriously eroded the place of the major networks as a source of entertainment in viewers' lives.[5] Other transformative developments emerged by the end of the 1990s, including the proliferation of cable, satellite, internet, and mobile systems of distribution. As these changes rearranged the television landscape, other aspects of the industry were taking hold behind the scenes, including the loosening of federal regulation of the industry and the expansion of foreign markets. Intrigued by these developments, we became interested in how they, alongside actions by industry participants and trends in program development and production, were consequential to the emergence of the international market for television and the contribution of syndicated television to the vitality of that market. We opted to study this market by focusing on elements of its social organization, including its participants and the products that are produced for it. Along the way we explore the kind of product that fills the international syndication market, and attend to the way different types of program genres are marketed and transformed to generate revenues under still-evolving business models. An essential part of the story is the marketplace where this business takes place, and that is where we begin.

Global TV's Marketplace

> Get them into the tent!
> —Dick Block, president of Block Communications Group, Inc., and
> UCLA instructor, highlighting the approach to selling
> at a television trade convention

Each year, four major international conventions or fairs bring together members of media industries for the marketing and purchase of syndicated television. Those gatherings, which serve as the international crossroads for the buyers and sellers of television programming, include the NATPE convention, which is organized by the National Association of Television Program Executives and held in the United States every winter; MIPCOM and MIP-TV, which are the Reed Midem Organization of France's annual fall and spring events located in Cannes;[6] and the by-invitation-only Los Angeles (L.A.) Screenings, which are held for two weeks in late May to early June in studios and hotel rooms throughout that city. Attendance at these venues can number in the tens of thousands, and they draw participants from every region of the globe. By way of illustration, MIPCOM 2000 had nearly five hundred exhibitors and twelve thousand participants,[7] and the NATPE convention that was held in New Orleans in January of 2000 had over 17,500 registered participants, including over forty-three hundred international attendees.[8] That year was one of the highest attendance records ever for NATPE, with over one-third of the exhibitors representing countries other than the United States.[9] Attendance at MIPCOM and NATPE fluctuates according to the vitality of the global economy, shifts in local tastes, and the impact of international crises such as the outbreak of the war in Iraq, but overall, participation stays robust. At MIPCOM 2004, for example, 3,557 firms participated, up 30 percent from 2003, and it registered the second-highest number of participants in its 20-year history after a 15 percent drop in attendees between 2000 and 2001.[10]

NATPE, established in 1963 to provide the syndication end of the domestic U.S. television industry an opportunity to gather program directors and other middle-level managers together in one place to buy and sell programming, has evolved to reflect the latest developments in the industry in order to stay in business. In response to the emergence of new media and other technological developments and institutional transformations in the marketplace, the annual conference and exhibition is now described as an "alliance of media content professionals" and as "the world's largest and most influential nonprofit electronic programming and software association dedicated to the continued growth and convergence of all content across all media."[11] And as international markets have become ever more important to the vitality of industry, NATPE has adopted an international perspective while still paying homage to its domestic roots. "NATPE was built on the King Worlds, Paramounts, the Sonys, Fox, Warners," observed its President and CEO Rick Feldman, "and their content continues to be in demand all around the world because that's the content people want to get their hands on."[12] Attendees are diverse, typically including executives from programming divisions of the networks, television station general managers, account executives, producers, and, increasingly, proprietors of Web-based businesses and purveyors of new technologies who promote the latest innovations in industry access, product, and distribution. As one participant describes it, "nowhere else do I see more decision makers in one place at one time."[13]

NATPE conventions are the site of important meetings and serious business, but in the glory days of the 1980s and 1990s the atmosphere was at its most festive and aspects of the convention itself could best be described as carnivalesque, even "sordid."[14] Television critic Howard Rosenberg, formerly of the *Los Angeles Times*, is said to have described the NATPE convention as "a gargantuan cocktail party abounding in food, booze, TV chatter and high-powered salesmanship."[15]

Fig. I.1. *Top*: Billboards at NATPE entrance
Fig. I.2. *Bottom*: Pedestrian "freeway" routes convention attendees

Fig. I.3. *Top*: Talk show host Sally Jesse Raphael greets attendees and poses for photos

Fig. I.4. *Bottom*: Assembling for NATPE seminar

Billboard-sized signs hawking new and successful ongoing series dominate the lobby space outside the exhibition hall, company "booths" include lavish bars and buffets in their reception area, evening events generate boisterous audience participation reminiscent of burlesque, and stars of hit series sit for hours at scheduled autograph and photograph sessions, where the lure of rubbing elbows with in-the-flesh celebrities turns even the most jaded of executives into attentive bystanders. The exhibit hall itself (which in some of the years we attended was located at the Ernest N. Morial Convention Center in New Orleans and in others, at the Las Vegas Convention Center in Nevada) is selected because of its capacity to accommodate enormous crowds. A vast network of wide, carpeted aisles organizes the exhibit hall into orderly rows and facilitates the flow of potential buyers, but those same aisles become virtually impassable near the more extravagant displays.[16] A more recent addition to the floor layout is the large international pavilions, collections of booths of exhibitors from a specific country, usually one with a well-developed industry, who group their displays together. Interactions (and the possibility of interactions) between major corporations and start-up companies struggling to make their first sale are managed in part by the "arrangement of the sales floor, the layout of sales stands, and security arrangements at certain stands [which] simultaneously construct and express power relationships among participants."[17] Because these conventions are a major site of trade, the importance of their physical organization is greater than it seems at first glance. At a more essential level they exist for the benefit of the industry's business and cultural functions, which include "facilitating efficient networking, concretizing power relations among participants, differentiating otherwise similar products, and providing the terrain on which distributors construct their corporate brand identities."[18]

While the primary function of this congested, frenetic atmosphere is to conduct business, the convention is much more than that. NATPE includes, for attendees who number in the hundreds, "seminars" about business strategies, new markets, and programming opportunities; morning "coffees" with successful producers; keynote addresses by the chair of the Federal Communications Commission and other industry leaders; demonstrations of new technologies; and concurrently running educational programs for television scholars from the world of academia. In short, while NATPE exists, first and foremost, to facilitate the business of buying and selling programs domestically and internationally, it is also increasingly a site for the presentation of leading-edge issues confronting the

Fig. I.5. Billboards and red carpet at MIPCOM

industry, as well as a major social occasion for celebration of the global syndication market.

At MIPCOM and MIP-TV the atmosphere is more focused and businesslike, albeit tempered by the affluent and sophisticated sensibility of Cannes. Held in the Palais des Festivals, the multilevel building located between the beach and the port filled with expensive yachts that ply the waters of the Cote d'Azur, it occurs at the same site as the star-studded, red-carpeted, photo-op-driven Cannes Film Festival. The convention hall is large and constructed at odd angles, and the layout of the MIPCOM and MIP-TV booths is very dense and mazelike, so much so that one can easily lose sense of direction and location. But it also contains plush, well-equipped theaters for the occasional panel session, free internet stations throughout, coffee bars, lounges, balconies, and terraces that overlook the Mediterranean, and ready access to the sweeping promenade along the waterfront for a quick breather. The only unexpected rupture in the feel of this otherwise well-mannered, all-business convention is the break for the two-hour lunch, which triggers a crush of well-heeled attendees pressing through the entrance of the Palais as if the building were on fire, followed by an equally frenzied return for afternoon meetings. There are far fewer

Fig. I.6. First floor schematic of MIPCOM convention hall

programmatic seminars and "all convention" events than at NATPE, with the end result being that the focus stays on conducting business.

The L.A. Screenings are an altogether different affair. Intended to showcase the pilots for prime-time scripted series picked up by the U.S. networks for the coming season, this international sales event is a two-week-long informal marketplace organized by U.S. sellers for overseas buyers that takes place soon after the broadcast and cable networks traditionally announce their fall lineups in late spring. Buyers number only about one thousand to twelve hundred, and while some attend in order to see the series their existing output deals are providing them (that is, the packages of programming they have already purchased), others come to bid on the new series for their program schedules. In 2005, there were just six major sellers—Warner, Fox, Disney, Paramount, Universal, and Sony—and a handful of smaller independent suppliers, including the now-defunct Carsey-Werner, Reveille, and E! Entertainment. The business of this marketplace focuses exclusively on the A-list series that the

U.S. broadcast and cable networks have deemed worthy for their own prime-time lineups, and that list is regarded by sellers as a key indicator of the competitiveness of U.S. products on the global market compared to the locally produced prime-time series of buyers' countries. Although this mostly all-business marketplace entails the buyers spending hours viewing pilots of marketed series, there are also studio lot parties, private cocktail gatherings, and extravagant dinners thrown by sellers at various locations around town.

The growth in the last three decades of industry gatherings such as NATPE, MIPCOM and MIP-TV, and the L.A. Screenings into major international marketplaces for the buying and selling of television programming is a direct consequence of the economic robustness of television production in the latter part of the twentieth century. Revenues generated are considerable, and the international market for programming is now a significant source of profit for major production companies.[19] Industry analyst Charles Slocum attributes the vitality of the international industry to the hyper-competitive state of the U.S. domestic industry, and the extraordinarily lucrative promise of financial return on programming. That return, says Slocum, is not anticipated to come so much from license fees (the revenue generated from the purchase of a series to air on a network anywhere on the globe) as from the asset value of the distribution network and the preservation of a market for productions. It is this vitality anchored in a vigorous profit-oriented logic that accounts for the considerable scholarly and policy debates worldwide about Hollywood's worldwide dominance.[20]

At this point, fundamental questions about exported television probably come to mind. What does such television look like? Sound like? Where does it go, how does it get there, and what accounts for its appeal elsewhere? How does U.S. television compare in quality to that produced in other countries? How are programs, or program concepts, transformed for the international market? What business practices underlie its trade? What policies, regulations, and other restrictions affect how and where it is bought and sold? These very same questions piqued our interest in the global market for television and guided us initially into studying a complex, lucrative, and often freewheeling industry comprised of a dizzying array of programming (some superbly creative, some downright embarrassing), eager celebrities and confident executives, and corporate hubris and hucksterism. Underlying that veneer, however, is a world of exceptionally hard-working and extraordinarily talented craftspersons and voice-over artists, shrewd executives, and clever agents and publicists who live and breathe their product in an intensely competitive business.

The Culture World of Television

Our focus in this book is the "culture world" of the global television marketplace, in particular, the social organization and institutional arrangements that underlie its logic. The concept of culture world is one we draw from Diana Crane, who devised it to take into account the myriad contributors to the production of popular culture and the arts, including gatekeepers such as policy makers who limit availability of content or products from particular sources, and audiences whose taste preferences influence producers and shape product trends.[21] In utilizing Crane's concept, however, our scholarly approach to the television industry is unique in several ways. First, we bring a sociological view to the study of an industry that has traditionally been the purview of communication scholars. While research by media specialists typically focuses on the efficacy and consequence of the communicative process, our perspective addresses the social, organizational, and interpersonal processes that underlie, construct, and inform television as a cultural product. Second, our work differs from most sociological research on the television industry. Whereas others analyze television as a market or as an industrial system, we focus on its micro- and interorganizational accomplishment. That is, we emphasize the social arrangements through which industry participants find practical solutions to cultural, policy, or financial constraints to transacting business with one another. Third, we draw upon humanistically grounded considerations such as genre and aesthetic elements, which allow us to investigate the way the content and properties of television programs function as cultural products and contribute to the organization of the international market. Finally, we consider the way attention to concerns of central importance to cultural studies, such as television's flow and distribution, broadens sociological understanding of the dynamics of the global marketplace.

Early scholarship on international television argued that the medium functions as a mechanism of cultural imperialism. Debates about this perspective have raged since it was proposed over forty years ago, and although this view still has adherents, many are engaged in a conscious reworking of it to complicate understanding of power, inequality, and disparate media flows. The most significant alternative view has come to be known as the active audience perspective, which reveals that audiences play an engaged role in selection of the media they consume and the textual readings they make of it. Although these opposing perspectives, which we discuss more fully in chapter 2, make important contributions to understanding what is at stake in the globalization of media, we are not directly contributing to either viewpoint. Instead, we adopt a middle-range theoretical approach, adhering to an examination of the industry at close range in order to achieve greater insight into the inner workings of television as a medium and an industry in the global marketplace.

There are several reasons for our particular focus on this industry that we treat in greater detail in subsequent chapters of this book, but the chief one is the fact that although the television industry is now global in scope, it is, first and foremost, a domestic industry born out of local concerns, a feature typically ignored by top-down theoretical perspectives. Nearly every country in the world produces television domestically within a distinctive national broadcast system.[22] The earliest systems, such as those in the United States, Australia, Japan, and Mexico, were adapted from their own existing institutional structures of radio.[23] Some early TV systems were state owned, such as Italy's and Great Britain's, while others were commercially supported through advertising, like the United States'. Many countries now have both state and corporate-owned systems operating side by side, some now well-established, such as in Great Britain, Italy, and Japan, and others just emerging, such as in Austria.[24] But whatever form the industry takes in a particular country, it operates within nationally specific state regulatory systems that might include censorship boards, cultural ministries, and broadcast licensing agencies. Where privatized systems operate, advertisers and network owners with proprietary interests are coparticipants who also come under formal or informal governmental oversight. In the United States, for example, the Federal Communications Commission limits extent of ownership, and in China the government tightly regulates the availability of satellite transmission systems (and the internet) into its populous areas.[25] In short, television is global, but also, all television is local. Thus, in order to comment knowledgeably on television's worldwide influence, in our view it is necessary to observe empirically how it operates as an industry.

Television's Culture World Components

We approach our study of television from the perspective of its key participants—producers, broadcasters, and syndicators—primarily those from the United States, but from other countries as well. We do so because the way participants orient toward global opportunities and constraints is fundamentally shaped by distinctive features of the U.S. industry. Before analyzing this culture world globally, first we draw upon our own knowledge of the television industry to describe how each of the five components of Crane's cultural world schema applies to it. Her schema is especially useful for our purposes because it was developed specifically to include analysis of so-called core culture organizations, such as television, film, and music. The five components are

(1) Culture creators and support personnel who assist them in various ways.

(2) Conventions or shared understandings about what cultural products should be like; these are important in providing standards for evaluating and appreciating cultural products.

(3) Gatekeepers, such as critics, curators, disc jockeys, and editors, who evaluate cultural products.

(4) Organizations within which or around which many of these activities take place, such as those in which cultural products are displayed . . . those in which they are performed . . . , and those in which they are produced. . . .

(5) Audiences whose characteristics can be a major factor in determining what types of cultural products can be displayed, performed, or sold in a particular urban setting.[26]

Each applies directly to the culture world of the U.S. television industry, as we explain below.

Culture creators. The production of television programs—half-hour situation comedies, hour-long dramas, movies-of-the-week, late-night talk shows, daytime soap operas—is the central activity of the culture world of the television industry. Key to this industry is the writer, whose creative imagination turns ideas into concepts, and concepts into scripts. Inspiration for a program concept can come from a variety of sources, including newspapers, a novel or film, a social trend or fad, or a writer's original idea. Like any artist, the television writer's "brief" is shaped by local wisdom and other familiar social expectations in place when the work is commissioned.[27] Program concepts compete with thousands of others each year, and if commissioned for development, go through an elaborate process within the network or studio to make them locally marketable enough to go into production. From inception to airing, the final product comes about through a set of collaborations among producers, production companies, actors, craft personnel, network executives, and advertisers. While writers draw upon what is familiar to them, some are aware of the potential global market for certain kinds of stories, especially in genres with widespread appeal abroad.

Artistic conventions. Those who collaborate in bringing a story concept to air are organized through interdependent tasks that network executives hope will yield a successful product. In Hollywood, the success of a production—its commercial viability—depends upon whether it is a hit with the audience. What makes a product successful is difficult to predict a priori, so network executives and other decision makers rely upon "conventions or shared understandings about what cultural products should be like," in the hopes that the final outcome will resonate with audience expectations for what constitutes entertainment.[28]

Because getting to that goal is so unpredictable, locally familiar cultural idioms of all kinds—metaphors, stereotypes, symbols, and discursive practices that signify social groups—are embedded in characterizations and plots in order to create the interpretive frameworks audiences rely upon to make viewing meaningful.[29] These conventions may include the already familiar images and portrayals, described above, that writers engage to tell their stories. But they also include the workplace arrangements through which the actual production work gets done, such as understanding what comprises "action" in a sitcom in contrast to, say, a game show, how cameras are used to record dramas in contrast to, for example, soap operas, and how editing is done in a variety show in contrast to an action adventure series. The way these conventions apply to audience understandings abroad is not well understood.

Gatekeepers. Acceptance of a television series depends not only on its resonance with audiences and the investments by producers but also on its endorsement by cultural authorities who designate a program of sufficient quality or innovation that it is worthy of viewers' time. Television programs do not go into production unless network or production company executives green light them as series. Once past that hurdle, a series becomes available for critical evaluation. In most art worlds, critics act as arbiters of taste whose judgments render particular works suitable for the public's attention. In many elite art worlds, those evaluations can make or break a product. Because television is a form of popular culture, the role of television critics is more ambiguous than for other forms of popular culture that have achieved more elite artistic status, such as film.[30] Early sociological research shows that television critics orient towards audiences in several ways; some attempt to advocate audiences' interests to the industry while others discount audiences' tastes as they pass judgment on program quality.[31] Subsequent research finds that in the absence of a well-institutionalized role for critics, audience members often fulfill that role for themselves, especially for genres such as soap operas, which are low on the cultural hierarchy.[32] Consequently, series that become successful may not be ones that receive critical acclaim. It is even less certain how critical evaluation in the country of origin contributes to acceptance by audiences abroad, if at all.

Organizations. The organization of production in Hollywood is highly complex. The worksites of television production are the studios, remote locations, and production company offices where the collaborative work of employees and their supervisors takes place. Filming or taping may occur in one location, editing in a second, and the laying of the sound track in yet a third. Not only can production be dispersed across locations, but the organization of work itself is fragmented across specialized crafts—camera operators, directors, writers, editors, sound technicians, and so forth. In addition, the administrative and corporate oversight of a series may be located some distance from the studio, or in a different city or country altogether.

Terms of employment in a culture industry like television are also distinctive. Since the demise of the studio system in Hollywood, writers and creative personnel are often employed by "single project organizations,"[33] formed for the duration of a single television or film project. And even when creative personnel are employed by a major studio or network, they are "life of project" workers,[34] temporarily employed for the duration of a single production. These terms of employment remain the same when series are prepared for export abroad. However, more organizational layers and craft specialists are involved when a series is exported, and these too must be supervised. Series are not necessarily sold in packages "as is"; they must be transformed for use in other countries.

Lastly, television programs are extremely expensive to produce, and historically, suppliers have sought a variety of ways to underwrite the costs of production. Given the lucrative after-life of television programs in secondary markets, ownership of a successful series is highly desirable, and to many, well worth the risk and expense. In the 1950s, television programs were owned and controlled by one or more advertising sponsors, and in the 1960s, they originated either as network in-house productions or through network co-ownership with outside suppliers. This changed dramatically in 1971 when the Federal Communications Commission instituted the Financial Interest and Syndication Rules (i.e., the Fin-Syn Rules) to prevent the networks, who control distribution, from also profiting from the syndication of series in which they had a financial stake. The logic behind the Fin-Syn Rules was that without such oversight, the networks would have little incentive to look to independent producers for sources of programming. During the Fin-Syn era, which ended in the early 1990s, nearly all prime-time programming (apart from news and sports) was supplied by the television divisions of the major studios and smaller independent production companies. Since the demise of these rules, the traditional broadcast networks, ABC, NBC, and CBS, have joined the major studios as sources of television programs, and now all five networks (including Fox and CW) increasingly rely on series they own to fill their schedules.[35]

Audience characteristics are crucial in determining which series executives consider commissioning for development (with the current emphasis obviously on the youth market). The industry relies heavily on advertisers' preferences and ratings services such as A. C. Nielsen that measure audience viewership of programs. These services are available in many (though not all) countries, and the statistics largely determine whether a series will remain in production or be canceled. Audience characteristics also reflect viewing preferences, which are crucial to the industry in other ways. In their quest to minimize uncertainty in finding new hits, network executives often rely upon imitation of already successful series that reach demographically desired audiences.[36] Consequently, audience characteristics, and the viewing preferences they are associated with, affect what producers and network executives perceive as likely to garner new viewing interest, whether the series are critically acclaimed or not.

How are these components that pertain to the domestic television industry relevant to the global marketplace? Although the business of domestic U.S. television is driven by writers' creative ideas, the business side of the industry is motivated by two related factors: (1) the search for financing to cover the costs of development and production; and (2) recouping on investments in production and realizing profits on those investments. Financing may come from a variety of sources for whom the investment return exists in the form of license fees (for a network) or license rights (for a foreign investor).[37] To executives who own or share in the rights to a series, a program is nothing more than a commodity, and the global market is nothing more than an additional potential revenue stream. High-level executives do not see it as their job to directly concern themselves with the particulars that make a series marketable in one country or global region but not in another. Instead, the international syndication industry is organized in such a way that those kinds of concerns are addressed at a much lower level, often at the sales level or even at the craft level. Those who do the actual selling of shows abroad are specialized personnel who cultivate personalized business relationships with buyers in foreign markets. Matters of production quality, such as dubbing, resolution of the screen image, and countless other technical and aesthetic considerations figure centrally in the interest a salesperson is able to generate among foreign buyers. Those who do the buying for networks, cable, or satellite systems in other countries are making decisions about the kinds of programming they need to fill out their broadcast schedules. Ultimately, however, buyers serve only "a surrogate function since the success of an internationally syndicated program lies with viewers. Though independent, buyers' choices are never wholly their own. Instead, they receive their authority because they lay claim to being privileged interpreters of viewers' tastes, much like book reviewers."[38] Thus, the nature and substance of the interaction between buyers and sellers in the global marketplace is rich and complex. While it may seem that international program flows are built upon simple business arrangements, their success is, in fact, sustained by a complex web of culturally bound business practices. Indeed, "networking among executives is perhaps the most commonly accepted business function of global trade shows."[39]

Despite the widespread interest in exported television, there is a surprisingly limited amount of scholarly research to guide our quest to understand the structure and dynamics of the global market for television. In the mid-1980s, Muriel and Joel Cantor were among a handful of social scientists conducting empirical analyses of exported television, and the only sociologists doing so. Although their work was motivated by the debate about the power and influence of U.S. programs circulating around the globe, they brought sociological insight to those arguments through an analytical description of the social organization of the international

component of the U.S. industry. Central to their discussion was their observation that the trade of products abroad was largely an afterthought
to domestic television production rather than an overt intent to dominate world culture. A chief concern for the domestic industry has always
been managing the costs of producing television programs. Having found
themselves participating in this new market and committed to it, U.S. exporters invented and improvised mechanisms for reaching and persuading
international buyers to consider their products as a source of programming. Thus, the development of the "contracting market," as the Cantors
referred to the export of existing series, was unsystematic and largely in-
cidental to the business of the domestic industry, and it drew attention
among domestic producers chiefly as an additional source of revenue.[40]
A watershed of sorts for this export market occurred in the inflationary
1980s as domestic program production costs escalated while audiences
shrank as a consequence of viewers seeking out alternatives on cable and
video. These shifts coincided with expansion of the European television
industry, which was driven by the consequences of industry deregulation and consolidation and the anticipation of trade barriers to outsiders
planned by the European Union. The upshot was that European television
production and distribution companies sought coproduction arrangements within the United States and other countries to increase programming for expanded broadcast options, and to circumvent looming trade
restrictions.[41] Thus, to a large extent, U.S. distributors were initially pulled
into the international market because of economic changes abroad, not
because of any coherent international strategy of their own.

The culture world of the international television industry that now
exists comprises a diverse group of program suppliers and buyers linked
through a vast, almost dizzying, amalgam of interconnected production,
financial, and distribution arrangements. While Crane's schema is useful for identifying key components of the culture world of the television
industry, it provides us less guidance about the mechanisms that shape
the business of buying and selling across borders. At its most basic level,
the elements of television's global culture world are not unlike those of
the domestic industry, where program suppliers and network programmers are mutually dependent in their search for new series that will be
financially successful. However, in the course of our research we have
observed that the international level differs from the domestic industry's
basic configuration in at least four ways. First, there are myriad avenues
by which series originate for the export/import market. Second, brokers

who constantly monitor the international scene for viable programming ideas are instrumental to the movement of programming concepts around the globe—sometimes these are truly innovative concepts in television while at other times they are new only to emerging markets. Third, reputation and the social networks that sustain it are key to the organization and operation of the market in particular ways. Fourth, although central decision makers are often attuned to the adaptations that are necessary to facilitate a program's ability to cross borders, an influential participant's role in the international market is often less apparent from his or her job title than from the way that participant is situated in social networks of buyers and sellers and the local cultural knowledge he or she possesses.

Because this market is organized through flexible arrangements—contracts—which supplant the bureaucracy of the firm,[42] many questions arise about how business is accomplished in this culture world. How do the cultivation of relationships of trust and strategies for gathering intelligence about local sensibilities facilitate selling abroad? How do syndicators evaluate the ways in which their products can be modified to meet the demands of specific markets? How does a change in the balance between foreign and domestic revenues affect the way series are produced and syndicated? At one level we are interested in these kinds of questions because they help us ascertain how this culture world is organized and its dealings accomplished across borders. But this culture world is further complicated by the fact that its product—the television programs themselves—must also cross borders, an aspect further problematized by the fact that television *itself* is a cultural product. In short, we are more interested in understanding how the culture of the business and the properties of the product itself complicate the process of buying and selling media products internationally.

Our decision to write this book was motivated in part by what we see as a limited appreciation for what there is to be known about television, in part by our abiding interest in understanding how television accomplishes being such a readily watched and widely enjoyed form of entertainment the world over. Therefore, a central focus of our book is understanding the contribution of television's properties to its appeal as a cultural product—not what values are embedded in it, but how and why it comes to take on the attributes that it does. In order to understand the way forces other than the market affect how, where, and why television programs are sold, our research analyzes the way the global market for television import/export is organized and conducted as a culture industry. To that end, we attend to the origins of the international industry in the domestic U.S. syndication market, and take a snapshot of its global organization by describing its participants, inner workings, and organizational mindset. We examine the kinds of products that are especially successful globally, focusing in particular on genres like game shows and soap operas/novelas that successfully transcend cultural differences. We also examine the attributes of genres that do not succeed internationally, and explore why. In the end, we seek greater insight into the way the development of the industry in the United States has contributed to the form and content of the worldwide television industry.

We limit our study to entertainment programs, not news, or sports, but rather the fictional worlds most viewers tend to think of when we say that we are studying the global market for exported television. Because sports events command considerable interest globally, our focus on television series actually eliminates quite a bit of programming that crosses borders. These kinds of programs, sports and news, are the ones that contemporary scholars tend not to think of first and foremost as exported television, even though news programs were central to early debates about the impact of the "free flow of information" across borders. Neither do we focus on the hyper-competitive activities of entrepreneurs such as Rupert Murdoch, Sumner Redstone, or Silvio Berlusconi to continuously expand their privatized systems of distribution. Nor do we concentrate primarily on the latest technological developments that contribute to furthering the development of new media. Finally, we note that issues of regulation and censorship, including those imposed by trade agreements and/or unions such as GATT or NAFTA, are important aspects of the context of what we are studying, but also are not the primary focus of our research. These various aspects of programming, and of industry and technological expansion and regulation, are central to debates about media globalization, but they are less central to our interest in programs as cultural products of a culture industry.

It may be surprising to some to think of the television industry as a culture world. Some scholars who study culture do not consider television to be highbrow enough to be included among those art forms worthy of analysis. To many, it is lowbrow because it is commercial, because it is entertainment for the masses, and because little training is required to understand it as a cultural form. The first two are true; the latter, however, is a presumption we would challenge. We think all are the very reasons television ought to be taken seriously. Moreover, although television is, indeed, low on the cultural hierarchy now, placements on that ranking system are historically fluid. Film, jazz, and Shakespeare once were pastimes as lowly as television is today.

In sum, our approach to the study of the global culture world of television is grounded in the study of the organization and dynamics of the industry and of the programs themselves. To date, scholars "have little understanding of the ways in which business practices concretize the general economic realities of international television trade."[43] The study of globalization by many sociologists tends to be abstract, detached, and theoretical. Instead, our approach is empirical, concrete, and oriented toward building a conceptual framework that reflects the complexity of the industry and its products. Similarly, understanding why television programs are received as they are in other regions of the globe can be equally abstract. While there is a rich scholarly literature on local viewers' reception of imported programming, the TV industry itself tends to rely on audience ratings systems that provide information about what shows are popular but not why they are popular. Syndication deals themselves are often based on word of mouth, unsubstantiated through audience research but legitimized through the credibility of individual sellers. Thus, the business uncertainty that contextualizes domestic television production and sales is magnified in the global context. What programming will prove successful in Holland? In Uganda? In South Korea? Who knows, and how do they know it? How do individual buyers and sellers conduct the business deals that shape a nation's televisual offerings? How do they come to trust (or distrust) one another and why? How does a country's international reputation impact what, how much, and to whom they are able to sell TV programming? Who, or what, fails to sell and why? Ultimately, this is a book about the various social and cultural factors that facilitate or hinder the sale of television programs and concepts for global syndication. TV sales are, of course, an economic transaction—but how is that transaction shaped by the relationships among individuals, companies, and nations?

Our book is organized into six chapters. Chapter 1 discusses the way the early domestic U.S. industry gave rise to the syndication end of the business, as well as the way the coincidence of industry growth, aspects of federal regulation, and the necessity for individualized business transactions fundamentally shaped the features of the international marketplace. In chapter 2 we describe the way the television industry navigates its increasingly bifurcated local/global focus by examining how the organization and mechanisms of this culture world extend early understanding of the export market. Chapter 3 analyzes one of the key components of television's culture world by exploring the role genre plays in the global syndication market. Using the most widely traded form of entertainment television as a case example—serial storytelling in the form of soap operas and telenovelas—we study the fluidity of genre in trading practices. Using the U.S. daytime soap opera industry as a starting point, we also examine the relationship between local production/global trade in understanding serials' function in the global market. Chapter 4 focuses on television's aesthetic properties for their particular contribution to the way the industry manages global buying and selling. In chapter 5 we address the ongoing productionist/consumptionist bias in most scholarly approaches to the study of global television by showing how the site of distribution connects sites of production and consumption to one another, and thus transforms TV texts and their meanings in the process. In the concluding chapter we suggest how our findings contribute to ongoing debates about globalization of media and to the analysis of cultural industries more generally.

1

The Syndication Market in U.S. Television

In syndication, programs are sold individually, market by market, meaning historically a series might play on the CBS station in Los Angeles, an NBC outlet in Detroit and an independent station in Nashville. —*Los Angeles Times* television industry critic and analyst Brian Lowry[1]

Highway Patrol was a gem. It was a terrible show. Broderick Crawford would get out the car and stand there and get the microphone and say, "10-4." And then he'd put it back and he'd drive off. That's the show. I've just given you a half-hour episode. But the audience liked it, so it was a gem.
—Dick Woollen, former vice-president, Metromedia[2]

It is much more fun to sell, because as buyers there is so much crap to consider.
—network executive at a Latino-themed cable network who has worked both sides of the industry[3]

The global market for the export of U.S. television programming was launched in the mid-1950s by the big three domestic broadcast networks—first CBS, followed by NBC and then ABC.[4] With airtime on newly established networks abroad needing to be filled, the market for the screening of "telefilms"—as the filmed series were called—outside the United States was thus realized. CBS, in 1954, was the first to venture into foreign distribution of its network programming with sales to other countries, with NBC and ABC following soon thereafter. Not only did the networks syndicate the programs they produced themselves, but they also syndicated abroad the series that were produced for their prime-time schedules by outside suppliers.[5]

The way the international export market that we know today emerged from the nascent television industry of the late 1940s and early 1950s was hardly the result of a well-developed business strategy for conquering the world. What eventually became a ubiquitous and popular form of entertainment abroad was, in its earliest version, a product that first had to be conceptualized, developed, and accepted in the United States by the industry, its audience, and government regulators.[6]

Commercial television broadcasting began in the United States in 1946, and a robust demand for programming to feed the burgeoning domestic market developed soon thereafter. In domestic television's earliest years, regularly scheduled programming consisted of a mix of live-interview, variety, quiz, and sports shows, and dramas appeared only during the evening hours.[7] As scheduling opportunities expanded to include daytime, late evening, and weekends, the networks scrambled to fill these additional time blocks.[8]

Live broadcasts were the preferred medium for the new industry, a taste that prevailed at the outset for several reasons. Chief among them was that recorded programs were not of good quality, and audiences that were used to decades of live broadcasts on radio were unwilling, at least initially, to modify their expectations. Another reason was that filmed programs could be distributed directly to local television stations and thus they represented a threat to the networks' control over distribution. In short, filmed broadcasts were regarded by the industry and the viewing audience as less desirable fare than live programming.[9]

Filmed Programming Enters the Picture

The filmed programming that existed between 1946 and 1951 originated from a handful of independent production companies that operated on the margins of the industry. This market began as early as 1949–50 with the appearance of series such as *Boston Blackie*, of 1940s B-movie fame, and *Hopalong Cassidy*, a reedited version of the 1930s and 1940s films that first screened in theaters. In 1951 and 1952, more reputable production companies emerged, including enterprises such as Desilu, which produced the still popular sitcom *I Love Lucy* for airing on CBS, and Four Star Productions, which produced the anthology series *Four*

		7:00 PM	7:30	8:00	8:30	9:00	9:30	10:00	10:30	11:00
SUNDAY	A									
	C									
	D									
	N					Various Special Presentations				
MONDAY	A									
	C									
	D	Small Fry Club	Doorway to Fame							
	N				Americana	Esso Reporter		Gillette Cavalcade of Sports		
TUESDAY	A									
	C									
	D	Small Fry Club		Western Movie		Mary Kay and Johnny				
	N									
WEDNESDAY	A									
	C									
	D	Small Fry Club								
	N		Kraft Television Theatre		*					
THURSDAY	A									
	C									
	D	Small Fry Club	Birthday Party		Charade Quiz					
	N		†	Musical Merry-Go-Round	Eye Witness	You Are an Artist				
FRIDAY	A									
	C									
	D	Small Fry Club								
	N			Campus Hoopla		‡		Gillette Cavalcade of Sports		
SATURDAY	A									
	C									
	D									
	N									

* In the Kelvinator Kitchen   † NBC TV Newsreel   ‡ The World in Your Home   A=ABC, C=CBS, D=DuMont, N=NBC

Fig. 1.1. Prime-time schedule: fall 1947. *Source:* Brooks and Marsh, 2003, p. 1354.

Star Playhouse, also for CBS.[10] Through diversification, coproduction arrangements, access to actors supplied by talent agencies, and creative financing, these companies came to dominate the industry throughout the 1950s.[11] Their programming, which was originally produced for broadcast on the major networks, subsequently expanded to include series that were sold via syndication to individual stations or groups of stations in lieu of airing over the networks.[12] Disney, in 1954, was the first of the major film studios to enter the television business. It wasn't until 1955 that the other major Hollywood studios began producing original filmed series for television. By 1960, they provided 40 percent of network programming.[13]

As the domestic television audience expanded, the emergence of independent (i.e., non-network-affiliated) stations generated a significant additional source of demand for filmed television programming. Independent stations had existed since the beginnings of television, with some of the earliest broadcast stations in large urban markets ultimately choosing not to affiliate with a network.[14] Most stations with low bandwidth became network affiliated[15] or, if they were in a large market, became stations that were owned and operated by a network.[16] Owned-and-operated stations are required to carry the network's entire program lineup, assuring the network exposure to all its offerings. Beginning in the early 1960s, the number of independent stations expanded considerably as high bandwidth was opened up by the Federal Communications Commission. According to Matelski, independent stations faced the same demands for finding prime-time programming as the networks did in the early days of television.[17] To fill their schedules, they relied heavily upon in-house production, syndicated off-network shows, repackaged movie serials, cartoons, or movies from the Hollywood studios' film libraries, and other similar kinds of recycled or independently produced filmed programming. Today's syndicated offerings are made up of an array of updated programming options that include the genres of game shows, talk shows, off-network sitcoms and dramas, court shows, and weekly action/science fiction shows, as figure 1.2 reveals.

The Financing of Production for Network Series

From its very beginning, prime-time television production operated under deficit financing, meaning that series were produced at a loss relative to the licensing fee the networks were willing to pay for airing the series. Procter & Gamble, a leading program underwriter in the early days of television, established the practice of paying only 60 percent of the production costs of the shows it sponsored, an arrangement that led to the owners/producers of telefilm productions sponsored by Procter & Gamble to seek other forms of compensation to recoup their losses, including reversion of syndication rights to themselves following broadcast in the domestic

Program Rank for Households	Program Rank by Advertising Revenue, 4ᵗʰ Quarter 2003	
1 Wheel of Fortune	1. Friends	$54,515,574
2. Jeopardy	2. Oprah Winfrey Show	$37,236,727
3. Oprah Winfrey Show	3. Will & Grace	$36,339,984
4. Friends	4. Entertainment Tonight	$34,543,621
4. Seinfeld	5. Seinfeld	$22,956,785
6. Entertainment Tonight	6. Everybody Loves Raymond	$21,496,699
6. Everybody Loves Raymond	7. Entertainment Tonight (wknd)	$20,184,135
8. Seinfeld (weekend)	8. That '70s Show	$17,774,797
9. Dr. Phil	9. Access Hollywood	$17,773,980
10. Judge Judy	10. Extra	$17,460,533
11. Wheel of Fortune (wknd)	11. Dr. Phil	$16,460,555
12. Live With Regis and Kelly	12. Wheel of Fortune	$15,106,972
13. Will & Grace	13. Jeopardy	$14,696,519
13. That '70s Show	14. Live With Regis and Kelly	$13,595,825
16. Entertainment Tonight (wknd)	15. King of Queens	$12,815,722
16. Who Wants to Be a Millionaire	16. King of the Hill	$12,730,450
16. Judge Joe Brown	17. Seinfeld (wknd)	$12,691,937
19. Home Improvement	18. Becker	$11,984,716
20. Access Hollywood	19. Steve Harvey	$11,143,377
20. Friends (weekend)	20. Ellen Degeneres Show	$10,646,500
20. Maury		
20. King of the Hill		

Fig. 1.2. Top 20 syndicated shows for September 2003 to January 2004 and their advertising revenue. Source: Nielsen Media Research and Nielsen Monitor-Plus, Broadcasting & Cable, March 8, 2004, pp. 2A and 11A.

market. Once the networks themselves began commissioning series,[18] they too adopted the practice of deficit financing, (i.e., paying a licensing fee less than the supplier's production costs). This financial arrangement led independent production companies who licensed their products to the networks to seek ways to recoup their losses from expenses incurred. In particular, it encouraged producers to seek out the secondary markets, domestic and international, beyond the network for additional revenue.[19] At the same time, due to the powerful bargaining position derived from control of the domestic prime-time schedule, the networks were often able to extract the right to sell those series abroad through their own syndication divisions.[20]

Regulations implemented in 1970 greatly expanded the participation of non-network companies, both large and small, supplying series to the networks under deficit financing arrangements. The Federal Communications Commission's Fin-Syn Rules, instituted in that year to broaden the diversity of perspectives on the airwaves, placed strict limits on the amount of prime-time programming that could be produced by the networks themselves and prohibited them from syndicating the series they broadcast. In the Fin-Syn era, most prime-time pilots and series were supplied by independent writer-producers working for outside production companies that retained ownership and syndication rights; consequently, the financial viability of virtually the entire community of program suppliers depended on success in the syndication market. And, indeed, syndication became immensely profitable for program suppliers, so much so that the networks lobbied vigorously for the removal of the rules so that they too could enter this lucrative market. The rules were phased out beginning in the early 1990s, and today the networks compete alongside the major studios and independent production companies in the syndication market. Networks may now own unlimited hours of the programs they broadcast and syndicate them abroad.

The end of the Fin-Syn Rules also changed the nature of deficit financing, since the networks now receive revenue from both advertising and eventual sale of series they own in the syndication market. Deregulation prompted the trend towards consolidation between networks and studios and a corresponding rise in in-house production[21] and direct participation by networks (via their parent corporations) in both domestic and global syndication. Program suppliers without an ownership relationship to a network are losing access to the prime-time network marketplace and to network licensing fees as a source of revenue.

The Prime Time Access Rule

Also implemented in 1970 was the Prime Time Access Rule, which further contributed to the expansion of the syndication market. Until 1970, "prime time" referred to the network-controlled broadcast period of 7:00 P.M. to 11:00 P.M. In 1970, the Federal Communications Commission's Prime Time Access Rule imposed two restrictions upon the networks and their affiliates: the rule limited network prime-time broadcasts to three hours each night (with an extra hour on Sundays), and it prohibited network affiliates in the top fifty rated markets from running off-network programming (i.e., syndicated reruns). The intent of the rule was to give back an hour of programming each evening to the local network affiliates for community-relevant shows. However, affiliates rarely programmed that hour with this kind of viewing, and instead, audiences developed a taste for the kind of syndicated entertainment programming that was being offered in its place. "With these new incentives, syndication companies proliferated to provide competitive first-run shows, franchised programs, co-op productions, and, of course, the ever increasing numbers of off-network TV fare."[22]

In sum, the market for syndicated television programming grew out of a need to fill ever-expanding program schedules at network, affiliated, and independent stations. The business considerations described above set in motion a quest to identify audiences, including audiences abroad, who were in search of additional choices for entertainment viewing. While syndicated television from independent suppliers originated to meet the networks' need to fill their prime-time schedules, the networks soon developed a demand for programming to fill other dayparts—daytime, early evening, and the late-night portions of the program schedule. The proliferation of cable channels has only intensified the demand for such programming. Those seeking to deliver programming that would appeal to these audiences were necessarily dealing with issues of content as well as finance, and our study of the culture world of the industry attempts to understand the interconnection between the two.

As we will see in later chapters, this history of the domestic syndicated market is centrally relevant to the contemporary international market for television in several ways. First, syndication suppliers built a large stock of programming that was outside of the control of the major U.S. networks. Second, the market created a cadre of independent, entrepreneurial producers and syndicators who were unconstrained by the bureaucracy and regulation of the networks, and who were free to locate and cater to untapped audiences wherever they could be found. Third, the spot-market concept upon which the syndicated domestic market was based created a model of sales distribution that could be adapted to any locale, domestic or foreign. We turn next to the origins and development of this market to illuminate just how the syndication end of the business grew out of these conditions.

Selling in the Domestic Syndicated Market: The Early Years

The man credited with originating the domestic syndication business as it exists to this day is Frederic W. Ziv, founder of Ziv Television.[23] Ziv's background was advertising, to which he introduced an early form of product syndication on radio wherein he audiotaped radio programs for time-shifted broadcast, a process known then as "transcription."[24] Transcriptions made possible the live-on-tape concept that, with improved technology, eventually became accepted by an audience and an industry that believed broadcasts had to be consumed in real time, at the moment of production, as noted earlier. According to Ziv, in the earliest days of television there were only nineteen cities in the United States with television stations. That left the remainder of the country poised for station development, each with a need for programming. This, in turn, motivated Ziv to produce his own series for syndication.[25]

This new business opportunity gave rise to the need for sales personnel who traveled from station to station selling syndicated telefilms (or "telepix," as they were referred to). These sales personnel, exclusively men, were known to those in the industry as "film peddlers" because of the format of the medium. Today, many of these veterans have attained legendary status, but as members of the "old-time syndicated television marketers," they are still regarded as merely sales personnel, a step removed from the more prestigious roles that exist in the industry.[26] Their careers, indeed their lives, were preoccupied by life on the road, with most of their time filled by calling upon regional lists of television stations, market by market, four to five days a week, forty-five to fifty weeks a year. Expense accounts were unlimited, which allowed them to dine well at expensive restaurants and overnight at comfortable accommodations, but this lifestyle meant long stretches away from family. In the tradition of booking agents for road shows, carnivals, and the like, these men were hawking wares in a manner that persists to this day: they rent "booths" at the annual NATPE meeting and talk about "bringing buyers into the tent" and "pitching" products. Selling also involved a healthy dose of showmanship.

Most veterans of those early days considered it a thoroughly energizing life. "I missed my family, but it comes with the turf," said George Back, former president of All American Television. "I mean, what could be better in some ways than taking a tape under your arm that you believe in and going to see people who are supposed to be open to ideas?"[27] In remarks to a 1998 seminar on the syndication market held at the University of California–Los Angeles, industry leader and veteran Dick Robertson, president of Warner Brothers Domestic TV Distribution, shared his motivation for this line of work:

> The difference was that you were selling programs versus selling time on programs that had already been bought. It's like the difference between the NASDAQ and the NYSE. At the NASDAQ, commodities are sold dealer by dealer, while at the NYSE, you have to qualify first to get on the board even before you can sell. In syndication, if one person doesn't like the program, it's not the death of the show, unlike at the networks, where one person can kill a show if they decide they don't like it. In syndication you have direct control of a lineup, which does not have to pass through a network gatekeeper making decisions for the affiliates.[28]

To all involved, the clear appeal of the job lay in the freedom from bureaucratic constraints—the openness of the market, the ability to set one's own schedule, having access to the source of the product and a direct line to the client, and being one's own boss while on the road. At its core was developing highly personalized, customized relationships with clients.

Despite the camaraderie, anecdotal accounts of the business indicate that from the very beginning it was extremely competitive. From the salesman's point of view, there was always the challenge of beating one's competitors to clear (sell) a market, to find a better time period for a show, or to make the most money on a sale.[29] "Each Monday morning I would set a goal to accomplish that week. It was hard, because there were no guarantees," stated Dick Robertson.[30] The zest for competition in this line of work was fostered by Ziv, whose ethos was one of "stay there until you sell," however long that took, which was sometimes months (or so the legendary stories go). Under Ziv, "you were forbidden to ever leave the market until you sold the show," recounts Stan Moger, president and CEO of SFM Entertainment.[31]

Overlaying this competitive orientation was a professionalism modeled by Ziv, who drew from his experience in advertising. Ziv pioneered for the syndication market the notion of a detailed and informed product pitch to the station or general manager. Although in its early days the show-and-tell aspects of the meeting were based on a cumbersome technology (the sales-call presentation literally consisted of a reel of 16 mm film screened on a projector in the manager's office), de rigueur were flip charts and, later, press kits outlining relevant information about the product. The content of the salesman's pitch itself evolved into a standardized body of information about the program—why the series was hot, why it would potentially work, and, if it was an off-network show, its network performance and demographic appeal. Other details included where the series would fit in the schedule, where the needs for such programming lay (i.e., what audiences the program would serve), and a list of similar shows that were successful in the marketplace.[32] The pitch often also included a good deal of showmanship on the part of the salesman—props, costumes, distinctive flashy wardrobes—and in some instances outright hectoring. If this sounds carnivalesque, to some extent it was. But by far, according to all accounts, the most important aspect of the sale resided in the personalized credibility of the salesman himself, reflected in his full knowledge of and absolute belief in the product.

Building a Business on Relationships

Salesmen pitched specific series as uniquely able to generate revenue by appealing to the right audience segment.[33] At the level of station staff, the relationship was customized through personalized interaction. Dick Robertson emphasizes that "the business is done through relationships."[34] Because the networks and the syndicator compete for the same customer—the television station—part of the ethos he promulgates to this day is that "the customer is king." Because stations "want to buy shows they feel good about, after all, it's human nature," Robertson's ethic is to establish the asset of credibility through honest dealings and treating the customer with the utmost respect. Ever the salesman, Robertson says key aspects of his job are "returning phone calls promptly, showing up on time for meetings, and selling quality shows that won't embarrass and hopefully will be a hit, a success." It also includes personalized relationships—specific investments cultivated though sending greeting cards for birthdays, surprising clients with their favorite foods at sales meetings, and the like.

This personalized approach to doing business is consistent with several defining characteristics of Hollywood more generally. First, everyone in Hollywood knows that business uncertainty rules (whether they articulate it in those exact words or not) and that predicting the success of a particular production is all but impossible. Referring to product development, as former CBS Entertainment president Jeff Sagansky once succinctly stated, "all hits are flukes."[35] This holds because audiences are the ultimate arbiters in determining whether a program is a ratings success. While Sagansky was referring to the inability to predict which series his network had picked up for the fall schedule would succeed, his observation applies to just about every product of Hollywood's markets.[36] In his interviews with network executives, Gitlin also found that they consistently expressed views like these and concluded that the "problem of knowing" is a key feature of program-development decisions.[37] If business uncertainty is true for a new series' success in the domestic market, it is compounded internationally. Structurally, this creates the need for "information brokers," individuals such as the sales personnel described above who can carry product information, market by market, to potential buyers.

Institutionalization of the Marketplace: The Emergence of Professional Associations

By the late 1950s, the business of syndication had grown to the point that syndicators, sales agents, and the station and program managers who bought programming saw the need for an annual convention where products could be made available at a single time and place on a regular basis. Not only did such gatherings consolidate marketing of their products to station managers from across the country; they also served to identify and represent their interests to the larger industry and to convey professional status. According to some in the syndication end of the television industry, establishing legitimacy as professionals was especially important, because sales agents were looked down upon by broadcast professionals who considered themselves part of the industry elite. The formation of trade associations such as NATPE and MIPCOM for this end of the business, besides centralizing the buying and selling of syndicated programming, also signaled a level of professional sophistication comparable to that of the broadcast professionals' organization, the National Association of Broadcasters.

Overall, the formation of NATPE and MIPCOM institutionalized several features of the syndication market. First, the annual conventions, where new and planned series were promoted to potential buyers, contributed to the formulation of "seasons" for development, production, and selling in the area of syndication. Although the syndication market's cycle does not coincide with that of the networks, it too now operates on a defined timeline.[38] Second, the annual conventions consolidated, to some degree, the availability of all series to the marketplace, reducing transaction costs associated with the process of selling. At the same time, however, the convention marketplace still required an individualized sales force that could tailor understandings about particular series to buyers from specific markets. Third, NATPE, in particular, strove to legitimate the professional identity of the syndication sales force, as the name of the organization, the National Association of Television Program Executives, makes clear.[39]

Consolidation of the Syndication Market

Although the viewing audience comprises hundreds of local markets served by local stations, the way in which individual series are sold to those stations has undergone significant change in the last decade. "Industry consolidation has altered that formula, creating vast station groups owning outlets in 20 or 30 cities that buy most of their programs collectively."[40] Specifically, over the last fifteen years most independent stations (as well as network affiliates) have been bought by so-called station groups. The creation of these groups was motivated by the potential profitability of local television stations, coupled with the economies of scale accruing from buying programming in bulk.[41] The station group business model has changed the way programming is bought and sold in several ways.

First, for the most part, consolidation has all but eliminated the need for an annual winter convention for the display and selling of new products. "Given the size and scope of station groups like Fox, Tribune, CBS, and Sinclair, syndicators are able to clear up to 40 percent of the country in a single phone call and more than 60 percent in two or three calls."[42] Conventions like NATPE are no longer essential for introducing buyers to new products, as most sales are now concluded prior to NATPE's annual winter meeting.

Second, the station's general manager no longer has responsibility for the acquisition of new programming for his or her local market. Instead, that responsibility lies with the head of acquisitions for the station group, who makes programming decisions for its member stations. Despite the shift in responsibility, however, the input of station managers has not been eliminated altogether, as the station group heads have found new ways to include them in the decision-making process, as follows. Often, a major group deal begins with the head of a syndication company contacting the head of a station group about a certain show. If the group head is interested, he or she will tell the syndicator to have his or her sales staff pitch the group's various general managers. Those general managers will then regroup and evaluate the pitch on a market-by-market basis.[43] "We're looking to gain a consensus among our general managers and program directors," says Dennis FitzSimons, president of Tribune Broadcasting Co. "We try to give our GMs as much autonomy as we can."[44]

Third, the station group model, with more centralized buying, would seem to reduce syndicators' need for a large sales force. "With that kind of instant access to their customers, it would seem that syndicators could cut back sales positions from the number that it used to take to get the job done."[45] Yet, as it turns out, that has not happened. In fact, the intense legwork and one-on-one negotiations that comprise the core of the syndication business still exist. According to Scott Carlin, former executive vice-president of Warner Brothers Domestic Television Distribution,

> the role of the syndication sales executive is more complex than just negotiating deals with the general managers in their markets. Once a show is sold, there is a constant push to see it upgraded, to make sure it is promoted properly and to seek renewals. There is also market research and analysis as to what each station is doing, how much various competing product is being sold for and what the clients' future needs might be.[46]

The information collected at the individual station level is regarded as essential local intelligence for use by syndication companies in negotiating the most complex of deals with station groups.[47]

Fourth, in response to the changing domestic market, NATPE has become more oriented towards international business. "The station guy in Boise, Idaho, today should be as interested in what is happening around the world as what is happening with digital television," stated NATPE's former president, Bruce Johansen, in 1998.[48] While retaining a focus on television programming content, increasingly, NATPE's objectives have been all but supplanted by efforts to sustain an effective business environment for syndication companies seeking international ventures.[49,50]

The Challenges of International Syndication

The extent to which these organizational and industry shifts represent a new form of selling is less clear-cut. Frederic Ziv brought sales practices to television from his career in advertising and radio, and their adaptation to the then-new medium of television was relatively straightforward. However, the product was domestic, as was the marketplace, and the customs and other understandings that framed the selling of series and their potential audiences, along with shared understandings of the revenue-generating goals of station managers, and the profit orientation of the industry more broadly, were readily understood outgrowths of other media industries. As we noted earlier in this chapter, television was an industry in which sales agents utilized product-specific and customer-specific information to tailor the utility of a series to individual markets; it was not an industry in which a commodity's (that is, an individual series') traits were equally knowable to all potential customers (e.g., like selling a piece of technology). However, when the international marketplace is introduced and coproductions or other joint ventures are added to the mix, the focus shifts to include not only how to sell but also *what* to sell. This development makes the uncertainty of what *will* sell all the greater.

This speaks, in part, to the enduring power of the audience in determining the value of the product, and ultimately, to the source of the uncertainty that pervades the industry. In the domestic arena, syndicated sales agents have systemized to a considerable degree how to anticipate and control that uncertainty—by developing social relationships within industry-based personal networks largely organized on trust and by relying upon trustworthy information about the local audience. But the way that localism translates to an international frame is largely unknown, and is what we turn to in our next chapter. An obvious question is how the attributes of a domestic series translate into desired viewing. But less obvious, and no less significant, in understanding that translation are the cultural aspects of the business contexts in which they are bought and sold: the reason why a given series is bought tells us something about what the receiving country values in entertainment, but what does that really tell us about local cultural interests, if anything? Equally interesting is how the competitive aspects of the syndication market translate abroad. Are competitiveness and profit as essential to the sale as they are in the United States? How do those similarities or differences translate to ways of doing business with other nations? Is doing business born out of localism as it is in the United States? We turn to these and other issues in the next chapter as we examine the international market for syndicated television.

2

Television in the Global Market

Television was born out of localism.
>—Barry Thurston, president of Columbia TriStar
>Television Distribution[1]

NATPE is now a foreign affair.   —*Hollywood Reporter* headline[2]

Reading the weekly International Edition of *The Hollywood Reporter* gives me a headache.
>—an aside by the head of a major studio's international division
>while speaking at a seminar on the syndication market[3]

The first two quotations reflect the complicated mix of parochial concerns and cosmopolitan considerations that make up the syndication market in the television industry today. In the first one we see the characteristically provincial origins of domestic television, remnants of which prevail to this day. The second quotation, a headline about the 1998 shift toward the importance of the international marketplace for television distribution, can only hint at the complexity underlying the change from its early focus on local markets to a focus on markets composed of locales never anticipated. The third quotation suggests the practical reality of working day to day in this segment of the industry. The two sociologists, Muriel and Joel Cantor, whom we mentioned in the introduction as among the first in our discipline to examine the international market for television import/export, described an environment that they could only "charitably" (their word) characterize as "chaotic, unruly, and unpredictable."[4] That statement is even truer today. Echoing that characterization nearly a decade later, Tom Keeter, director of advertising and publicity for Columbia TriStar International Television, said, "I couldn't tell you why in one country a show is a big hit and it's not in another."[5] Given the inability to predict the success or failure of series abroad, other aspects of business come into play when it comes to making sales. For business to be accomplished, it is essential that a viable co-orientation be established among the many different players who interact across many organizational levels and in many industry arenas.

In this chapter, we examine how the industry navigates its increasingly local/global bifurcated focus. To examine this aspect of the industry, first we discuss foundational scholarship on international television, identifying both its contributions and its shortcomings. Then, we discuss the organization of this complex culture world. Finally, we elaborate on the importance of attending to its underlying mechanisms in order to understand how work in an industry so far reaching and aptly characterized as chaotic is accomplished.

Scholarship on Program Flows

Communication scholars have led the study of exported television. Consistent with their interest in understanding the exchange and impact of information, their scholarship has focused almost exclusively upon identifying the flows of programming from one country to another and the major national exporters in the global arena.[6] The earliest attempts at systematic documentation of exported television programming revealed that by the early 1970s the United States, Britain, France, and the Federal Republic of Germany were leaders in its origination. According to that research, the United States led this group with an estimated 150,000 hours of programming per year, followed by the United Kingdom and France, estimated at twenty thousand hours each. The Federal Republic of Germany exported approximately six thousand hours.[7,8] The UNESCO report that produced these findings relied upon questionnaire data collected from over fifty countries and analyzed the general content and percentages of imported versus domestic programming. In that first-ever study of the exchange patterns of exported television, entertainment programming comprised a greater portion of the imported product than other forms, such as news.[9]

To some extent these statistics merely reflect the number of hours of airtime that needed to be filled in newly emerging national television systems.[10] For the most part, the leaders in exported programming sent their programs to countries whose systems of broadcast reception were sufficiently developed to have schedules to fill, or who shared the same language. Moreover, by no means did the number of hours reported indicate that programming from any one exporter dominated the globe. In the early 1970s, for example, the United States exported programming primarily to Canada, Australia, Japan, and Western Europe (Varis, 1974). Programming from the French commercial group went to Europe, North America, Japan, and ten French-speaking African countries, with Zaire and Tunisia being the major receivers on that continent. West Germany was a major exporter within Western Europe but had more limited presence beyond that sphere because of the relatively few countries globally where German is spoken.

While these nations were the largest exporters, several other countries were major producers of programming for international distribution in other regional markets. For example, programs from Mexico were widely distributed throughout Latin America and in areas of the United States where Spanish is widely spoken, and Lebanon and the United Arab Republic were major producers for the Middle East. Analyses of flows among non-Western countries published a decade after the first UNESCO report show that among developing countries there was no substantial change in the use of foreign programming.[11] Among those flows was, however, a trend toward greater intraregional exchange, especially among Arab countries and also within Latin America. And, since Varis's work of the mid-1980s, additional patterns have been observed. Countries with large internal markets, such as Brazil's television and India's film industries, now not only supply their own markets but also send exports internationally.[12] Japan is a major supplier throughout Asia and South Asia, especially of animation, and its global reach includes Western nations.[13] In short, since the pioneering work by Nordenstreng and Varis, vital regional markets based on geolinguistic, cultural, and geographic similarities have developed.[14]

Still, though, the United States remains the dominant television exporter; one study estimates that 85 percent of all children's programming, 81 percent of television movies, and close to 75 percent of dramatic television programs sold in the global television market are of U.S. origin,[15] while another estimates that over 60 percent of the global trade in television, about $4 billion, is controlled by U.S. companies.[16] Statistics documenting the degree of U.S. influence over television markets abroad are often provocative and compelling; and they can be a helpful starting point for trying to understand key questions about the power of U.S. media culture around the world and about the landscape of diverse media markets. Indeed, some of these statistics helped to launch a debate about media domination that has now raged for three decades. However, too often discussions of global media ownership end rather than start here. This is a problem because these broad statistics about the distribution of shows, while interesting and obvious, also lock us into assumptions and narrow our explanations and understanding of the way the global market operates. For instance, important questions are missed when we focus only on the broad picture of television trade flows, such as how television programs are transformed by touching down in diverse international contexts of reception and interpretation. The problems are not isolated to the level of reception and audiences, though. A focus on television trade flows also obscures understanding of the particulars of production and distribution processes. Why are specific programs, for instance, marketed, adopted, or rejected by distributors? To understand the concerns about U.S. domination of global television markets (and, more recently, the increasing consolidation and integration of global media megaconglomerates) requires a much more fine-tuned understanding of the organization and cultural logics of these markets than can be gleaned from such crude evidence of program flows alone.

The Debate over Cultural Domination

> By most measurements, American television is the world's leader. It's bigger, more popular, more profitable, flashier, and at times, *at times*, better than almost any form of television in existence on the planet. America is to television what Switzerland is to clocks and banking, what Holland is to tulips, and what France is to wine. If we could export our other products to the rest of the world as successfully as we export our television programs, we'd have a[n enviable] balance of trade surplus.
> —introductory remarks by Ron Alridge of *Electronic Media* at NATPE's 1999 seminar, "How We Do It: A U.S. Television Market Primer"

Still debated among scholars is the question of whether expansion of international media flows is a mechanism for both economic and ideological cultural domination, specifically by the United States. The so-called cultural imperialist view refers to "the domination of one country's system of symbolically producing and reproducing constructed realities over another's production and re-production of self-identity,"[17] or, more succinctly, to a "system of exploitative control of people and resources."[18] This view assumes that ideological power resides within the media as part of the cultural superstructure that emerges within economic relations of dependency between industrialized and peripheral countries. "This idea is similar to (but in many formulations less sophisticated than) Gramsci's concept of hegemony, in which elites and sometimes others compete to use media and other cultural or information structures to set a dominant ideology."[19]

Debates about this macro–structurally oriented perspective have raged since it was proposed over forty years ago, and although this view still has adherents, many are engaged in a conscious reworking of it to complicate understandings of power, inequality, and unequal flows in the global market. Contemporary approaches to the effects of global media refocus attention, instead, on its political economy, in particular, the political and economic workings of media industries. This later tradition, represented by scholars like Garnham, McChesney, and Herman, is more nuanced in its analysis of presumed media effects.[20] For instance, work from this viewpoint by Toby Miller and his colleagues directs attention to the so-called New International Division of Cultural Labor (NICL), the global commodity chains that underlie capitalist market production, to account for Hollywood's long-standing international dominance in global media.[21] By attending to such matters as the inner workings of copyright and intellectual property law, coproduction arrangements, marketing strategy, and industry employment practices, Miller et al. explore the political contexts that shape the economics of media production through a social scientifically oriented analysis of media industries and organizations.[22]

The most significant opposing view has come to be known as the active audience perspective. Ethnographic study of viewers' reception reveals that audiences play an active role in selecting the media they consume and the textual readings they make of it; those readings produce meanings that connect with viewers' own social experience.[23] Audience studies research has demonstrated, for example, that cultural products such as television, music, and film are engaged by audiences through the local cultural frames they bring to viewing, listening, or seeing.[24] Some of the early work on reception among international audiences identified similar factors at play. For instance, gender can be pivotal in shaping the way audiences respond to foreign media, and culturally specific beliefs can evoke active resistance to the values portrayed in imported programs.[25] Because the response of actual viewers at the point of local reception is both complicated and nuanced, it problematizes any straightforward notions of domination, and to assume otherwise, assert these scholars, vastly oversimplifies the "power" of an industry on an audience, *even* if the industry is global in reach and *especially* if that audience is international.[26] As some of these scholars have pointed out, the "fallacy of internalism" of the cultural imperialism approach is "a tendency to try to 'read off' the impact of capitalist-dominated media systems at the level of individual cultural experience from an analysis of the structures themselves, without paying attention to the complexities of cultural reception."[27]

It is not our goal to resolve this debate over cultural imperialism but instead to recognize its importance to the field and its usefulness as a starting point for understanding key questions about the presence of U.S. media culture around the world and the landscape of diverse media markets. Certainly, discussion of the export of television needs to be placed in the context of broader debates about global media, and as we have shown, much important work has been done in recent years, and it is a burgeoning field. At the same time, though, sometimes it seems as if the debate has reached an impasse. There is a too-easy way to caricature contrasting sides and approaches to critical analysis of the globalization of media. This caricature, which pits macro-structural analyses focused on issues of economics and power writ large against more micro-oriented analyses of media texts and audiences within localized contexts, oversimplifies the outlooks of each. The problem is not that these two positions have no basis in reality, but revisiting critiques does not get us very far. Moreover, as work on both sides of the debate has grown increasingly theoretically sophisticated, there seems to still be a bit of an impasse with regard to translating theoretical calls for integrative approaches to global media into concrete, empirical analyses that are able to move the discussion forward. Such an endeavor requires the difficult task of truly interdisciplinary engagement as well as drawing on the unique strengths of different disciplines to fit various pieces of the global media puzzle together. Our discipline of sociology—though it has too often been missing from critical engagement with questions of global media in the past—has something to offer such a project. The key aspect of such a project is engaging meso-level analysis and middle-range research.

Moving to the Middle Range

Nearly overlooked in the debate over cultural domination are middle-range social-structural factors that complicate the flow of television across borders and its impact at the point of reception. Less developed and organized as a unified viewpoint, this perspective attends to industry practices globally and locally to account for variation in international audience responses.[28] For example, following Nordenstreng and Varis's 1974 UNESCO report came a study of Latin American television broadcasters in Mexico, Peru, Argentina, Brazil, and Venezuela, in which Antola and Rogers argued that examining "audience-hours" (i.e., number of hours divided by size of audience for each program) provides a more realistic assessment of exposure to imported programming and demonstrated that it is substantially lower than proponents of the dominance thesis imply.[29] Within Mexico in 1982, the year of Antola and Rogers's study, the 50 percent of programming hours filled by imported programming translated into one-third of the total possible audience-hours of viewing. Moreover, of four available channels, only two carried a high proportion of imported programming.

The significance of these figures for Mexico was borne out through interviews conducted by Antola and Rogers with Latin American television broadcasters in Venezuela, Brazil, Argentina, Chile, Mexico, and Peru regarding viewers' preferences for domestically produced versus imported programming. According to the executives interviewed, audience preferences ranked in the following descending order: locally produced programs, imports from other Latin American countries, and, last, programs from the United States (which was the source of the greatest percentage of imported programs). Davis found a similar pattern of viewing preferences in Ecuador, a smaller and less developed country than those studied by Antola and Rogers.[30] These findings support notions of a cultural discount; that is, "A particular programme rooted in one culture, and thus attractive in that environment, will have a diminished appeal elsewhere."[31] The discount is less in the entertainment genre than in other categories, which Hoskins and Mirus argue is the single biggest reason why entertainment-based programming (rather than education- and/or information-based programming) dominates international flows.

The relevance of research on television's textual properties to the cultural domination debate is more complicated. Liebes and Katz suggest that some genres originating in Western cultures, such as serialized dramas, have an inherent cultural power that makes them accessible and appealing in almost every region where they are imported.[32] Their narrative structure, which leaves them open to a wider variety of cultural readings than other forms of programming, also contributes, it is argued, to serials' success in the global syndication market.[33] Although much of the literature on serials' global success focuses on content or genre characteristics, recent scholarship indicates that concrete and local programming practices may be equally instrumental in shaping viewing preferences. For example, Stuart Cunningham and Elizabeth Jacka identified factors other than genre that accorded success in the U.K. of the Australian soap import *Neighbours*. On one hand, they recognize that certain cultural themes (e.g., the youthfulness and "whiteness" of the cast, and the historic ties between Australia and Britain) resonated with the audience. On the other hand, they emphasize that crucial to the success of *Neighbours* were aspects seemingly as mundane as placement on the network schedule (early and late afternoons, five days per week) and the ability to reach the target demographic (the youth audience).[34] In this instance, specific programming strategies were successful in placing the series before an audience that would both find it and appreciate its meaning.[35,36] Conversely, *Neighbours* failed to catch on with U.S. viewers for reasons partly related to content/genre (e.g., the show's "non-exceptional realism"), but mostly due to factors such as gridlock scheduling and the brevity of the show's run.[37]

While issues of genre continue to be relevant, as we shall discuss in chapter 3, these findings further underscore the importance of examining middle-range factors in understanding how and where imported programming comes to dominate audience preferences. Cantor and Cantor advocate this strategy in the conclusion of their exploratory study of the international marketplace of U.S. television. They noted that "the production and distribution of American programs abroad is a complex and intricate process, involving many players both in the United Sates and abroad—including the audience." They go on to conclude that "the time has now arrived for communication researchers to move away from a model of direct, single-centered, and worldwide influence to one that functions as interactive, multicentered, and regional."[38] Making a similar point, Schement, Gonzalez, Lum, and Valencia argue that middle-range approaches avoid applying "a single interpretation to diverse cases."[39] Recent calls by television studies scholars in the humanities also point to a continued lack of progress on this front and to the importance of attention to industry and other intermediate-level factors.[40]

The point we wish to underscore here is that there is burgeoning research on exported media that identifies numerous intervening market-level factors and industry-related practices that potentially affect the direction and extent of its flow and that those factors may occur either in the production or in the distribution of a media product.[41] In advocating this alternative approach in the context of debates about global media, we concur with Mowlana and Cantor and Cantor, who also take into consideration that the market is shaped by formal, legal, and technical constraints, on the one hand, and by informal rules and understandings rooted in culture and ideology, on the other. Our interest in understanding this marketplace directs us to the practices that make possible its concrete functioning and cultural logics: the features and operation of the marketplace rather than the market per se; the cyclicality of the forms and practices of the business of the industry rather than a presumed teleological development; industry participants who are located at all levels of organizational settings rather than just industry leaders or other highly visible decision makers; and the possibility that television series are malleable cultural products rather than immutable texts with inherent meanings. In short, we are interested in the *mechanisms* that make this culture world operational.

Opening Up the Culture World of International Television

The Main Players in Global Television Syndication

Wrestling with the complexities of the international television industry today can be as frustrating as time spent with a Rubik's Cube. It's a spider's web of complicated co-productions and multiplex partnerships that span borders and government regulations.
— *Hollywood Reporter* international market reporter Steve Brennan[42]

The international market for exported television is made up of numerous interconnected organizations, institutional actors, and products. Firms in the global syndication business are extremely diverse, ranging from complexly structured production companies with international syndication divisions to small, one-person operations selling a single product.

Many different organizational entities make up the industry—from the studios and other program suppliers to the networks to companies that specialize specifically in the preparation, handling, and distribution of television products for the international syndication market. Institutional actors range from company presidents of large, multinational media conglomerates to owners of local, community enterprises in developing nations. Ancillary to these key participants in the market are other players, including advertising agencies (whose clients generate the revenues that sustain the business), law and/or government regulatory agencies and ministries (which set policies such as import or content quotas), and ratings companies (whose measures of audience size provide the basis for advertising rates). All participants pay close attention to the health of local, regional, and global economies, which shape overall demand and the terms of trade for international commerce in television programming.

These players co-orient to one another through the buying and selling of television programming as a cultural product. The buyers include national and privately owned broadcast, cable, and satellite networks, cable systems, digital broadcasters, pay-per-view operators, station group owners, and independent television stations. Their representatives rely upon accumulated knowledge about what the television industry is expected to provide as a source of entertainment. That knowledge includes an understanding of the qualities that constitute desirable programming, the audiences they want those programs to reach, the parts of the broadcast schedule that need to be filled, and the balance acquired programming must strike with other, already scheduled programming in order to round out a broadcast day, week, or season. Of course, everyone knows that the ultimate goal is bottom-line profit, but it is those who understand the subtleties of buying and selling cultural products who are most successful. Indeed, because television programming is so culturally/symbolically laden and its success and failure so difficult to predict, the particular challenges it presents as a matter to be managed lie at the very center of this marketplace. In figure 2.1 we schematically present components of the global television marketplace.

Thinking about Television as a Cultural Product

Conventional economic approaches are of limited utility for understanding television as a cultural product. According to media economists, television is a public commodity that is consumed as a private one.[43] The

INDUSTRY	**Sites** Trade conventions, private meetings, subsidiary offices
	Marketplace Features and Practices Business/licensing models
	Industry participants **Producers/Sellers**[a] **Distributors/Buyers** Majors/network studios Broadcast networks Independents[b] Cable/satellite networks Cable system/MSO/DBS Station group owners Station representatives
	Ancillary Participants/Services[c]
	Products Television series, concepts, formats; films
NON-INDUSTRY	**Contexts** Audience History, ownership, and development of national industry Cultural and legal policies and practices of government agencies and ministries National/regional economies Global economy

[a] Some content producers are also distributors; for example, CBS Broadcast International/King World International Productions is a unit of CBS Enterprises.

[b] For example, GayDateTV, Inc., which produces a television show that "chronicles the gay, lesbian, and bisexual dating experience through a series of televised blind dates" (NATPE 2002 Conference and Exhibition Directory, p. 83).

[c] For example, Swiss Film Center, which represents independent Swiss producers, and USA Dubs & Replication, which provides broadcast duplication, standards conversion, video editing, etc.

Fig. 2.1. Structural components of the global television industry marketplace

public/private distinction has nothing to do with who produces the product; public goods can be produced by private sources and private sources can produce public ones. Instead, the public/private distinction pertains to how many individuals are able to consume the product before it is used up. Many products have both public and private aspects, and this dual quality characterizes television, just as it does other cultural products such as films, radio programs, and books. As a public good, a television program is a commodity that is not depleted by any one viewer as he or she "consumes" it through viewing. The public good concept also applies to buyers and sellers in a syndication market. The fact that a series is sold in one market does not decrease its availability to other markets. Of course, the utility a given program provides to an individual viewer is affected by the fact of viewing. In most instances, after a program has been viewed once, the consumer will derive less utility from subsequent viewings. That is, the act of consumption has "used up" (at least for the time being) the experience of entertainment that the product provides for the viewer.

The distinction between public and private goods as it applies to television is usually employed by media economists to determine how best to ensure that the quantity of a commodity that is produced meets the needs of audience members and program providers in the marketplace. However, our interest in the buying, selling, and consumption of television programs is somewhat different. Whereas to the media economist "utility" is a static concept related to a consumer's willingness to pay for a commodity or to his or her preference for one good over another, our interest is in how the viewer's process of consumption involves actively creating value in the product. That is, the viewer plays an active role in transforming the product to something that has meaning and value to himself or herself. While this is true to some extent about every commodity[44]—e.g., a bicycle, a can opener, or a box of cereal—it is especially true of cultural products whose value resides in part in aesthetic properties. As a cultural product, television's value to its audience lies in its ability to entertain in intangible ways that provide satisfaction.

In contrast to economists, cultural studies scholars have focused almost exclusively on understanding the active process through which audiences engage cultural products and create meaning. In his influential analysis of the institutional structures of broadcasting, Stuart Hall challenged the assumed linearity between producers and consumers through which a cultural product like television has impact, and made clear that the consumption of television is also a site of production by the viewer. In identifying the discursive practices through which television products can be encoded with meaning, Hall argued that for those meanings to be brought to bear on the viewer, he or she must decode them during reception. "If no 'meaning' is taken, there can be no 'consumption.'"[45]

Subsequent work in the cultural studies tradition elaborates the ways that cultural meanings are made "in usage" through the practices that make up consumption. In placing emphasis on practices at the level of the individual, however, cultural studies scholars have focused almost exclusively upon audience activity and the material conditions, social identities, ideologies, and related factors that viewers bring to the act of viewing, all but neglecting institutional practices that also contribute to meanings of cultural objects.[46] The prevailing view among these scholars seems to imply that audience members are largely unconstrained in the meanings, satisfactions, and pleasures they can derive from a cultural object.[47] Commanding less scholarly attention in the study of the global television marketplace, but greater interest from our sociological vantage point, is the way the properties of cultural objects themselves attract consumers' attention in the first place. Cultural sociologist Wendy Griswold has written that cultural objects are themselves social constructions; they are, as she describes, "shared significance embodied in form, . . . an expression of social meanings that is tangible or can be put into words."[48] Including analysis of the attributes or properties of cultural products like television is centrally important to understanding the operation of the culture world comprising the global television marketplace because, as we have argued elsewhere, the very process of attribute selection by series creators or producers implies cultural valuation, and the very process of rendering meaning occurs through a cultural process itself—aesthetic appraisal —which renders relative worth to audiences.[49]

To some readers it may be inconceivable to regard television, as well as other popular art forms, as being aesthetically valued by audiences or worthy of aesthetic valuation by critics.[50] However, noted cultural sociologist Herbert Gans makes a strong argument for extending the application of aesthetic criteria to such forms. In discussing the place of aesthetics in popular culture, he says,

> I use the term aesthetic broadly, referring not only to standards of beauty
> and taste but also to a variety of other emotional and intellectual values
> which people express or satisfy when they choose content from a culture,
> and I assume, of course, that people apply aesthetic standards in all taste
> cultures, and not just in high culture.[51]

Gans raises two important considerations by including popular art, such as television, in the world of so-called legitimate art. The first is that there are recognizable and observable aesthetic standards by which consumers assign value to popular art, although those criteria may not be readily articulated (even by industry participants, as we shall see in chapter 4). Second, those standards are aligned with the expression of emotional and intellectual values. Thus, even though a cultural object is popular, individuals are applying aesthetic judgments in their selection and engagement of those objects.

To illustrate just how central television's aesthetic properties are to the business of global television, we focus briefly on the relevance of genre to program exportability by examining how different genres fare in the global marketplace. As we shall see, the level of cultural specificity inherent in three familiar ones—soap operas, situation comedies, and action/adventure programs—in combination with local concerns of viewers can affect acceptance, rejection, or indifference by audiences abroad in ways that are highly consequential to the business of buying and selling programs.

Audiences and "Their" Serials: Why Do Soaps Translate across Borders?

One often hears about the passionate followings that develop abroad around American soaps airing in other countries. *Santa Barbara*, which aired in the United States on NBC from 1984 to 1993, was one of the most watched programs worldwide in the 1990s and was the first U.S. program to air in Russia after the collapse of the Soviet Union.[52] Telenovelas, the Latin American relative of American soaps, are often spotlighted as well by the American media, but, understandably, they receive less attention because they originate elsewhere and are not viewed by a large English-speaking audience in the United States. For example, in late 1997, several articles appeared in the industry trade publications about the intense fan following that had developed in war-torn Bosnia for the Venezuelan telenovela *Kassandra*. According to a story in the industry trade publication *Electronic Media*, "the locals were getting restless" because the series, which was being rebroadcast illegally in Bosnia, had been taken off the air. The punch line of the article was that *Kassandra*, a "riches to rags and back to riches" story of an heiress sold to a band of gypsies, illustrated that even in the most unlikely of places, "TV is stronger than ideology."[53] In a similar example, a Mexican telenovela export featuring a "profoundly philosophical dog . . . whose thoughts are audible to the audience," took the Philippines by storm in 1996. The series, *Mari Mal*, "caused motorists to abandon their cars in the middle of the street, provoked a murder, baffled psychologists," and so captivated the country's 1.3 million public employees that they ran the risk of losing their jobs if caught watching the program.[54]

Soap opera scholars are well versed as to why the genre transports so well across borders. Serials have a unique ability "to explore apparently global themes in more specifically local ways."[55] In terms of content, their shared focus on family, romantic relationships, emotions, and conflicts seems to hold universal appeal. Through the reliance on melodrama as a stylistic form, action located in the real world is pushed toward the symbolic activity of metaphor.[56] Soap viewers around the globe are familiar with this stylistic form, and they recognize that encoded in the personal talk that comprises soaps are the psychic and social dilemmas that constitute soaps' fictional world of family and personal relationships.

Additionally, serials are able to adopt a variety of strategies to appeal to both their own and other cultures and still be considered soap operas. Brazil's phenomenally successful TV Globo, for example, has based serial narratives on internationally known works of literature. In other cases a serials' fictional community might be located in a non–nationally specific setting or a well-known expatriate hub; stories might focus on characters who are internationally mobile; a serial might be produced in multiple versions, one for domestic consumption and the other for export; or co-production arrangements might lead to simultaneous airings of culturally specific versions of the same narrative (*Ugly Betty*, for example).[57] While the basic features of the serial genre are universal, particular stylistic emphases depend on the country of origin. For example, telenovelas often tell romantic stories of social class mobility, and when coupled with their standing as prime-time programming for a general audience, they are much more than a form of entertainment—they engage the politics, economics, and culture of Latin American nations as a whole.[58]

British and Australian soaps are an interesting contrast to telenovelas. According to Geraghty, while British soaps, too, capture a strong sense of place and class, they do not do so through melodrama or through exemplification of social issues, but rather by an emphasis on the mundane realism of social community.[59] What each of these examples illustrates is the importance of specific nationally and culturally associated properties of the genre in its many variations. As one Russian viewer explained to us, his country preferred *Santa Barbara* over the Mexican telenovela *Los Ricos Tambien Lloran* then airing in his country (translated into Russian as "The Rich Cry Too"). "While there is a similarity in social values between Mexico and Russia, with both nations placing value on not bettering oneself at the expense of others, 'Los Ricos' is less popular because it was all talk about small things and no action."[60]

Our discussion thus far has foregrounded the importance of content to the international appeal of the soap opera genre. However, the genre's narrative structure—the serialization of story over an extended period of time—also affects the translatability of soaps across borders, as illustrated by the intense interest in Latin American telenovelas that has developed in China over the last two decades. According to Michelle Sie Whitten, president and CEO of Encore International and an expert on Chinese culture, in the 1980s U.S. series were among the first international programming broadcast on Chinese television.[61] Initial forays included *Dynasty* and *Dallas*, some of the earliest prime-time soaps in the United States. They were eventually pulled, and very few other U.S. TV series were allowed by the Chinese government to be imported at that time. However, telenovela imports from Mexico and Brazil were permitted and became hugely successful, filling the void for entertainment programming. With TV ownership becoming more widespread in China in the 1990s, the country's burgeoning commercial television industry was eager to acquire series that would have mass appeal. Building on the success of imported serialized dramas, domestically produced versions featuring Chinese locales and stories have come to dominate entertainment programming.[62] Nevertheless, Latin American telenovelas remain extremely popular among Chinese audiences as their content and narrative forms continue to resonate with local tastes.

The Challenge Facing Situation Comedies in the Global Market

The example of soaps illustrates how specific cultural properties of the serial genre shape series' success or failure with audiences in other countries, and the relative ease with which they cross borders. The distinctive properties of the situation comedy genre, in contrast, do not transcend cultural differences as easily. As one media journalist put it, "despite the influence of world TV, there isn't a growing global sense of humor."[63]

Writing about the dominant forms of American mass humor in the late twentieth century, David Marc identified two primary forms.[64] The first is stand-up comedy, which is built around the talents of an individual performer, usually delivering his or her own material to a live audience (e.g., Jack Benny, Bob Hope, Dean Martin and Jerry Lewis). The second is the situation comedy, written by a team of staff writers, usually set in a fictional domestic setting, and filmed before a live audience and/or overlaid with a laugh track. In the decades since television was launched, these forms have sometimes been combined, with the premise for a specific situation comedy built around the fictionalized life of an established comedian (e.g., Jerry Seinfeld, Ray Romano, Tim Allen, or Margaret Cho).

The content of specific shows may differ but is always a variant of what Marc calls the "domesticom" theme. That is, regardless of premise, in general these shows "depend on familiarity, identification, and redemption of popular beliefs." Series are successful because they manage to achieve what Marc refers to as the "art of the middle" by avoiding extremes in psychology or politics and focusing instead on day-to-day human foibles. Even *All in the Family*, considered adventuresome for its time, conforms to this structure, according to Marc. By definition, then, in order to succeed a situation comedy has to engage beliefs and conventions that are widely shared by a mass audience.

For this very reason, however, situation comedies are often *too* culturally specific and as a result do not transport well across borders. Their characteristic humor "may have audiences roaring in Atlanta, but falls totally flat in Rome."[65] (Or as Steve Askew of Star Entertainment succinctly put it in reference to the most popular U.S. sitcom of the 1990s, "Two thirds of the world's population has no idea what Jerry Seinfeld is going on about.")[66] Still, that does not completely deter distributors from finding ways to sell their product abroad. Indeed, for series to work in other locations, it is not uncommon for adaptations to be made to a fundamental premise of the show, making it, in effect, more local. Sometimes, however, an imported series finds an audience without any accommodation to local tastes. For example, Australian audiences have embraced the class-bound humor of British imports such as *To the Manor Born* and *Absolutely Fabulous*, and distinctively American sitcoms such as *Friends* and *Fresh Prince of Bel-Air* have succeeded there as well. These series work in the Australian context because audiences are sufficiently familiar with the cultural context and conventions of British and American series that they can enjoy what might otherwise be seen as highly culture bound. It clearly is *not* that the themes of these imported series resonate with local culture, because nearly every attempt to develop a domestic Australian sitcom with similar themes and conventions has failed miserably. So, for example, Australian audiences are comfortable with laugh tracks on imported American sitcoms but are offended by them in homegrown series. As Australian actor-writer Tim Ferguson put it, "we won't cop an Australian producer telling us, 'This is a joke.' . . . We can forgive the Americans for doing it, but we can't forgive Australian producers."[67]

The bottom line is that situation comedy, unlike soap opera, is situationally specific in the fullest cultural sense. That is, while soap opera is based upon widely shared assumptions about the elements comprising human social bonds, the premise of situation comedy often resides in the temporary social rupturing of those bonds. Because cultures vary in their tolerance of the social contrasts exposed by humor and in solutions to those contrasts, the resolution proposed in comedic narrative itself is very localized. Moreover, some cultures and nations vary in their interest in situational humor, as one media journalist observed about Germany (which she attributed to "a lack of a cohesive sense of 'German-ness' at which to poke fun").[68] American distributors recognize that these differential tolerances translate into a limited appeal of American comedy on the international market. Stated Armando Nunez, president of CBS International, which was selling the U.S. hit *Everybody Loves Raymond* in 2001, "American comedy is definitely on the second tier."[69] They also recognize that different types of comedies—sophisticated satire, those with family appeal, or ones that rely more heavily on a visual telling of the narrative —sell differently depending on local tastes and sensibilities.

Action Adventure as Universal Storytelling

In contrast to situation comedy, the genre of action adventure, or action drama, transports extremely well. Series such as *Rescue 911, Xena: Warrior Princess,* and *Baywatch* (which is one of the most widely syndicated U.S. series in the world, at one point airing in 140 countries and thirty-three languages)[70] emphasize action and plot over dialogue and character. They export well because they do not rely upon dialogue to advance the narrative. More so than situation comedies or dramas, meanings in action-adventure are encoded visually.

The popularity of action-adventure television series and films worldwide influences what kind of programming gets produced for domestic consumption in the United States and other countries that are active in the global market.[71] Production costs alone in television have risen over the past decade. A typical episode of an hour-long series costs approximately $1.2–$1.3 million to produce in 1990, and by 2005 that figure often exceeded $2 million (excluding marketing and studio administration expenses), while over the same period, sitcoms roughly doubled, to $1.25 million.[72] With ultimate profitability of a television production increasingly dependent upon foreign sales, as syndication executive and Universal Television Group chairman Greg Meidel put it, "the [domestic] shows wouldn't get made unless we felt there was a very strong international component."[73] Syndicators have come to subscribe to a clear hierarchy in the marketability of genres in foreign markets. Media journalist Richard Covington observes that "soap operas travel tolerably well, but action series and films move with the speed of light, proving no-brainer hits in nearly every country. Animation, documentaries, game shows, and science fiction cross borders with relative ease. Comedy does not."[74]

In sum, cultural properties of television series are centrally important to the popularity (or, in industry terms, the ratings or sales success) of a television series abroad. For those in the industry, selling abroad entails recognizing, as best as can be understood, what has appeal and what does not. In myriad ways, buyers and sellers both reference and orient to the attributes of the product that shape its entertainment value to audiences (a topic we explore more fully in chapter 4). In the following section, we describe the implications of this for specific practices in the culture world of television import/export.

Business Strategies for Crossing Borders

Since the emergence of the international market in the 1950s, larger exporters in the United States and elsewhere have developed business strategies that strive to minimize the unpredictability of demand for individual series and to regularize revenue in the global arena by relying upon specific kinds of contractual arrangements with buyers. One approach is output deals—packaging programs with motion pictures. Feature films, especially those produced by the United States, are very popular on the global television market, and by bundling them with series, the seller guarantees a demand, at a prenegotiated license fee, despite uncertainty over the appeal of specific series in foreign markets. These packages might combine a hit television series and a box-office-hit film with one or more failed series and some less successful films, and they often consist of multiyear agreements. One such deal, between Disney/CapCities and Germany's RTL Television in 1995, was described in the industry trade publication, *Mediaweek*:

> For its $240 million, RTL Television got the exclusive broadcast rights to 500 hours of library and future TV product—including 100 hours of TV series programming, 75 made-for-television movies and 60 specials—as well as 46 feature-film titles for the next five years. Among the feature films is last summer's top-grossing hit "Batman Forever," "The Fugitive" and "Interview with the Vampire."[75]

Describing the state of the international market in 2000, industry journalist Elizabeth Jensen observed, "Those deals, which commit foreign
broadcasters to take the good along with the bad, remain a huge part of
the overall market."[76] Another approach is to sell in a single package the
distribution rights of a given property across multiple viewing outlets,
such as theatrical release, videocassettes, and cable. "What we're trying to
do now is quicken the windows and put multiple [broadcast and cable]
windows together so that we can cycle the product through, which is one
way to make [revenue] up," said Gary Marenzi, president of Paramount
International Television.[77]

A third, increasingly popular approach is to sell a program concept
or format rather than the program itself, a strategy that substantially
reduces the costs incurred by the seller. As president of CBS Broadcast
International and U.S. syndication executive Armando Nunez, Jr., put it,
with these kinds of arrangements, the seller is "controlling the software,
whether you're producing locally [i.e., abroad] or in the U.S."[78] Compared
to the outright sale of programming abroad, the selling of program concepts allows for a more sophisticated adaptation to localized tastes and
preferences. This strategy has been used with great success by British exporters, with the U.K. presently producing and distributing 45 percent of
this business (and being anointed the "king of formats" globally).[79] Among
the most successful were the sale of program concepts, for example, *Step-
toe and Son* and *Till Death Do Us Part*, which became in the United States
Sanford and Son and *All in the Family*, respectively. More recently, the international licensing of the concepts for the quiz shows *Who Wants to Be
a Millionaire*, *The Weakest Link*, and *American Idol* (which began as *Pop
Idol* in the United Kingdom) earned millions for their British syndicators.[80] British media scholar Tom O'Regan notes that these strategies are
components of a much larger set of approaches developed to cultivate and
sustain the international presence of British television. He elaborates that
these also include

> overseas investment in British television and British investment in tele-
> vision production outside the U.K. This presence also involves the in-
> digenizing of British formats and productions by foreign producers, the
> adaptation of British policy models, the use of British precedent and
> programming to organize public discussion and debate, and the role of
> British television in supplying personnel and training for other television
> systems.[81]

Australian exporters pursue similar strategies. For instance, between 1978 and 1995, the Grundy Organization maintained an office in Los Angeles to concentrate on coproduction arrangements and the sale and placement of Australian series such as *Paradise Beach* on U.S. off-network schedules.[82] Successfully syndicating *Paradise Beach* in the U.S. market required Grundy to enter into a complex web of business alliances. That series, produced by Australia's Nine Network and the independent Village Roadshow, was distributed in the United States through a collaborative arrangement between these companies and the American distributor New World International–Genesis. Commenting on Australia's success at establishing international demand for its products through its business arrangements, Australian industry scholar Stuart Cunningham concluded that as a result of its efforts, "a taste for Australian television has been established internationally, and producers are increasingly building this into their financing and production strategies."[83]

Not surprisingly, U.S. suppliers and distributors imitate these strategies. For example, as the demand for American series has declined abroad, U.S. companies have developed original programs in other countries or have invested in the production of non-U.S. versions of their series. In 1998, for instance, All American Fremantle International was producing localized versions of the 1950s Jackie Gleason classic *The Honeymooners* in Denmark, Spain, Portugal, Norway, and Sweden, by relying on the scripts used decades ago for the U.S. series.[84] That same year, the now-defunct independent production company Carsey-Werner, which created and produced such hits as *Roseanne*, *Cybill*, and *Cosby*, signed a deal with the U.K.'s ITV network for the sale of format rights of Carsey-Werner's *That '70s Show* in the U.K., to be produced in the U.K. with "an English twist and English cast."[85] In its arrangement with ITV, Carsey-Werner was able to retain almost complete control over the production. Although *That '70s Show* was produced by the British company, Carsey-Werner took responsibility for financial and production oversight, and retained all ownership rights to the new episodes. In this example, Carsey-Werner is not simply seeking maximum advantage in its contracting arrangement in response to global economic constraints. It is also experimenting with new ways to take the programming concepts it owns and adapt them to other cultural contexts.

However, even these strategies involve some of the same kinds of risk and uncertainty associated with conventional export strategies. The all-important cultural discount still needs to be addressed, even when a series concept from one country is produced in the importing country's facilities. Referring to coventures, where partners from different countries collaborate in producing a series, Stuart McFadyen and coauthors concluded,

> We think [our analysis] shows that it is not enough to attend to the cultural distinctiveness of cultural products themselves. Cultural differences also play a critical role in providing an understanding of the process by which such cultural goods are produced. Not only do co-production partners in different countries experience different benefits and drawbacks in the production of feature films and television programs, but there is evidence that many, but certainly not all, of these differences can themselves be traced to the cultural characteristics of each partner and the extent of the cultural difference that exists between the partners of a given project.[86]

In short, successfully overcoming the matter of cultural discount that we discussed earlier requires developing an intuitive sense of what appeals to audiences abroad (and, conversely, what concepts from other countries will work in the United States) and what kinds of collaborative arrangements are viable when partners come from different cultural backgrounds.

Industry participants are to varying degrees sensitive to the cultural nuances involved in these complicated cross-border transactions. Speaking in 1998 of Paramount International Television's plans to develop international partnerships, President Gary Marenzi said, "We are getting to know the best producers in each territory and are matching what they want to do with what broadcasters' needs are in local markets."[87] Marenzi's comments reflect insight about who are likely to be the most knowledgeable and effective informants for creating new programming that would appeal to foreign audiences. In describing the success of Discovery Networks International in markets around the globe, President Dawn McCall stressed the importance of recognizing and understanding regional differences in tastes. Said McCall,

> We could not have achieved the expansion we have by simply throwing our programming up on a transponder. It does not work that way anymore. Local intelligence is crucial, and we always have to forge a local connection to the viewer.[88]

McCall's comments are all the more interesting in that Discovery International exports documentaries and nonscripted entertainment programming, which presumably should have an easier time crossing borders. But in today's sophisticated international market, McCall observes, "Every region has its individual tastes. . . . It seems incredible, really, that such subtlety is applicable to factual programming."[89] To detect cultural differences and nuances from region to region, McCall designed into her business operation a core element that relies upon on-the-ground personnel to do key audience research in their local territories, sound out local advertisers, and carry out focus group missions.

Not all industry participants do their cultural homework, however. In the following extended quotation, Gary Carter of Endemol Entertainment (the company behind Holland's smash global hit *Big Brother*), takes his American counterparts to task for the culturally biased presumptions they carry into business transactions:

> The European format trade is pretty evolved in terms of its customs and practice, and one of the biggest problems that I experience when I'm dealing with American colleagues, both as a buyer and as a seller, is a fundamental misunderstanding about how *our* television market works, and what you as American producers can necessarily bring to the table on our side. And that's a big problem, because it means that there's a lot of explaining that has to go on before our American colleagues understand the bases on which we *can* do business. It's not a question of whether we *want* to do business that way, it's a question of our economic imperatives on our side. So if you're . . . looking to license into Europe, *do* take the trouble to understand the basis on which format trading goes on in Europe because once you start talking co-production and those kinds of things in the sense that you as Americans mean them. . . . [I]t is a fundamental misunderstanding of the position of European producers, and it just mires the conversation down in needless arguing before we all have to say, "I'm sorry, we can't do business like this."[90]

In sum, to operate successfully in the international export market for television, sellers need to adapt their product for use in other locales, and they need to understand how audiences engage television's cultural attributes, deriving pleasures and constructing meanings through aesthetic valuation. Industry participants understand this, with varying degrees of insight and accountability, and formulate a wide range of arrangements that seek to retain creative control and ownership over products while simultaneously adapting them sufficiently to transcend cultural differences.

Thinking Sociologically about the Industry: Going beyond Market Economics

The rich cultural content we see in participants' comments is not adequately captured by most scholarly approaches to the study of international media markets. Understanding the international industry of television as a culture world requires going beyond strictly business considerations such as risk, transaction costs, and profit, and instead focusing upon the forms of cooperation and patterns of collective activity that create television as a cultural product and render it available and accessible to audiences worldwide.

To economists, a television series is merely "an asset consisting of a bundle of broadcast rights,"[91] but it is clearly much more than that. Television is a product that embodies cultural substance reflecting interests and values, it originates in the creative process of writers, and it is evaluated by critics and audiences who apply aesthetic criteria that ultimately determine the fate of individual series. Hirschman describes distinctive features of artistic products that differentiate them from the kinds of commodities that are amenable to conventional marketing principles. They are "more abstract, subjectively experienced, nonutilitarian, unique and holistic."[92] Artistic products are "abstract" and "nonutilitarian" in that they "invoke something other than themselves" and are not valued because of specific tangible features. They are subjective in that they are experienced differently by each consumer and unique in that their creators strive for novelty. Finally, artistic products are holistic in that their value cannot be easily disaggregated into constituent parts. While Hirschman's analysis pertains to principles of marketing as applied to consumers, the same point could be made about the promoting and selling of television series to buyers in other countries.

Schudson makes a further distinction in discussing the issue of resonance, the extent to which a cultural object is relevant to its audience. Schudson says,

> What is resonant is not a matter of how "culture" connects to individual "interests" but a matter of how culture connects to interests that are themselves constituted in a cultural frame. . . . Relevance or resonance, then, is not a private relation between cultural object and individual, not even a social relation between cultural object and audience, but a public and cultural relation among object, tradition, and audience.[93]

By "tradition," Schudson is referring to the customs, rituals, practices, habits, and beliefs surrounding the use and valuing of a cultural product. So, for example, telenovelas, a product originating from Latin America, are viewed in unique ways by Latino families in the United States. Typically, prime-time viewing of telenovelas in the United States is an evening routine shared by all family members. This routine, adapted from practices in viewers' country of origin, takes on additional significance because of its depiction of familiar locales, styles, traditions, and speech. Watching novelas allows U.S.-based viewers to "re-experience that which is familiar," and thus maintain strong cultural and emotional bonds to Latin America.[94]

Thus, buyers and sellers of international television, motivated by profit, must take into account the unique properties of the products they sell, the cultural systems that shape their use abroad, and the complications that arise from doing business across borders. They are operating in a culture world that involves collaboration among individuals with disparate understandings about the cultural product and how it shapes production, distribution, and reception globally. Thus, from our perspective, key questions to ask include the following: How is it that the participants involved in this industry understand what it takes or what it means to do business with cultural products that are produced in one distinctive cultural context and exported, distributed, and consumed in another? What are the practical problems that need to be solved? What are the organizational and institutional mechanisms that are used to solve those problems? How are they enacted and understood in the course of everyday business?

The Matter of Trust

Especially useful here is Granovetter's conceptualization of markets as embedded in social relations, which has been widely applied in the area of relational contracting in labor markets and business-to-business transactions, including international commerce.[95] DiMaggio and Louch summarize his key idea succinctly:

Granovetter (1985) argued persuasively that economic transactions are embedded in social structure. That is, the structure of our social relationships, and not simply a transaction-specific maximization rule, determines our choices of economic trading partners and how we interact with them.[96]

How this might pertain to the international market for television is the question. Without doubt, buyers and sellers of syndicated television are guided by bottom-line concerns; within that constraint, however, embedded social relationships are pivotal to making the industry work. And because the commodity being exchanged is a cultural product, with complex aesthetic properties that resonate differently in different contexts, the challenge of establishing meaningful social relationships among buyers and sellers is especially important. But it can also be particularly daunting.

Illustrating this point in the extreme is *Hollywood Reporter* journalist Steve Brennan's account of the challenge facing Western syndicators who wish to do business in China, where connections, or *guanxi*, are both essential and difficult to establish. Brennan quotes Michelle Sie Whitten, president and CEO of Encore International, a company that acquires programming for and supplies it to China Central Television:

> When doing business in China, there are mistakes that I see being made over and over again. You need strong relationships, but don't think that those relationships will open a million doors. For 5,000 years in China, culture has been founded on connections (*guanxi*), and a lot of people make the mistake of thinking that being in China for a year or two or treating someone to a trip to the U.S. represents *guanxi*. *Guanxi* exists between friends who went to school together or who suffered through the Cultural Revolution together. That's the kind of relationship which seems to supersede all others.[97]

Nevertheless, foreign syndicators are able to establish relationships and do business with Chinese buyers. As Brennan himself notes, "The fact that *Baywatch* airs in Canton is testimony to that."

Somewhat surprisingly, there is not a great deal of scholarly research to draw upon for understanding the interorganizational complexities introduced by cross-national business transactions in the television industry. Paul Hirsch's influential work of three decades ago on culture industries pointed to the key role of product distribution in linking producers to audiences, and the importance of organization middlemen (and women) to the flow of products in the production and sale of popular culture. Then, as now, in a recent revisit to his original conceptualization, he directs attention to the "interconnections and interdependencies" among the firms and individuals comprising industry systems.[98] Although Hirsch's emphasis is largely on the functional organizational elements of culture industries, including gatekeepers and so-called distributor organizations, he also underscores the contribution of individuals in key roles and the actions they take as an important element to the business of culture industries. More recent research by Havens emphasizes the networking function of global syndication conventions and the importance of personalized relationships in rationalizing such a chaotic and unpredictable business:

> The challenges of national, regional, racial, ethnic, and historical differences associated with international trade make it tough for buyers to figure out which imported series will work in their markets. . . . Because buyers function as surrogate consumers . . . distributors can focus their promotional efforts on courting their favor, rather than trying to create programming that appeals to viewers around the world with far-flung tastes. This practice rationalizes the process of international television trade and makes manageable the otherwise insurmountable task of trying to understand the cultural affinities and dislocations between specific national and sub-national groups and specific television series or films.[99]

Referring to the many actors involved in the interorganizational flow of cultural products, Hirsch states, "How this sequence is organized and traversed remains a fascinating forest of power plays and techniques, employed by role-occupants in the same positions as have existed since the advent of mass media."[100] In short, the business of buying and selling is inextricably linked to the nonroutine actions of and relationships among key individuals involved in the process, and in an industry that remains so personality driven, those individuals (such as Rupert Murdoch) come to wield an enormous amount of cultural influence.[101]

Those who buy and sell television programs understand these fundamental facts at an intuitive if not a practical level, and they do business accordingly. Trust is one of the social relationships accomplished through nonroutine actions. Interorganizational trust is widely regarded as a mechanism that economizes on transaction costs among firms that do business in contexts of risk and uncertainty. Organizational scholars consider it a "key enabler" because it increases the predictability of others' behavior and performance.[102] In the international syndication of television programming, trust becomes crucial in surmounting the cultural discount encountered by programs as they cross borders.

In the global marketplace for television, in our view the matter of trust figures in two central ways. The business relationship is one, as participants seek arrangements though which they co-orient to one another's cultural understandings of how (and who) to conduct business with, as we discussed above. Another centrally important one is participants' co-orientation to television's cultural properties, which pose an equally complicated management issue because they are so culturally/symbolically laden and their success or failure so difficult to predict. Although there is considerable scholarly interest in the mechanisms of market embeddedness,[103] very little attention has been paid to the way the attributes of the products themselves contribute to it. Unlike most industries, where product uniformity is the norm and variation tends to occur instead in the arrangements for buying and selling, the television industry, in contrast, deals with a product in which almost every unit is unique. How then are the properties of specific television series understood in the process of buying and selling?

Up to this point our discussion has focused on defining some of the key elements of the culture world of the global market. As we have seen, early scholarship on this media market attended to global flows—broad sweeps of exports—that were able to reveal that some sort of cultural transfer was occurring but offered little else in the way of insight, resulting in unresolvable debates about television's cultural impact. Useful conceptual refinement that has developed since then, and that we touched on in a limited way in this chapter, is increasingly empirical and conceptually nuanced, and yet the field is still marked by an analytical disjuncture that leaves latitude for further unresolvable debate. Our interest in seeing the field move to a more meso-level approach that engages middle-range theoretical concerns relevant to the concept of culture world is guided by our goal of being able to take into account the myriad sources of concrete evidence of the industry's institutional and organizational structures, practices, customs, and modes of operating. These, in turn, open up opportunities for us to observe how culture world participants in the global marketplace directly co-orient around the content of media as a *cultural* commodity.

Television genres and aesthetic elements are central to the challenge of successfully marketing cultural products across borders, and these cultural properties are reflected in the ways in which programs are characterized in brochures and demo tapes, and the kinds of information marshaled for buyers abroad. One would assume that to some extent, sellers have to know how best to frame product marketing itself in terms that not only are understood by those in other cultures but are also meaningful to the way a buyer may want to use the product. But how is that accomplished? In the next three chapters we explore these issues in depth by examining empirically how cultural properties of television, genre and aesthetic elements, and the industry discourse about them figure into the operation of television's global marketplace.

3

The (Continued) Relevance of Genre

I don't think hits are made by genre. I don't think people watch
genre, they watch good shows and I don't think it makes a
difference whether it's a police show or an action show or a game
show or a talk show, people watch good programs. And I don't
think you can say that [a particular show] works and so this
genre works, and so we're going to duplicate it and we'll be a hit.
That's foolish.   —Steve Rosenberg, Domestic TV Production at
        Universal Television Group/USA Networks, Inc.[1]

You have to give the audience what they want. Previous regimes
at Telemundo tried to force-feed programs down the throat of the
Hispanic U.S. and it simply didn't work. We found that what the
Hispanic U.S. really wants is novelas. And so we've given them
novelas at seven, novelas at eight, novelas at nine, novelas at ten,
and they've reacted very well.
   —Jim McNamara, president and CEO of Telemundo Network[2]

From 2000 to 2005, reality shows dominated the world mar-
ket, with *Pop Stars, Survivor, Big Brother,* and *Queer Eye for the Straight
Guy* (among others) successfully adapted to numerous countries around
the world. Reality programming was so popular in the United States
during this time period, particularly among the youth demographic, that
the genre was predicted to alter the economics of the domestic television
industry in fundamental ways. For example, analysts forecasted the end
of traditional seasons on ABC, NBC, and CBS so that these networks
could avoid summer reruns and enhance competition with Fox's year-
round programming philosophy and its top ratings for reality offerings

such as *Joe Millionaire* and *American Idol*.[3] Industry insiders also anticipated fewer orders for comedies and dramas in subsequent seasons, a move that would put both actors and writers out of work. Most significantly, network executives foresaw a radical restructuring of the economic model that has guided network programming since TV's inception, replacing revenue based on commercials with product placement.[4] Indeed, the 2005 introduction of the Fox Reality Channel suggests the entrenchment of reality programming on prime-time television.

But as history reminds us, television tastes and predictions of radical change come and go. To draw on examples from the U.S. domestic market, the rise of daytime talk shows in the early 1990s and producers' efforts to one-up the competition with controversial story premises spurred a series of lawsuits "until advertisers fled and the genre withered."[5] In the late 1990s, newsmagazines were thought to herald industry restructuring as multiple weekly episodes of *Dateline NBC*, *Primetime Live* (ABC), and *60 Minutes* (CBS) dominated network prime-time television, but the genre's popularity declined as swiftly as it rose.[6] Today, the frenzy for reality programming in the United States has been tempered following several ratings flops (e.g., ABC's *Are You Hot?*), flat ratings for the genre's flagship offerings (e.g., CBS's *Survivor*), an increasingly skittish advertising sponsorship, rising costs of production, out-of-control competitiveness on some programs, potentially rigged contest shows,[7] and growing concerns about format piracy. The genre is certainly not dead, as the current success of ABC's *Dancing with the Stars* attests, but the dominance of reality programming was supplanted in the 2006–2007 season by serialized drama thrillers such as Fox's *24* and *Prison Break*, and the big story of the 2007–2008 pilot season is close-ended dramas.[8] This brief historical review and the quotations opening this chapter reflect conflicting industry perspectives regarding the importance of program category for ratings success, and illustrate more broadly the fundamental uncertainty among programming executives as to what makes successful television. As the world market shifts from the import/export of existing shows to coproductions to licensing of formats for local adaptation, what is the continued relevance of *genre* to global television syndication?[9]

As noted in the previous chapter, genres are best thought of as constructs created through social relationships between creators and audiences that delineate the similarities and differences among cultural objects.[10] In terms of Crane's cultural world schema, genre can be thought of as one of the conventions or shared understandings that provide "standards for evaluating and appreciating cultural objects."[11] Consensus between artists and audiences over genre boundaries is probably greater in television than in any other area of popular culture, partly because of the industry's aversion to the risks that accompany innovation and partly because of the audience's preference for familiarity when seeking popular entertainment. Since the late 1950s, the TV industry has recognized two basic genres of prime-time entertainment programming, sitcoms and dramas, with reality shows now accepted as a separate, third genre. (There are, of course, numerous subgenres and hybrid genres of these basic types.) Different genres of programming air at different times in different world markets. For example, U.S. networks' daytime offerings include morning news shows, game shows, talk shows, lifestyle shows, and soap operas, while Japan's feature morning news, cartoons, soap operas, and cooking shows.

In many ways, local television markets, including the U.S. domestic market, seem remarkably genre bound, with familiar program types shaping the pitches that are made (and thus the programs that ultimately air), the organization of industry award shows (e.g., the Emmys, the Golden Globes), and the function of local publicity industries and trade publications (e.g., *The Hollywood Reporter, Soap Opera Digest*), among other factors. Importing markets are attuned to genre as well, as programming executives aim to acquire certain types of programming for specific schedule slots. If a program or format is sold for syndication abroad, publicity industries in export and import markets cooperate with one another to generate cross-border promotional campaigns that help secure local fan bases and increase profitability. This cooperation among publicity machines exists even though there is no necessary relationship between the domestic scheduling and genre identification of a program or concept and its status as an export product (see chapter 5). The world of TV distribution appears much less genre bound as compared to domestic and receiving markets, and as compared to the discourse of genre permeating the industry press and scholarly works. While genre is certainly a component of individual product pitches and promotional campaigns (as will be discussed below), the more frequently heard rhetoric at NATPE, MIPCOM, and other trade conventions focuses on *quality* as the key criterion that facilitates a deal or sale (see chapters 4 and 5). While genre might matter to viewers, as the opening quotations debate, it is "good" programming or ideas that purportedly matter most to those who distribute products on the global market—even though trade conventions "have few pretensions to art."[12]

We explore issues of aesthetics and perceptions of quality television in chapter 4. In this chapter, we focus on the ways in which genre categorizations remain relevant to the world market for export television. More specifically, we are interested in the ways genre is (or is not) attended to in the buying/selling process and the preparation of products for export. In general, we argue that classification by genre continues to be relevant as a *programming strategy* or a means of economic planning for import markets, though it is not an accurate predictor of the local success or failure of imported shows; as a *rhetorical strategy* in the promotion, marketing, and sales of programs and formats on the world market; and as a set of *storytelling considerations* around which domestic producers orient as they create and/or prepare programs for export.[13]

As middle-range perspectives have gained prominence in scholarly writings over the past decade, genre as a method of analysis has been de-emphasized in television studies. However, genre continues to connect "industry, academic, fan and promotional discourses about television: everyone uses some sort of genre-speak when they describe what they make, sell, consume, enjoy, or dislike."[14] We argue in this chapter that the social construction and *fluidity* of genre—as a system of categorization and as an organizer of understandings—are taken for granted in middle-range approaches. Television scholars seem to agree in principle that genres evolve over time and are modified as they are produced and received, but then often simply proceed to treat genre as a static label assigned at the level of domestic creation, to remain attached to a television program/concept/format throughout the import/export process.[15] We argue instead that genre classifications and understandings are dynamic—visibilized, invisibilized, and routinely contested during the process of cultural meaning making.

We explore genre's relevance to the global syndication market by focusing in this chapter on serial narratives as an extended case study, specifically U.S. daytime soap operas, Latin American telenovelas, and other comparable programming. We chose this focus for several related reasons. First, as noted earlier, serials in the form of Latin American telenovelas are the top entertainment television export in the world. The generalized content of the genre is argued to have global appeal, with the shows' narrative structure leaving them open to a wide variety of localized readings.

Moreover, as will be discussed below, serials have historically been important in opening new commercial markets because they allow large blocks of airtime to be filled at relatively low cost. Consequently, serial narratives were central to some of the early debates about cultural imperialism (regarding flows of U.S. prime-time soap operas in the 1980s) and to subsequent debates concerning so-called reverse cultural imperialism (regarding flows of Latin American telenovelas). Serial narratives have also been a central nation-building enterprise in all regions of the world, raising complex questions about the impact of imported television on national identities.[16] Finally, the popularity of serial narratives globally coincides with a sustained decline in the popularity of daytime soap operas in the U.S. domestic market, allowing us to examine the relationship (if any) between different levels of success at different levels of the marketplace. Part of our aim in this chapter is thus to explore local-global connections by examining the extent to which the fate of soaps in the United States is tied to changes in the global TV market.

In the following section we describe the serial genre, focusing on its various global manifestations and its status as an export product in different world markets. We then turn to an exploration of the three ways genre remains relevant to the export market—that is, as a programming strategy, as a rhetorical strategy, and as an essential set of storytelling considerations. In the concluding section we return to the question of the social construction and fluidity of genre categorizations, offering an extension of middle-range approaches that reincorporates genre as a central factor in global television distribution.

Serial Narratives on the Global Market

The major distinction between television *serials* and television *series* is that in a serial, the narratives continue across episodes, often taking weeks, months, or even years to resolve, and the characters evolve and change over time. In contrast, the characters in a series remain fairly stable, with little growth or development, and each episode contains an independent storyline that is typically resolved at the end of the show.[17] Theoretically at least, episodes in a serial must be aired chronologically in order for the narrative to make sense, but series episodes can be shown in any sequential order. The distinction between series and serials has become increasingly blurred over the past decade, with elements of seriality now appearing across a wide variety of television programming worldwide, but the distinction remains important in terms of the narratives' ability to generate different relationships between programs and viewers.[18] For our purposes, it is important to note that the serial/series distinction originates in factual elements of content and/or structure, but the designation or interpretation of a program as one or the other is made by individuals (e.g., producers, distributors, programmers, promoters, etc.) who are engaged in different social networks at different stages of the buying/selling process. The designation, in other words, is socially constructed by individuals who may or may not have the "appropriate cultural competencies" in order to deal successfully with the particular narrative form at hand.[19]

There is a rich diversity of serial forms globally, and the genre itself is increasingly difficult to define. While every serial remains "a product of the culture within which it is made and initially broadcast,"[20] in general terms the genre depends upon "the use of multiple, simultaneous plots, unending narrative strands, the absence of a hero, a focus on dialogue rather than action and the use of domestic and romantic plots."[21] Offering a pragmatic definition that incorporates elements of content, structure, and middle-range factors, Livingstone suggests that television programs classified as serials manifest most or all of the following characteristics:

> They are transmitted at regular and frequent times, often daily. They are aimed predominantly at female viewers, and thus occupy daytime or early evening rather than prime-time slots. They use a fairly constant and large cast and continue for years, building up a faithful audience. They have cheap production values (except American prime-time shows) and are regarded as low prestige entertainment. [Serials] tend to concern the day-to-day activities, the minutiae of the everyday lives of characters who center on a small community and/or large family. They attempt simulation of real time and realistic events, with several interweaving narratives whose resolutions overlap rather than coincide with episode boundaries. They make use of "cliff-hangers" to ensure continued viewing and focus predominantly on female characters and "feminine" or domestic concerns.[22]

This set of criteria accommodates many serial forms worldwide, including U.S. daytime and prime-time soaps, Latin American telenovelas, India's devotional serials, Japan's *oshin* dramas, and Britain's naturalistic serials. Within the criteria, however, there are several useful ways to distinguish serial forms from one another. For example, they can be divided into two thematic categories, one engaging primarily with emotions or melodrama (such as Mexican, Venezuelan, and U.S. serials) and the other engaging more explicitly with social and political realities (such as Brazilian, Colombian, and British serials).[23] They can also be categorized by creative origins. For example, U.S., British, and Australian soaps are rooted in domestic novels and screenplays whereas Latin American serials are rooted in nineteenth-century serialized stories and literature intended for the theater.[24]

Another method of categorization focuses on elements of familial and relational structure. In an ethnographic examination of the diversity and evolution of the serial form in Europe, Liebes and Livingstone studied British, Scandinavian, and European soap operas and identified three distinctive genre subtypes: dynastic serials (focusing on one powerful family), community serials (focusing on a number of equal, separate families and characters), and dyadic serials (focusing on romantic couples).[25] Britain has a long tradition of specializing in community soaps whereas Germany produces all three subtypes. Greece and Italy tend to produce dynastic serials, the Netherlands focuses on dyadic serials, and Denmark, Norway, and Sweden tend toward community-based narratives. As Liebes and Livingstone point out,

> One wonders how accidental this pattern is. . . . [B]oth the choice of a particular soap opera model and the way in which each pattern is elaborated is likely to be dependent on the different cultural settings in which it is produced. . . . [W]hile there are many successful formats available for import across national boundaries, certain choices are made, and these surely reveal the cultural assumptions and audience expectations of a particular nation.[26]

This point is relevant to the global syndication market as a whole, in that it can be difficult to understand why certain styles or formats of programming resonate with viewers in some cultural contexts but not others. The dyadic model, with U.S. daytime soap operas the originator and prototype, became the dominant serial form in the global market in the 1990s;[27] we discuss the implications of this trend later in the chapter.

Most significant for export purposes is the categorization of serials into two main types based on the presence or absence of narrative closure. Continuing (open-ended) broadcast serials originated on U.S. radio in the 1930s and moved to television in the 1950s in the form of daytime soap operas. Today, the continuing format is most closely associated with serials produced in the United States, Britain, and Australia, though it has been copied and/or adapted in all regions of the world.[28] The other main type of TV serial follows a noncontinuing (closed-ended) format, in which narrative closure is achieved in anywhere from fifty to two hundred episodes. Noncontinuing television serials originated in Latin America in the form of telenovelas, with Cuba broadcasting the first in 1952. The novela format remains characteristic of serials produced throughout Latin America and has been copied and/or adapted around the world.

Both continuing and noncontinuing serials sell very well on the global market. Novelas produced in Latin America have a strong presence in Asia, Eastern and Southern Europe, countries comprising the former Soviet Union, and even Israel, where viewers have access to Argentinean programming along with *Novela News*, a 10-minute clip program showcasing the telenovela world.[29] Novelas also serve as a staple of Spanish-language programming in the United States, as will be discussed in greater detail below. The United Kingdom, with England leading the way, has the longest tradition of serial production in Europe, dating from the early 1950s. Germany and England are the most important distributors of serials within the European Union, but European serials are rarely exported outside the region (a fact generally attributed to language barriers and regional boundaries, among other factors). In the Pacific, only Australia and New Zealand are major producers and distributors of serials, with Australia's exports being particularly successful in the United Kingdom and the Pacific. Asian and African countries' presence on the global serial market, to date, remains limited.[30]

Genre as a Programming Strategy

The concept of genre has been a central element in economic planning since the early days of television, in part because (as noted earlier) the industry relies so heavily on imitation over innovation. In a context of ambiguity and uncertainty over what constitutes "hit" television, network programmers rely on genre as a central framing device to legitimize and rationalize their actions.[31] In general, genre classifications serve an economic need by standardizing production and stabilizing audiences. "Genres are production formulas that allow the routinized production of television series and provide heuristics for estimating the potential success of proposed programs based on the success of previous programs in the same genres."[32] From the industry perspective, serials are appealing programming due to their comparatively low cost of production (excepting prime-time serial programming) and their unique ability to generate habitual viewing and a dedicated viewership. In his classic book on the U.S. daytime soap industry, *Speaking of Soap Operas*, media scholar Robert C. Allen writes,

> The economic structure of [commercial] television is predicated upon habitual viewing. . . . The name and superior qualities of a product must be available to an advertiser on a regular and predictable basis. . . . [Therefore], in the soap opera, broadcasters have found the ideal vehicle for the reinforcement of advertising impression, and the best means yet devised for assuring regular viewing. . . . [The genre's] longevity and remarkable resilience derive from its ability to serve the same economic function today it first served nearly a half-century ago.[33]

In addition to providing a strong content staple for local television systems, serials work well as export products by offering considerable benefits to both sellers and buyers. As discussed earlier in regard to entertainment programming in general, sellers benefit in that the monies earned from export are typically pure profit since costs of production and distribution are recouped domestically. The serial genre is particularly attractive to buyers "in a marketplace where national producers—however zealous—cannot fill more than a fraction of the hours they feel they must provide."[34] Important to nations without the infrastructure to produce their own programming, or with limited budgets to purchase all genres of programming, serials offer a large pool of episodes at relatively low cost. Moreover, many contracts allow serials to be broadcast several times each day, "taking up the slack for otherwise empty air space."[35]

Since television's inception, then, serials' good economic value and broad appeal have made them central in efforts to open new commercial markets around the globe. As with other genres of entertainment television, however, serial imports tend to be replaced by local programming as markets mature. One of the first instances of this pattern occurred with the displacement of U.S. daytime soap operas by locally produced serials in Latin America. As has been well documented, television systems in Latin America were originally developed in accordance with the North

American commercial system. In 1947 the president of Mexico elected to model the nation's TV system on CBS rather than the BBC. Due to long-standing trade and investment ties with the United States, most Latin American countries followed Mexico's lead by importing organizational commercial media models from the United States.[36] While relying primarily on U.S. imports to fill schedules in early years, most Latin American countries quickly developed their own inexpensive programming, including variety shows and telenovelas. As noted above, Cuba broadcast the region's first novela in 1952, dominating in early years over Mexico, Brazil, Venezuela, and Argentina, whose serial production also dates to the 1950s. The development of telenovelas lessened the influence of U.S. soap operas, and they slowly transformed into uniquely Latin American products. Telenovelas were key to opening local markets and reducing dependence on U.S. imports, and remain the core of television production and consumption throughout Latin America.

Building on their domestic success, telenovelas quickly became important in the global market. Brazil's TV Globo effectively internationalized the serial form when it exported its first novela to Portugal in 1975. As worldwide demand for programming of all types increased in the 1980s and 1990s due to the expansion of satellite and cable, Latin American production centers (especially in Mexico and Brazil) benefited significantly, and telenovelas became the dominant Latin American TV export.[37] TV Globo was the first company to establish an expansive global distribution network though Telemundo; Venevision and others quickly caught up. Telenovela producers, along with producers of other forms of entertainment television, looked to the emergence of commercial television in Western Europe as offering a prime export market. Major companies such as Globo and Televisa developed new business strategies to sustain foreign program distribution by gaining control over or participating in foreign broadcasts.[38] "The central programming strategy in this all became, more than ever, long running fictional material with the capacity to attract a large audience for a longer time."[39] Telenovela imports fit the bill perfectly, offering good economic value, seriality across a large number of episodes, and generally good technical quality.

As commercial television took hold in the late 1990s, however, Western European nations began moving away from novela imports toward domestically produced television and (to a lesser extent) U.S. soap operas. Continuing their strategic reliance on serial programming, Latin American companies shifted attention to emerging markets in Eastern Europe.

Biltereyst and Meers observe that the situation in Eastern Europe "clearly illustrates the commercial strategy of Latin American producers, who are keen to respond to the higher demand for cheap entertainment. Globo, for example, explicitly chooses to gain a presence with telenovelas in these opening markets; though not profitable in the short term, they prove to be highly profitable in the long run."[40] The profitability of novela imports throughout Europe lies less in high ratings, since they tend to be broadcast in off-peak slots, than in respectable market shares over a long period of time.

U.S. soap operas have also been utilized as part of strategic efforts to open new commercial markets, though they came relatively late to the international scene. Audiences in other countries did not associate U.S. television with serial narratives until the worldwide success of *Dallas* in the early 1980s.[41] It took another decade for U.S. daytime soaps to become viable competitors to Latin American telenovelas, with *The Bold and the Beautiful* (CBS) being the first to attract a major international following in the early 1990s.[42] As of 2005 *Bold* aired in over 130 countries and was the most watched daily dramatic series in the world.[43] Five of the nine daily soaps currently airing in the United States enjoy significant international sales: *The Bold and the Beautiful* (CBS), *The Young and the Restless* (CBS), *Days of Our Lives* (NBC), *Passions* (NBC), and *All My Children* (ABC).[44,45] In most cases, however, their profitability as export products, like that of Latin American novelas, lies in good market shares in off-peak schedule slots. Ultimately, the U.S.– and Latin American–produced serial imports that flooded Europe in the shift to commercialization were more of a short-term solution to fill rapidly growing schedules than a long-term transformation of local programming and viewer tastes.[46]

A final example of the power of the serial genre to open new commercial markets is the prominence of telenovelas on Spanish-language television in the United States. The long-standing insularity or ethnocentrism of U.S. network television meant that viewers rarely saw the diversity of serial forms produced in other parts of the world (see below), but the rapid growth of the U.S. Hispanic population has caught the attention of advertisers seeking to capture their potential purchasing power.[47,48] Cable channels were telenovelas' entrée into the U.S. market because "they have more need than networks for inexpensive imported programming and a much smaller and demographically narrower audience to please."[49] As of this writing, Televisa's Univision is the largest Spanish-language channel in the United States (available in nearly 95 percent of all U.S. Hispanic households), with Telemundo, a subsidiary of NBC/GE, being its close competitor (available in nearly 91 percent of all Hispanic households).[50]

The youthfulness of the U.S. Hispanic population, half of whom are under twenty-seven years of age, has programmers increasingly uncertain about their reliance on imported telenovelas as a content staple. In the mid-1990s Telemundo tried to vary its prime-time lineup by replacing novelas with other genres of programming. As the opening quote by CEO and president Jim McNamara reveals, the move was a ratings disaster. Novelas were quickly returned to the schedule and now comprise about 75 percent of Telemundo's prime-time offerings.[51] But industry insiders continue to voice a need for new programming opportunities for the youth audience. Beatriz Acevedo of HipTV recently argued that while novelas have been successful at targeting older Spanish-speaking viewers and recent immigrant populations, Hispanics born in the United States are not well served by the programming of either Telemundo or Univision.[52] According to Acevedo, the growing population of young Hispanic viewers wants access to different genres of programming both on network television and on Spanish-language channels that resonate with their unique cultural location. Telemundo and Venezuela's Venevision Productions have responded to this challenge by writing and producing more shows in the United States with content that features the realities of U.S. life—programming designed to appeal to a younger audience while still retaining the core audience of older Hispanic viewers.[53,54] It remains to be seen whether serial narratives can buck conventional wisdom by not only opening this new commercial market but also sustaining it over time.

Genre and Promotional Marketing

As noted earlier, genre remains the common language that connects industry, academic, audience, and promotional discourses about television.[55] While we focus attention in the next chapter on the varied promotional materials used to sell products for export (in particular on how the aesthetic properties of programs are marketed), we explore here ways in which genre is attended to in the buying/selling process. For example, genre has been a key piece of information included in product pitches since the early days of television sales. As discussed in chapter 2, the content of pitches has gradually evolved into a standardized body of information about the program itself, including length of program, potential schedule location, basic plot points, and merchandising potential. Genre is a necessary ingredient in successful pitches, whether named explicitly (e.g., "sitcom"), through hybrid reference (e.g., "a cross between action adventure and romantic comedy"), or through now-clichéd reference to other successful cultural texts (e.g., "It's *The Real World* meets Kerouac meets *The Simple Life 2*—in Mandarin.").[56] The annual pitch sessions at NATPE, MIPCOM, and other trade events are highly educational for industry newcomers who find their two- or three-minute pitches interrupted, questioned, criticized, and modified by seasoned insiders. If program genre is omitted by the pitcher, that omission is quickly corrected by the pitch receiver as it remains a key source of information about the product and its potential audience.

The promotion of genre is also crucial to developing a global corporate identity. Suggests media scholar Timothy Havens, "Programming genres and subgenres form the primary product in international television, around which many distributors build their corporate identities. . . . Perhaps the most effective brand identities in international television come from a combination of proven ability in a programming genre and a clear national image."[57] So Brazil gains a reputation for producing quality serials or novelas, Germany is known for action-adventure, and Scandinavia is heralded for its reality programming. Branding is much more difficult for nations and regions "without readily identifiable images or those that do not have expertise in a particular programming genre."[58] While some distributors resist being pigeonholed in this way, the importance of building a brand presence is undeniable.

How is genre made visible in promotional materials? As case examples we look at the online marketing of two U.S. daytime soap operas, *All My Children* (ABC) and *Spyder Games* (MTV), by the Fremantle Corporation; print materials obtained at NATPE and MIPCOM for *The Bold and the Beautiful* (CBS), distributed internationally by BBL Distribution, Inc.; the Australian serial *A Country Practice*, distributed by Southern Star; and the Argentine telenovela *Los Angeles no Lloran* (Angels Don't Cry) from Telearte International.

In its online product catalog (www.fremantlecorp.com), Fremantle categorizes shows by genre, country of origin, and language. At present, twelve broad genre categories are listed: Children/Animation, Documentary, Educational/Instructional, Entertainment, Events/Performances, Fiction/Drama, Film/Telefilm, Formats, Late Night, Magazine, Sports, and Youth.[59]

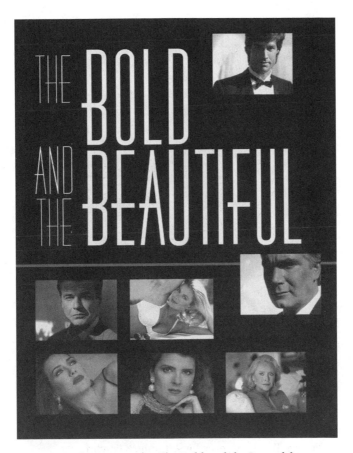

Fig. 3.1. Brochure cover for *The Bold and the Beautiful*

Fremantle features twenty-four products under five different genre headings: Fiction/Drama (n = 5), Children/Animation (n = 6), Entertainment
(n = 4), Documentary (n = 6), and Events/Performances (n = 3). The products originate from the United States, the U.K., Canada, and Australia,
with twenty out of twenty-four being produced in the United States. All
are in the English language. Of the five Fiction/Drama programs featured,
two are designated as "soap operas," two as "films," and one as a "historical drama." One of the soaps is MTV's *Spyder Games*, a 30-minute noncontinuing daily serial that debuted in the United States in 2000; episodes
from 2000 are for sale. The other is ABC's *All My Children*, a 60-minute

Fig. 3.2. Brochure cover for *A Country Practice*

program that debuted in 1970 and continues to air daily in the United States. Episodes from 2000–2003 are for sale. Site links to *All My Children* specify its target audience as teens, young adults, family, and adults (its target audience domestically is women 18–49), and its target gender as both male and female. *Spyder Games*'s target audience is specified to be teen/young adults (similar to its domestic marketing) and its target gender to be male and female. While both shows are designated as soap operas under the Fiction/Drama genre category, *All My Children*'s link further specifies the program as Fiction/Drama/Drama whereas *Spyder Games* is Fiction/Drama/Soap Opera. What distinguishes the two subcategories (or subgenres) is not clear from the online information.

To explore how genre is made relevant in the distribution of products

Fig. 3.3. Brochure cover for *Los Angeles no Lloran*

for export, we reproduce in its entirety *All My Children*'s program description from Fremantle's website:

> The legendary TV success continues! Now in it's [sic] 33rd year, AMC wins top ratings and holds it's [sic] viewers because it's got the hottest characters and the most compelling stories! AMC has won over 30 Emmy Awards including Outstanding Drama Series and, in 1997, it won it's [sic] 4th Emmy for Best Writing. AMC star, Susan Lucci, was nominated 19 consecutive years for Best Actress in a Daytime Series and, in 1999, she won. AMC has shown it's [sic] unique ability to captivate viewers with a blend of social issues, satire and emotional realism. The program has undertaken story lines on abortion, drug abuse, incest and interracial

romance, always in a well-informed and sensitive manner. The characters and storylines of AMC win loyal fans each and everyday as this legendary series, created by Agnes Nixon, continues to define the successful
modern soap opera.[60]

We note here the emphasis on popularity (as indicated by ratings and
longevity), quality (as indicated by awards and award nominations), and
celebrity (through mention of actress Susan Lucci, well known in the
domestic context), among other marketable characteristics of the show.
These emphases are interesting in that, as discussed earlier, it remains unclear how critical evaluation in the domestic context contributes to acceptance by audiences abroad, if it does so at all. Genre is referenced indirectly through the program's continuing serial format (i.e., its thirty-third
year on the air) and through story style and content (e.g., social issues,
satire, emotional realism, story lines on abortion, drug abuse, etc.). Genre
is referenced explicitly through the claim that *All My Children* "continues to define the successful modern soap opera." Only those readers with
a personal viewing history of U.S. daytime soap operas (which may or
may not include potential program buyers) would recognize how *little* the
description of story content and style captures the uniqueness of *All My
Children* compared to other representatives of the genre shown domestically in the United States. [61]

Compare the promotional materials for *All My Children* to the online
program description for MTV's *Spyder Games*, which reads (in part),

> Once again, MTV is at the forefront of a totally new genre in television.
> . . . This is a new kind of entertainment for the MTV generation. In 65
> titillating half hour episodes, each filled with fast, hard, twisting plots, the
> story follows the Carlisle family, owners of the cool "Spyder Videogame"
> empire. The series features all the attractions of a successful soap opera
> or a young telenovela [sic]: there's a murder mystery, sibling rivalry, a
> hot love triangle, an unspoken crush, cat fights, a torrid top-secret fling
> with a hot boy a few years below the legal limit, bare abs and closeted-
> gay action. . . . [This is] an addictive daily series for the young "GenXer"
> audience. . . .

The show is heralded as a "totally new genre in television" and a "new
kind of entertainment for the MTV generation," but with the same "at-
tractions" (defined through story content) as traditional soaps and novelas

—so what makes it new is not very clear. The description is both more specific than that of *All My Children* in its reference to the core family and their line of work and equally nonspecific in its reference to the type of story content that stereotypically (in the U.S. context) defines the serial genre. Most central to *Spyder Games*'s export potential, at least as implied through Fremantle's online description, is its format (noncontinuing, stripped daily) and the association readers will (hopefully) make with its parent company, MTV (e.g., youth, hipness, diversity, etc.).[62]

Promotional materials on display at the annual NATPE and MIPCOM meetings offer additional insight into the relevance of genre to export marketing. Available to anyone wandering the vast convention spaces are tens of thousands of glossy brochures describing programs to potential buyers. Consider a recent brochure for *The Bold and the Beautiful* (CBS) distributed by BBL Distribution, Inc. The four-page brochure includes seventeen photographs, sixteen of which depict characters on the show. The front cover depicts only the title of the show and photographs. The back cover features additional photos with a one-sentence description that emphasizes the show's format (continuing), key characters, and worldwide success: "Since 1987, the exploits of the Forresters, the Spectras, the Logans, and assorted friends, lovers, and foes have made 'The Bold and the Beautiful' a global phenomenon." The lengthier description inside notes the show's fictional setting (Beverly Hills), the wealthy core family (the Forresters), their line of work (fashion), and details about characters and storylines. Compared to the descriptions of *All My Children* (ABC) and *Spyder Games* (MTV), this is a very program-specific description that could *only* refer to *The Bold and the Beautiful* (CBS). Significantly, *Bold* is not marketed here as a representative of the serial genre despite the overt reference to its continuing format. Rather, it is marketed as a television *series* with its genre type unspecified. This potentially allows programmers in the import market greater flexibility in its schedule location and frequency of airing, though it also risks mystifying new viewers if aired out of sequence.

In another example, the flyer for Australia's popular *A Country Practice* features on one side a photograph of a young heterosexual couple, the title of the show, the teaser "A magnificent ensemble cast. . . . A picture-perfect setting . . . and the everyday drama of life in Wandin Valley," and the words "Long Running One Hour Drama Series" at the top of the page. The lengthier description on the back features the show's setting in Wandin Valley ("Fresh air, clean water, friendly neighbors and enough time to stop, catch your breath and enjoy the simple things"), its recognizable cast ("including a few very familiar faces"), a bit of story content ("Whether it's bushfires, vandalism, or just good old fashioned romance, there's always a story to be told and quite a few willing to tell it"), and the show's self-stated "successful formula of 'tears and laughter' as it celebrates the drama of everyday life in the country." Genre is referenced indirectly through the program's continuing format (i.e., long-running) and story content. Like *Bold, A Country Practice* is marketed here as a drama *series* rather than a serial or soap opera.

Finally, the brochure for Argentina's *Los Angeles no Lloran* (Angels Don't Cry) offers yet another example of the way genre is (and is not) represented in international marketing materials. The brochure is six pages long, and its cover is a picture of two adult women superimposed over a softer picture of a woman behind bars. In addition to the title of the program, the cover contains the phrase "Love, Hatred and Revenge." The inside pages include the following synopsis (in both English and Spanish):

> "Angels don't cry" is a captivating story of lonely souls entangled in a web of deceit and fear. The dramatic turning point in the lives of people who belong to opposite ends of society: The arrogant, wealthy upper classes of Buenos Aires; The harsh life of people who make their living at a neighborhood market and the horrors of a prison pervaded of [sic] violence and hate.

This very generic description, which could apply to any number of Latin American telenovelas featuring the familiar tale of love across socioeconomic classes, is followed by a longer description of the plot of the novela —from beginning to end—which includes reference to the primary characters and their role in the story. All of the novela brochures we obtained offer similar plot detail. Promotional materials for continuing serials, in contrast, routinely include information about story content but not in *temporal* language, since by definition they are stories that do not end. The marketing of novelas, then, centers on the overall narrative tale in a way not possible for continuing serials. Most interesting, however, is that the brochure for *Los Angeles no Lloran* does not contain any reference to genre. The length of the show is indicated (180 hours), but nowhere does the word "telenovela" (or "novela" or "serial" or "soap opera") appear. The same holds true in promotional brochures for many other Latin American telenovelas.

These examples offer insight into the function and meaning of genre in television import/export. Of all the ways in which genre might be conceptualized or understood—in terms of program content, format, target audience, narrative structure, visual style, production values, aesthetic criteria, etc.—the two that hold most relevance at the level of global distribution are *content* and *format*. The more subtle differences between serial offerings that local viewers and critics can readily identify tend to be reduced in promotional materials to stock descriptions of story content/plot, length of episodes, and number of episodes available for purchase. The differences between programs are reconstructed, in a sense, through reception and evaluation in new cultural contexts—but is something lost in the process? If so, what? We return to this question in the concluding section of the chapter.

Storytelling Considerations: Local-Global Connections

We are interested here in the connections between domestic and global markets—more specifically, in the ways in which, and the extent to which, domestic producers are oriented toward the world market and the potential for foreign sales when creating programming for audiences abroad. How do business decisions at the local level speak to emergent trends at the global level? We suggest that one of the ways genre continues to be relevant is as a set of *storytelling considerations* around which the domestic industry orients in order to position its products effectively on both the domestic and the world markets. Following the theme of the chapter, we explore this aspect of genre by using the U.S. daytime soap industry as a case study. Soaps have historically served as cash cows for U.S. network television. Despite their low cultural status, soaps' enduring appeal and resulting profit-making potential have consistently paid for other forms of network programming. In recent decades, however, U.S. soaps' domestic ratings have declined steadily, and the daytime industry has begun to reexamine the meaning, boundaries, and adaptability of the genre—including its status as an export product.

We noted in the introductory chapter that central to Cantor and Cantor's early research on global television syndication was their observation that the trade of products internationally was mostly an afterthought to domestic production.[63] That is, U.S. distributors entered the market primarily due to economic changes abroad, not because of an internationally focused business strategy. That changed dramatically, however, with grow-ing industry recognition that "an endless 'ancillary afterlife' [is] now a possibility for all shows. . . . Syndication possibilities and foreign distribu-tion in particular are now always very much on the mind of producers and executives."[64] The U.S. daytime soap opera industry is increasingly oriented toward global sales as a deliberate strategy to counter declining domestic revenues. We begin with a brief description of the current state of the industry and its struggles to retain a dwindling domestic audience. We then discuss four ways the domestic industry appears increasingly oriented toward trends on the world market: (1) through transformations in story content; (2) through transformations in story format; (3) through courting the U.S. Spanish-speaking market; and (4) through local organi-zational decision making.

An Industry in Crisis

Compared to past decades, the U.S. soap industry is in serious economic straits. The genre's popularity has dropped considerably, from an all-time high of nineteen network soaps on the air in 1969–1970 compared to eight currently airing. While still economically viable in the domestic market, with ABC, NBC, and CBS generating about $2 billion in daytime adver-tising revenue in 2004,[65] audience ratings have declined steadily over the past thirty years. The ratings decline was particularly dramatic in the 1990s as soaps lost an average 35 percent in mass, unduplicated household audi-ence between the 1993–1994 and 2000–2001 television seasons.[66] In 2004 alone, marquee shows such as *General Hospital* (ABC) witnessed ratings drops of about 10 percent.[67] The soap audience is also getting older—the median age of viewers grew an average of seven years between 1991 and 2001, making advertisers increasingly concerned about the future profit-ability of the genre.[68] While audience erosion has occurred throughout network television over the past two decades due to increased entertain-ment options, soap operas were uniquely affected in the 1990s by several factors, including increased competition for daytime viewers generated by talk shows and lifestyle shows, extensive daytime coverage of the O. J. Simpson preliminary hearing and murder trial in the mid-1990s (which permanently drove away some viewers), and by ongoing changes in the paid labor market that led greater numbers of women between the ages of eighteen and forty-nine to work outside of the home during the day.

This audience erosion has generated considerable debate in the industry over ways the genre can adapt or evolve to secure its viability in the U.S. domestic market. Compared to prime-time, soaps face unique constraints to developing innovative programming, with a narrower audience, more conservative advertising sponsors, and genre restrictions that emphasize continuity and respect for history over innovation.[69] Given that continuing serials are designed to last forever, and the degree of audience loyalty generated for the characters and communities depicted onscreen can be intense, any significant genre transformations must be more carefully balanced with maintenance of history than is required of prime-time. In the 1970s, the key strategy to attract viewers involved updating narrative content to meet changing viewer tastes. Producers across daytime introduced more socially relevant narratives, younger characters, and more career-oriented female leads in the hopes of attracting new (and new kinds of) viewers.[70] In the early 1980s Gloria Monty, then executive producer of ABC's *General Hospital*, was widely credited with expanding the male and youth audiences for soaps through the introduction of action, adventure, and science fiction elements into the genre. However, these changes did little to address the overall decline in viewership among soaps' target audience.

The increasingly troubled state of the industry has insiders predicting radical change in the genre.[71] As in past decades, some of these predictions involve storytelling itself. Certainly the narratives of the past twenty-five years represent a new and not altogether successful effort to compete with story content available on prime-time and cable, with vampire communities (on ABC's now-defunct *Port Charles*), witches and talking dolls (on NBC's now-defunct *Passions*), and storylines involving gay, lesbian, and transgendered characters (ABC's *One Life to Live* and *All My Children*). Indeed, gay and/or lesbian characters were featured on all three networks in 2006–2007 for the first time in daytime television history. However, industry efforts to sustain profitability have gone far beyond storytelling modifications. Virtually all shows slashed production costs by trimming casts and salaries, recycling sets and wardrobes, and canceling on-location shoots. There have been increased efforts to identify new ways of promoting and marketing the genre, ranging from ABC's strange-at-the-time promotion "Shop the Soaps" (which allowed viewers to purchase jewelry and clothing worn on-screen by favorite characters) to CBS's arrangement with American Airlines to feature its programs in the airline's in-flight magazine.[72] More significant is daytime's increasing use of (or return to) product placement, with Wal-Mart, Frosted Flakes, Nice 'n Easy hair coloring, and OnStar featured in recent soap storylines. Indeed, advertisers are explicitly targeting the genre because of the deeply felt loyalty (potentially experienced over the course of decades) that many viewers have for the characters and communities depicted on-screen.[73] In another move to attract viewers, CBS's *Guiding Light* became the first daytime soap with an accompanying online series with 2002's launch of *Misguiding Light*, and in 2005 became the first soap to offer podcasts. Cashing in on the reality craze, CBS's *As the World Turns* took a different approach; the network just greenlighted the second season of the original Web series *InTurn*, in which aspiring actors compete to win a 13-week role on *ATWT*.[74,75]

Certainly one of the most significant attempts to enliven the genre was the 2000 launch of SoapNet by Disney/ABC. SoapNet offers same-day repeats of *All My Children* (ABC), *One Life to Live* (ABC), *General Hospital* (ABC), and *The Young and the Restless* (CBS), next-day repeats of the same four shows plus *Days of Our Lives* (NBC), prime-time and daytime series from the past (e.g., *Dynasty*, *Ryan's Hope*, *Port Charles*), and other soap-compatible programming. As of February 2007, SoapNet reached about fifty-eight million subscribers, attracting an upscale audience employed in paid labor outside the home during daytime hours.[76] In an effort to appeal to younger viewers (the channel's median age is forty-six), the network recently acquired rights to *The O.C.* and *One Tree Hill*, both of which appeal to a younger demographic, and launched a spin-off of ABC's *General Hospital*. Titled *General Hospital: Night Shift*, the show featured self-contained episodes and younger *GH* actors and characters.[77] Finally, SoapNet has capitalized on the popularity of reality programming with *I Wanna Be a Soap Star*, a contest show with the winning prize being a contract role on an ABC soap. The show just completed its third season.

Orienting toward the Global Market

I don't think that you sit down and write a show or create a show that you think is going to be uniquely suited for Germany or Italy, I think that you have to write a show that is going to appeal to U.S. audiences first and foremost, but there is no question that when you're dealing with the production cost level that hour shows are dealing with now, that you have to consider [the global market]. Is there a way to get additional revenue streams on foreign sales two or three years out? It's very crucial.

—drama producer Dick Wolf[78]

There is a lot of pressure from . . . the business community to cut costs, to pare down the shows, maybe to get rid of the shows that aren't doing well. I don't see a lot of planning and development for new soaps. . . . If that is the case then [*Days of Our Lives*] needs to find new areas of income. The international culture still believes in soaps, even more so than the American culture.

—Ken Corday, executive producer of NBC's *Days of Our Lives*[79]

As the above quotations suggest, while TV producers do not traditionally create programming solely for the export market, in the current economic climate they are motivated to develop programs and program concepts that speak to *both* local and global audiences. Historically, in order for a production company to prepare an existing program for distribution abroad, a fairly predictable series of alterations might occur, from dubbing or subtitling to changing the show's title to better resonate with the import country's value system (e.g., the game show *Family Feud* airs as *Family Fortune* in India, and *The Bold and the Beautiful* airs as *Rich and Beautiful* in Germany) to changing a show's lighting and music to reflect local cultural tastes. While such alterations are still routine, organizational decision making at the local level is increasingly oriented, up front, to the possibility of a globally dispersed viewership. We discuss below four manifestations of this global orientation as it exists in the context of serial production.

One way local-global connections are manifested is through strategic efforts to internationalize (or deculturize) narrative content to enhance portability across cultural borders. The point made by Martin-Barbero more than a decade ago, that "production for a global market implies the generalization of narrative models and the thinning out of cultural characteristics,"[80] continues to hold true today. Without question, the historical success of the U.S. television industry on the world market rests (in part) "on its ability to produce a type of entertainment that appeals to large, anonymous, undifferentiated audiences and that is unencumbered by forms of cultural content that might be an obstacle to portability."[81] As the revenue to be generated from international trade rises, this strategy is increasingly shared by television industries worldwide. Certainly, the debate over whether local industries' orientation toward the world market leads ultimately to homogenization of cultural products addresses all forms of entertainment programming, not just serials. In the U.S. serial context, this strategy is most apparent at CBS's *The Bold and the Beautiful,* the top U.S. soap opera export. Explains Bradley Bell, executive producer and head writer of the show,

> I am definitely aware of our international audience when I develop story lines. Romance—the focus of our show—is the international language. . . . I stay clear of long, drawn-out trials because I think that international viewers may get bored with endless details of how the American legal system works. . . . I don't think comedy translates very well to different cultures, so if we stick to romance and love triangles and love stories, we maintain a broad, universal appeal.[82]

But as with everything else in entertainment programming, this has not proven to be a sure-fire strategy. For example, a similar approach with *Bold*'s sister show, *The Young and the Restless,* did not result in comparable global success. Explains Bill Bell, Jr., of Bell-Phillips Television Productions, Inc.,

> The international market is very unpredictable. Even though *The Young and the Restless* and *The Bold and the Beautiful* are very similar in tone and style, and American audiences see them back to back and occasionally with characters crossing over, the international audience doesn't really know the relationship between the two. Interestingly enough, almost consistently, when one show is a huge success the other show does rather poorly. For example, *Bold and Beautiful* became an undisputed hit in Italy and *Young and Restless* had been on there for years and was always struggling along and never developed a solid audience. . . . We have yet to find a market where both shows are a home run. . . .[83]

Liebes and Livingstone argue that serial producers worldwide are moving toward a singular model of storytelling characterized by the absence of cultural content—the serial narrative as "empty form." As explained above, in their analysis of domestically produced serials in Europe, they categorize programming into three prototypical models: dynastic, community, and dyadic. The dyadic model, originating with U.S. daytime soaps, focuses on a network of densely interconnected, interchanging romantic couples who are generally unaffected by larger social or political realities. They argue that this model, which is not very expressive "of any particular cultural environment," has come to represent the global form of the soap opera, making it "increasingly difficult for nationally produced soap operas to reflect the cultural concerns of their country."[84]

The rise of the dyadic model speaks less, perhaps, to narrative *homogenization* than to narrative *transparency*, with transparency being defined as "any textual apparatus that allows audiences to project indigenous values, beliefs, rites, and rituals into imported media or the use of those devices."[85] To elaborate,

> Transparency is the capability of certain texts to seem familiar regardless of their origin, to seem a part of one's own culture, even though they have been crafted elsewhere. The commercial advantage to a movie or television program of this type is that it has the potential to garner a large global market. [A media product] that lacks transparency has much more limited commercial possibilities.[86]

For example, in his study of a development-oriented radio soap opera in Afghanistan, Skuse finds that producers are deliberately vague in their storytelling in hopes of enabling a very diverse listenership (e.g., linguistically, culturally, and economically) to make their own narrative meanings.[87] In this perspective, the global success of locally produced media products speaks to elements both textual (e.g., polysemy)[88] and nontextual (e.g., foreign policy, media pricing structures, etc.), and the historical dominance of U.S. media on the global market rests primarily on its cultural transparency.[89]

Concern over product homogenization and/or transparency is not limited to U.S. exports alone, as regional markets around the world create programming made for export. In reference to Latin American telenovelas, Biltereyst and Meers observe that there has been a "hybridization and neutralization of the telenovela content for export objectives. Its contingent cultural and national characteristics tend to dissolve into a universal export-formula."[90] For example, the boom of novela production in Miami has been accompanied by the emergence of local classes for telenovela writing and production, including one led by Telemundo. One of their efforts is to train actors in a "neutral" accent to play to the broadest Hispanic/Latino audience possible. Explains a Telemundo spokesperson,

"You can't have a believable show if the mother speaks like a Cuban, the father like an Argentine and their child like a Mexican."[91] Not all serial creators are oriented to the export potential of their programs, of course,[92] and the degree of deculturization that exists in the world market is debatable. However, recent transformations in serial programming produced in major regional markets suggest that we are witnessing a new global soap style, characterized by high production values, appealing visual appearance, quick pacing, a Hollywood-style narrative mode, and an emphasis on melodrama over realism as the dominant narrative style.[93]

In addition to shaping story *content* to enhance portability on the global market, local producers are also attuned to the traditional *forms* in which television programming unfolds. As noted earlier, serial narratives can be divided into continuing (open) and noncontinuing (closed) formats. Continuing stories face challenges as export products, in part because it is difficult to delineate the boundaries of the narrative. Continuing stories are also increasingly incompatible with the needs and desires of viewers in the U.S. domestic market. As soap analyst Joanna Coons noted more than a decade ago, "The pace of life is faster, we want different things, our time is limited and many of us crave a payoff in our fiction—and then we want to move onto the next story."[94] In a recent *Soap Opera Digest* feature, *The Bold and the Beautiful*'s executive producer and head writer, Bradley Bell, was asked if the show's declining domestic ratings were tempered by the show's global success. His reply speaks to perceived cultural differences between the United States and elsewhere that shape viewing habits:

> It does help to know our worldwide audience is still there and very strong, but the U.S. is our most important market. . . . The serial format is embraced differently in other cultures. In South America and Italy, people have more time. We have gotten so busy here [in the United States] and there are so many alternatives. We're so wired with cable, the Internet and satellite that our culture has dramatically changed. But cultures that are more relaxed and family-oriented are where our serial thrives.[95]

Since the mid-1990s, the industry as a whole has begun to replace the traditionally "brain-meltingly slow" pace of U.S. daytime soaps[96] with shorter story arcs guaranteeing quicker payoffs for viewers.

One of the most radical attempts occurred at ABC. The network's half-hour soap *Port Charles* debuted in 1997 as a spin-off of the long-running *General Hospital*. Faring poorly in the ratings since its premiere, *Port*

Charles made an unprecedented shift to a telenovela-like format in March 2000, telling stories in 13-week story arcs or "books." Felicia Minei Behr, senior vice-president for programming at ABC daytime, said at the time that the network planned to bring the new format to all its daytime serials,[97] though that transformation never took place. There are clearly costs and complications with introducing a different genre form into a long-running and established genre concept, including the potential alienation of the domestic audience.[98] The executive producer of *Port Charles* at the time, Julie Hanan Carruthers, acknowledged the risk and potential payoff of "telenovela-izing" the U.S. serial genre:

> I do think there's a value to the short-arc in this genre. I think it's taking it to the next step of whatever our genre is going to end up being. We're still trying to hone in on what works best, not only for the audience with the payoff but also for the show, so that you're not giving people a chance to disconnect, but leading into the next evolution. It's very easy to talk about; it's very difficult to accomplish and get everything we need out of it.[99]

Port Charles's transformation was clearly in response to the show's own poor ratings and the decline of the U.S. domestic soap audience as a whole. However, one distinct economic advantage the new genre form holds in comparison to continuing narratives is its exportability. While the show does not have significant sales outside North America as of this writing (and was canceled in the domestic market in October 2003), its formatting could allow each book or chapter to be exported as a self-contained package. This could have been particularly significant if ABC had followed through with the idea to reformat its entire daytime lineup, since its three remaining serials (*General Hospital, One Life to Live,* and *All My Children*) specialize in the kinds of culturally and/or politically specific topics that tend to be less popular in the export market.[100] Another version of the telenovela-ization of U.S. serials was recently proposed by soap writer Patrick Mulcahey, who suggested that soaps take the summer off, giving viewers a respite from a 52-weeks-per-year viewing habit and generating new enthusiasm for the resumption of storytelling in the fall. Soaps would still be told in a continuing format but with an unprecedented three-month annual interruption.[101]

A local-global orientation is also manifested through U.S. network efforts to court the domestic Spanish-speaking audience so as to better compete with telenovelas airing on Spanish-language television. For example, in attempts to expand the Hispanic audience for *Days of Our Lives* and *Passions*, NBC began close-captioning the shows in Spanish in July 2001.[102] More significantly, CBS's *The Bold and the Beautiful* began simulcasting in both English and Spanish in May 2001, representing the first time a network used Secondary Audio Program (which provides Spanish translation) for a daytime soap opera. The move made *Bold* accessible to almost 50 percent of the Hispanic homes in the United States.[103] As CBS daytime executive Lucy Johnson explained at the time, "We're working to bring [our shows] to the attention of a particular core of the Hispanic audience who we know are already telenovela viewers and are bilingual or English-speaking."[104]

A more intriguing transformation is the emergence of English-language telenovelas in the U.S. television landscape, but in prime-time rather than daytime. While a number of cable networks have aired English-language novelas in the past (e.g., Australia's *Neighbours*), U.S. networks have generally avoided the globally successful format in favor of preexisting genres and modes of storytelling. ABC enjoyed good ratings for the first season of its dramedy *Ugly Betty*, an adaptation of the global smash hit *Yo Soy Betty La Fea*, which originally aired on Colombia's RCN network in 1999. *Ugly Betty* was very aggressively marketed prior to its debut, particularly to Hispanic/Latiño/a audiences.[105] However, the U.S. adaptation has been de-telenovela-ized in at least two significant ways. First, the program airs one night per week despite initial predictions that it would mimic the traditional novela format and air two or three times per week.[106] More importantly, *Ugly Betty* is not designed to be close-ended. Explains executive producer Silvio Horto, "As far as having it be a close-ended show, no. We really want to see this grow, and see her evolve—hopefully for a very long time."[107] A more radical attempt was made by the new Fox-owned U.S. "weblet" MyNetwork TV, which in 2006 launched two all-English telenovelas (*Fashion House* and *Desire*) stripped five nights a week. Ratings were dismal, however, and the fledgling network was forced in a matter of months to switch to programming more palatable to U.S. viewers. Meanwhile, active talk of a prime-time novela at ABC, CBS, NBC, and Fox has died down.[108] Explains marketing executive Derena Allen, "It's one of the big questions of television, why Spanish-language viewers love telenovelas so much, and English-language viewers won't watch them at all. Everybody's trying to figure it out."[109]

At this point it is not clear how U.S. daytime soap operas might be impacted by English-language novelas, if the format ever emerges as a true competitor to daytime.

Finally, a local-global orientation can be manifested in major programming decisions. For example, in the summer of 1999 NBC debated whether to cancel *Sunset Beach* or *Another World* to make room in the schedule for its new show *Passions*. While both shows fared poorly in the Nielsen ratings, *Beach* had been on the air only two years (it debuted in 1997) while *World*, drawing higher total ratings than *Beach*, was a fixture of American daytime television, with thirty-five years of continuous storytelling. In canceling *Another World* the network risked losing a loyal domestic audience as well as its long-standing relationship with Procter & Gamble, the show's owner and one of the industry's largest advertisers. Canceling *Sunset Beach*, which NBC co-owned with Spelling Entertainment, also meant losing revenue. While domestic ratings were low, NBC profited from the show's lucrative foreign distribution. Before final casting of the show had been completed and shooting had begun, Spelling's export subsidiary had already concluded sales of the entire first year of the show to England, France, Germany, Greece, Sweden, Norway, Israel, Belgium, Denmark, the entire Middle East and North Africa, and all of Latin America.[110]

NBC elected to cancel *World* in June 1999 and gave *Beach* a six-month extension before canceling it in December 1999. The network invested instead in the development of *Passions*, which debuted in July 1999 and is wholly owned and produced by NBC. Created by soap veteran James Reilly, *Passions* was designed to be the lead-out for Reilly's popular *Days of Our Lives* (produced by Corday Productions in association with Sony), a slot previously held by *Another World* in most domestic markets. An explicit concern in these programming decisions was to make NBC's lineup easier to promote by broadcasting its programs in a set day-and-date sequence, as ABC and CBS do. (In the mid-1980s NBC began to allow network affiliates to juggle their schedules, which disrupted the sequence.) U.S. viewers of both *World* and *Beach* were dismayed at the cancellations,[111] but they were ultimately profitable business decisions for NBC both domestically and globally. Not only did they allow NBC to promote its domestic lineup more effectively but also, as noted earlier, *Passions* is one of the five U.S. soaps with significant international sales. In spring 2002 NBC closed a deal to export the show to over eighty different countries, including Russia, Yemen, and more than fifty countries in Africa.[112] Unlike the situation with *Sunset Beach*, the profits from this deal benefit

NBC, who produces the show in association with Outpost Farms Production, Inc.

As is evident from these programming decisions, producers' efforts to compete effectively on the world market are necessarily shaped by larger industry ownership patterns. *The Young and the Restless* and *The Bold and the Beautiful* air domestically on CBS but are wholly owned by Bell-Phillips TV Productions, Inc. This means, in part, that the "internationalization" of narrative content can be made at the level of production (not at the network level), with the considerable profit from export sales going directly to Bell-Phillips. Similarly, ABC (through Disney) owns all its own soaps, which allows them to experiment with programming (such as telenovela-ization) in ways that NBC and CBS cannot. NBC's programming decisions, as described above, favored network-owned shows, allowing NBC to operate more effectively in the domestic market as well as to profit from export sales.

Conclusion

We have suggested in this chapter that serial narratives remain an important topic of inquiry in the study of global television syndication. They are the most exported televisual product in the world, and their relatively low economic cost, large number of episodes, wide viewer appeal, and reliable profitability continue to make them attractive import products. They play an important role in programming strategies for opening new commercial markets, but due to cultural discount, quotas, and other regulatory policies, they tend to be replaced by local programming as markets mature (again, this trend is not unique to the serial genre). Serials also remain an important focus of inquiry due to their centrality in ongoing debates around the influence of exported cultural products and the construction of national identities.

More broadly, we have argued for the continued relevance of the concept and construct of genre to television export. Classification by genre remains a central programming strategy (a means of economic planning), a central rhetorical strategy (in the marketing and sales of programs to foreign buyers), and a central set of storytelling considerations around which producers and distributors routinely orient as they create and/or prepare programs for export. In recent years, however, media scholars have argued that the relevance of genre as a mechanism for understanding the world television market is overemphasized by both academicians and the industry itself. One version of this argument holds that genre is relevant to television export *only* because broadcasters and/or the press make it so. According to this perspective, articulated by Steve Rosenberg in one of the opening quotations to this chapter, viewers could care less about genre conventions or classifications—they simply want to be entertained by what they see on-screen.[113]

A related perspective holds that focusing on genre obscures the significance of other middle-range factors (such as scheduling) as more accurate determinants of a product's saleability, its success with local viewers, and the very construction of the meaning of genre as a concept.[114] For example, Bowles argues that recent media scholarship has conceptualized genre in large part on the basis of audience studies: what viewers report they like or dislike in a program becomes the (sole) lens through which genre's meaning is constructed. In reference to serials she writes that

> the study of serial television itself contributed significantly to the shepherding together of a set of textual features which were considered to be hallmarks of the genre—no matter how the results were skewed by the selection of interview subjects and by the interviewers' own preoccupations with particular content. . . . However, there is [another] position, which suggests that soaps are watched not primarily because of their content or sociological accessibility, but because they are conveniently scheduled, and that they were therefore watched by those for whom the scheduling is convenient.[115]

In this latter perspective, serials "as serials" do not have global appeal. Rather, programs that air at 2:00 P.M. (or 4:00 P.M. or 8:00 P.M.) have appeal to various groups of people in various parts of the world who can access television at those times, and since there is a strong connection between program type and program time,[116] what "looks like" genre popularity may be better understood as an outcome of scheduling practices. According to Bowles, analysis of scheduling reveals the "frailty" of genre categorization, "just as it offers a new, market-based justification for it."[117]

To a certain extent, we agree with this argument. Research on the significance of program content to viewers' TV choices offers mixed conclusions. In general, viewers' motivations and tastes do matter in choosing what to watch, but structural features of programming are better predictors of program choice.[118] In addition, research on the success of particular serial programs as export products has demonstrated the importance of middle-range factors for success in local markets.[119] However, we believe scholars who emphasize scheduling to the *total* exclusion of genre as a relevant construct overlook several key points. First, genre loyalty clearly exists among television viewers, as the opening quotation from Telemundo's Jim McNamara attests and as ethnographic and survey research confirms. For example, in his study of programs, schedules, and the viewing preferences of Israeli adults, Cohen found that viewing patterns are best explained by channel loyalty, language loyalty, and genre loyalty, with viewer loyalty much higher in some genres (including serials) than in others.[120]

In addition, we remind that the development of pay television was explicitly structured around niche marketing to viewers' genre preferences for soap opera, sport, music video, cooking, documentary, etc. On one hand, the success of single-genre channels such as SoapNet would seem to bolster scholars' emphasis on scheduling, since the channel allows those who cannot (or choose not to) access *General Hospital* at 3:00 P.M. to access it at 10:00 P.M. instead. On the other hand, however, anyone who has access to SoapNet also has access to dozens if not hundreds of other channels, and thus is choosing specifically to watch a one-genre channel over other televisual offerings. Despite the range of options created by new satellite and cable capabilities, most viewers limit their TV choices to a mere handful.[121] According to Nielsen Media, U.S. households that receive about sixty channels typically watch only fifteen of them; households with the capacity to receive ninety-six channels also watch only fifteen.[122] Channel loyalty does not always reflect genre loyalty, but in some cases it does.

We also suggest that the current focus on scheduling over genre is somewhat misleading in that programmers or schedulers are themselves influenced by their understanding of genre (which admittedly may be a very different understanding than that held by scholars).[123] As Turner points out, "One would imagine that an understanding of the pattern of differences and similarities that help define the individual programme must be built into the strategic structuring of a schedule that will match the competition and maximize audience capture."[124] While Turner goes on to state that there is little evidence that the term "genre" (or an equivalent abstraction) is actually used in the scheduling process, Ellis finds that scheduling grids maintain traditional slots for programs or program types that rarely alter because they are "required by the regulators or are simply habitual. Such arrangements have a great solidity."[125] Our own observations at NATPE, MIPCOM, and other industry events reveal that sellers, buyers, and distributors regularly rely on the discourse of genre in their admittedly elusive search for the "right" show in the "right" time slot for the "right" market. Genre does not guarantee hits but remains a key ingredient in efforts to produce, distribute, and program successful television worldwide.

Ultimately, genre is relevant to the global market for television because it is, in a sense, a middle-range factor itself, though it is rarely considered as such in television studies. Genre classification by content and form (the two conventions most oriented to at the site of distribution) is not static but rather is interpreted, contested, and reinterpreted by many different social actors at many different points in the process of "moving" a program or format from one cultural context to another. Those points include (but are not limited to) local production, distribution, programming/scheduling, promotion, reception, and critical evaluation; dubbing, subtitling, reformatting, or reshaping for export; promoting and selling as an export product; regulatory officiating; and distribution, scheduling, promotion, reception, and critical evaluation in importing markets (see chapter 5). The U.S. domestic soap opera *All My Children* (ABC) is transformed into Fiction/Drama/Drama for the export market, *Spyder Games* (MTV) becomes Fiction/Drama/Soap Opera, *The Bold and the Beautiful* (CBS) and Australia's *A Country Practice* become "series" rather than "serials," and Argentina's novela *Los Angeles no Lloran* is given no explicit genre designation in the promotional materials available at trade fairs. To the extent that gatekeepers are among the industry participants who are actively oriented toward genre conventions in the buying/selling process, those conventions *become* one of the institutional and cultural preconditions for the success or failure of TV programs internationally.[126]

Mittel argues that the "textualist assumption" in traditional media studies (i.e., that genre is ultimately a component of the text) has contributed to the decline in genre analysis: "as cultural media scholars have moved away from textual analysis, genre has been left behind with topics like narrative and style as perceived relics of extinct methodologies."[127] He reminds us, however, that genres are not intrinsic to texts; rather, they emerge from and are constituted by highly *social* processes:

Genres emerge only from the intertextual relations between multiple texts, resulting in a common category. But how do these texts inter-relate to form a genre? Texts cannot interact on their own; they come together only through cultural practices such as production and reception. . . . Texts themselves do not actively link together without this cultural activity. . . . The boundaries between texts and the cultural practices that constitute them . . . are too shifting and fluid to be reified.[128]

Social activities at multiple levels of the global syndication process thus work in complex (and sometimes contradictory) ways to categorize and recategorize TV programs into genres, and this fluidity is central to understanding the movement of television around the world.

4

Managing Television's
Cultural Properties

Content Is Still King!
—2005 NATPE advance registration brochure

Whether the jump in production quality leads to an international
sales payoff for the studios will depend on the capricious tastes of
foreign TV viewers.
—quotation from leading industry journalists[1]

The first quotation, from an advertisement for the 2005 NATPE
convention in *The Hollywood Reporter*, features a recent mantra in the
marketing of American television programming at home and abroad.
Declaring that content is "*still* king" harkens back to when marketing in
other countries meant that the content of a series—its presumed quality
or the universality of its themes—could sell itself as the bread and butter
of the international market. But it also refers to a resurgence in the global
market for U.S. products such as *Desperate Housewives* and *Lost* precisely
because of their local hit status and critical acclaim as an outgrowth of focused attention to narrative quality. Emphasizing the relative importance
of quality storytelling may well be a useful strategy for marketing 2005's
U.S. offerings, but television that is sold for viewing in other countries
typically has to register first with local tastes in order for its appeal to be
understood and rendered marketable to potential audiences elsewhere, as
the second quotation makes clear. How, then, does the industry attend to
the importance of product attributes of television programs as an aspect
of the export/import business? What mechanisms and other devices or
practices do industry participants use to facilitate local receptivity of imported shows? What practical solutions does the industry rely upon to

adapt series for crossing borders? In this chapter we focus on these and related questions in order to explore industry strategies and practices that attend to the cultural properties of television. To arrive at an understanding of these practices, we focus in depth on the aesthetic elements of television's cultural properties. In particular, we focus on what is entailed in transforming, framing, or representing programs as cultural products for airing in other regions of the globe, and what such strategies and practices reveal about the industry itself as it draws upon television's attributes as a resource in the business of television export/import.

Although it may seem unusual for sociologists like ourselves who are studying global television even to talk about aesthetics, our fieldwork at industry conventions and monitoring of the industry more generally found that attending to such factors is essential for attaining a deeper understanding of the organization and dynamics of television's global marketplace. Consideration of aesthetic elements permeates this business in myriad ways. For instance, commentary about "quality" routinely figures into media coverage of program offerings for upcoming conventions, and a key aspect of advertisers' work entails appraising program features in order to price their value. Consideration of aesthetic elements is also necessary, we found, for another important reason: contrary to prevailing criticism of television as an overly homogenized mass culture product whose programs are virtually indistinguishable from one another, product differentiation is, in fact, a characteristic feature of this culture industry, and industry participants depend on information that reliably identifies product uniqueness and differentiates one product from another in their decision making about the thousands of products available.

To casual observers, television programs can appear to be anything but different from one another. One need go no further than to count the many knock-offs of the U.S. daytime hit *Judge Judy*, the weak imitations of prime-time's audience-grabbing *Grey's Anatomy*, and the similarities across the 2005–2006 season's aliens-focused *Invasion, Threshold*, and *Surface* to make the point, and it is relatively easy to segue from there to complaints about how unoriginal and (thus) lacking in aesthetic value much of television is. While undoubtedly true in some respects, such hasty appraisals close off understanding of the role of proven success in a culture industry like television. In short, imitating or recombining elements —"copycatting"—is prevalent because it functions well as a strategy to attract viewers who have already established a taste for a particular style, content, or format, much as in other culture industries, such as fashion.

In France, for example, locally produced detective series such as *Jug et Flic* created a taste among French audiences for similar shows, opening the door to U.S. series that include *CSI*, *Without a Trace*, and *Law and Order: Criminal Intent*.[2]

What is important to understand in considering the function of imitation in relation to the aesthetics of commercial culture industries like television is that it does not preclude the potential for innovation or novelty, or the search for quality. Indeed, as we have discussed earlier in this book, sufficient novelty is essential in the midst of so much imitation, precisely so that viewers *can* differentiate one show from the next but still know that they can expect to be entertained as they make program or series selections. Typically, novelty originates from creative workers within the industry as they search for new series concepts or produce an episode, although scholarly analyses of other commercial media such as popular music, romance fiction, and children's books indicate it can also be directly affected by changing audience expectations.[3] Our point here is that television programs are by necessity sufficiently different from one another, within the constraints of given genre conventions, so that they continue to attract the interest of potential viewers within constantly evolving cultural tastes and preferences.[4,5] The way product differentiation, or distinctiveness, is understood and managed, often within the confines of established genre conventions, effectively complicates the business dynamics of the global television market, and that is what we focus on in this chapter. As we shall see, the management of differentiation in the sale and purchase of products in this diverse and complicated marketplace goes a long way toward explaining how the characteristic "chaos" of the global market becomes more systematized, or at least more routinized.

Valuing Product Differentiation

Economists who study the transactions of cultural products in arenas like the global market for television typically equate product uniqueness, its infinite variety, with desirability, or the value of what a buyer (such as a country or a satellite distributor) is willing to pay to air a program in his or her locale. Particular attributes, properties, or qualities that differentiate one series from the next, such as a series' subject matter, its production quality or techniques, or its longevity, contribute to the infinite variety of products, and these become important considerations in the

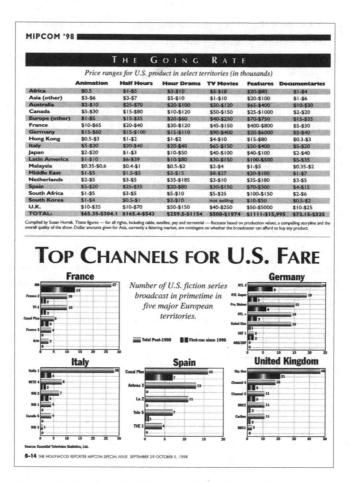

Fig. 4.1. Going rates for U.S. product in select territories, 1998

calculation of relative value or "rent" that may be extracted at the auction of programs in the marketplace.[6] Program value, or rent, sought by sellers is affected by factors we have explored in earlier chapters, such as genre or the celebrity of the actors in the series, and these in turn contribute to demand; the considerations that go into demand are, in turn, further complicated by the social, political, economic, or cultural contexts in which product appraisal is undertaken by buyers.

"Going-rate" rents that program producers/sellers would like to obtain are provided for market participants in industry trade publications as the opening date of an international television convention approaches, and they offer starting points for negotiations between program buyers and sellers. By way of illustration, figure 4.1 presents the list of such rates in thousands of dollars for U.S. products in selected territories in advance of the 1998 MIPCOM convention.[7] Figures 4.2 and 4.3 present more recent lists for MIP-TV that reveal the cyclical nature of the market.[8] But if one were to examine these illustrations no further than the asking price provided in the rate lists, one would have a relatively incomplete understanding of the underlying complexity that product differentiation brings to the business of this marketplace. Although going rates offer interesting detail about some of the sources of variation in relative value among particular products or across specific regions of the globe, they are merely a point of

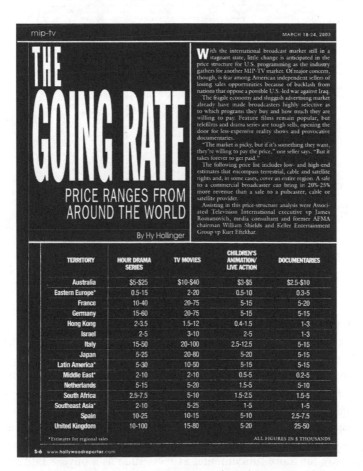

mip-tv — MARCH 18-24, 2003

THE GOING RATE

PRICE RANGES FROM AROUND THE WORLD

By Hy Hollinger

With the international broadcast market still in a stagnant state, little change is anticipated in the price structure for U.S. programming as the industry gathers for another MIP-TV market. Of major concern, though, is fear among American independent sellers of losing sales opportunities because of backlash from nations that oppose a possible U.S.-led war against Iraq.

The fragile economy and sluggish advertising market already have made broadcasters highly selective as to which programs they buy and how much they are willing to pay. Feature films remain popular, but telefilms and drama series are tough sells, opening the door for less-expensive reality shows and provocative documentaries.

"The market is picky, but if it's something they want, they're willing to pay the price," one seller says. "But it takes forever to get paid."

The following price list includes low- and high-end estimates that encompass terrestrial, cable and satellite rights and, in some cases, cover an entire region. A sale to a commercial broadcaster can bring in 20%-25% more revenue than a sale to a pubcaster, cable or satellite provider.

Assisting in this price-structure analysis were Associated Television International executive vp James Romanovich, media consultant and former AFMA chairman William Shields and Keller Entertainment Group vp Kurt Eftekhar.

TERRITORY	HOUR DRAMA SERIES	TV MOVIES	CHILDREN'S ANIMATION/ LIVE ACTION	DOCUMENTARIES
Australia	$5-$25	$10-$40	$3-$5	$2.5-$10
Eastern Europe*	0.5-15	2-20	0.5-10	0.3-5
France	10-40	20-75	5-15	5-20
Germany	15-60	20-75	5-15	5-15
Hong Kong	2-3.5	1.5-12	0.4-1.5	1-3
Israel	2-5	3-10	2-5	1-3
Italy	15-50	20-100	2.5-12.5	5-15
Japan	5-25	20-80	5-20	5-15
Latin America*	5-30	10-50	5-15	5-15
Middle East*	2-10	2-10	0.5-5	0.2-5
Netherlands	5-15	5-20	1.5-5	5-10
South Africa	2.5-7.5	5-10	1.5-2.5	1.5-5
Southeast Asia*	2-10	5-25	1-5	1-5
Spain	10-25	10-15	5-10	2.5-7.5
United Kingdom	10-100	15-80	5-20	25-50

*Estimates for regional sales
ALL FIGURES IN $ THOUSANDS

S-6 www.hollywoodreporter.com

Fig. 4.2. Going rates for U.S. product in select territories, 2003

between the lines [April 11-15 Cannes] APRIL 5-11, 2005

THE*GOINGRATE*

Price ranges for U.S. TV product in selected territories

By Hy Hollinger

Prices for U.S. television programming are holding up as the international broadcast industry continues to recover from the crisis that plagued the first few years of this decade and century. Networks and stations around the globe are showing profits for the first time in years, advertising revenue continues to increase slowly, and new technology is helping to advance or develop new revenue sources for buyers and sellers of content.

As MIPTV 2005 gets under way, Germany is still on the comeback trail, Russia and Eastern Europe are becoming more active in the TV marketplace, Latin America is stabilizing, Japan remains highly selective, and the stalwarts of Europe — the United Kingdom, France, Italy and Spain — remain willing buyers of the "right" product. In addition, the weak U.S. dollar can be a tremendous help to U.S. sellers when deals are consummated.

Still, making a sale usually is extremely difficult. U.S. sellers say they are facing one of the most selective markets in years as they encounter stiff competition from local

programming, reality formats and homegrown cultural-content pressures.

Prices are not an overriding factor in the TV marketplace because they largely "depend on how badly (buyers) want a show," according to one veteran seller. The BBC, for example, is reported to have bid $3 million recently for a six-hour Sci Fi Channel miniseries.

The estimated prices listed below are ranges for all rights and uses including terrestrial, cable, satellite and pay TV. They are meant to be negotiation starters and in no way carry official status. It should be noted that some shows cannot find buyers in all markets, and some fail to make a single sale.

Territory	Hour Series	TV Movies	Children's Animation/ Live-Action	Documentaries
Australia	$15-$40	$20-$60	$5-$10	$2.5-$12.5
Eastern Europe*	10-40	10-30	2.5-10	2.5-7.5
France	15-60	25-75	5-15	5-20
Germany	20-60	25-75	5-15	5-15
Hong Kong	3.5-7.5	3-7.5	1-2.5	1-3
Israel	2-5	3-10	2-5	1-3
Italy	20-60	25-60	2.5-12.5	5-25
Latin America*	15-50	25-75	10-20	5-15
Middle East*	5-10	5-10	1-5	1-5
Netherlands	10-25	15-40	2.5-7.5	5-10
South Africa	2.5-7.5	5-10	1.5-2.5	1.5-5
Southeast Asia*	20-40	20-50	2.5-10	2.5-10
Spain	20-40	20-40	5-15	5-15
United Kingdom	25-150	25-100	10-30	15-50

*ESTIMATES FOR REGIONAL SALES   ALL FIGURES IN THOUSANDS

24 www.hollywoodreporter.com

Fig. 4.3. Going rates for U.S. product in select territories, 2005

entry because of the many other factors that can come into play as buyers evaluate programs for purchase and seek adaptations for their particular programming needs.

In conducting our fieldwork at television conventions, we found that quantifiable information such as the expense associated with the production of big-budget A-list series, robust audience ratings, commanding advertising rates, and even schedule placement and network promotion budgets can be crucial to a potential client's willingness to consider going rates, as are far more fundamental aspects such as a buyer's budget. Note, for instance, the important additional qualification in figure 4.1 that going rates in 1998 "are contingent on whether the broadcaster can afford to buy a product" and in figure 4.3 for 2005 that rates "largely depend on how badly [buyers] want a show." But we found these considerations to be, in fact, merely indicators of far more elusively represented attributes or qualities of a show—its aesthetic elements—and that such elements themselves are crucial to buyers' appraisals of a product's desirability. Consider the comment by Hans Seger, one of Germany's chief program officers in attendance at the 2005 MIPCOM convention, about the upsurge in interest in U.S. products after years of disinterest in his country: "It started last year with *Lost* and *Desperate Housewives*, where we saw a real jump in quality—in the storytelling and in the production look. The money was on the screen."[9] In short, attributes by which quality can be perceived and registered are important to a series' desirability, even though they may be less apparent to the casual observer. Thus, television's aesthetic elements —its production values, storylines, and overall quality of a show—are not only central to differentiating the infinite variety of products available; they are also central to their product valuation by buyers and sellers. Note also how genre, which we discussed in chapter 3, is included among the illustrative details, in particular that the rates listed are organized by genre and within genre by country. But most important for our purposes here, these illustrations capture the caveat that going rates may vary according to the properties or qualities of a particular program's aesthetic elements. To routinize business in the global marketplace, these aesthetic elements have to be managed systematically like other product features, and in the remainder of this chapter we examine how such matters are represented, utilized, and transformed for the international import/export market.

The Aesthetics of Television

Television critics and scholars have understood the medium's artistic potential ever since it was commercially launched in the late 1940s.[10] Calling for greater insight into the aesthetics of television, industry scholar Horace Newcomb identified three distinguishing features.[11] Observing that television is "something more than a transmission device for other forms," Newcomb clarified, first, that the medium's small screen (compared to the cinema's) and its embeddedness within the household create a distinctive sense of *intimacy* or direct involvement between the viewer and the characters and plots; second, that the *continuity* generated by the episodic structure of series facilitates a density of character and plot more characteristic of literature; and third, that the medium's reliance upon social issues for its stories embeds viewers within a sense of *history* that foregrounds personal and other local concerns. Taken together, these features of television are instrumental to fostering an engagement by the viewer that is intimate, intense, and emotional.[12] Since Newcomb's initial observations of over three decades ago, the venues in which television viewing takes place have expanded considerably because of advances in distribution technology, and there are now many more forms of nondomestic viewing that also include geographically dispersed locations. Media studies scholar Anna McCarthy characterizes television as "ambient" in presence because of this expansion in viewing options and venues.[13] Regardless, in our view, whether reception takes place among members of an informal group in an airport, dormitory, bar, or prison, or via video-on-demand on one's personal computer, cell phone, or other device, and whether its transmission is via satellite beamed to another country or is time-shifted through a DVR or a TiVo recording, the features of the medium of television identified by Newcomb remain the same, underscoring television as "a community of imagination" constituted by "a common *affective* [emphasis added] tie and not merely as a common and therefore immediately visible instance of media consumption."[14]

Compared to other aspects of television and the more established medium of film, far less has been analyzed about the connection between television's aesthetic properties—its visual and aural compositional elements—and the way television entertains. Aesthetics is "knowledge of [a cultural object's] qualities in their immediacy and their immediately grasped relations," and aesthetic analysis is the demonstration of the relations among elements comprising a scheme or "structure."[15] The field of film studies, in contrast to that of television studies, has established that a film image is "a complex function of its visual qualities (composition, angle, lighting, screen size, camera movement, etc.), the content of the image (acting, stars, iconography, etc.), its juxtaposition to surrounding images, and the context of the narrative."[16] Along with "ever-enlarging contexts, such as the conventions of a particular genre, of film generally, and of the time in which the film is made and in which it is viewed," these elements contribute to the social construction of meaning among audiences.[17]

Film is based on self-contained narratives that achieve closure, and the visual action that conveys the story is technically photographed frame by frame. Arguably, that very aspect of the medium, its characteristic construction through individual, sequential frames, is central to the analysis of film as an art form. The compositional elements of each frame and their visual interrelationship lend themselves readily to formal artistic analysis, much as one would approach analysis and interpretation of a painting or a photograph; thus, principles from art history and art criticism provide many of the theoretical bases for film's aesthetic interpretation, with consideration of perspective, foreground, background, lighting, and shading lending further insight. This composition of frame elements in space and time, and the cinematography that captures the movement of these elements across a span of film, is under the creative control of the director (perhaps in interaction with a cinematographer), and for that reason film is widely regarded as a director's medium (and relatedly, it is why auteur theory, which credits the director as the chief creative agent in a film's production, long dominated the discipline). Another, central aspect of film's aesthetic is its viewing context. By taking place in the "sacred" space of the darkened theater (or through a "personal appointment" with a VCR or a DVD player), film viewing is segregated from the mundane activities of everyday life. The distinctiveness of this constructed setting sets the aesthetic experience of film viewing apart from the experience of other media and positions the viewer as a spectator who, distanced from reality, becomes subjectively embedded within the narrative and action onscreen.

Television, in contrast, is a producer's medium.[18]

> Coordinated by the television producer, guided by the television director, and with the work of the crew (floor manager, lighting engineers, camera operators, audio engineers, microphone operators, switching operators, etc.), the various production techniques in lighting, framing, editing, and sound are achieved. . . . The television production principles are generated by the cooperative effort of the television production crew and are unique to the medium.[19]

Given the time constraints in which television is produced—an hour a week for a prime-time show and five episodes a week for daytime television—and budgetary constraints imposed to maintain its profitability, there are limited opportunities for creative workers to consistently inject unique stylistic features. Another chief difference between the medium of film and television is television's format—its episodicity and its ongoingness—which foregrounds the importance of creative control over the structure of the unfolding narrative across a broadcast season and the years a series is in production (if a series has acceptable ratings or audience demographics). Responsibility for implementing the concept for a television series into ongoing action falls on its producer, who is usually the writer who created the concept on which the series is based. Typically, this individual is appointed to the lead staff position of executive producer, the "show runner," who oversees a series' implementation by its production team.

Other pertinent differences between film and television are that its technology—the videotape on which television is recorded and the electronic equipment used for its production—are constantly evolving, and that television's moving images are created and framed electronically, line by line, at the very moment of enactment (rather than as a historic photograph of action captured frame by frame on segments of film that are later edited together). As an artistic form, television's production also differs from that of film in that it is largely studio bound, and while film to a considerable degree is also produced indoors, television's technology introduces particular constraints on visual movement and setting that are consequential to its "look."[20] In particular, television's characteristic studio boundedness, its camera's small visual angle and resulting trademark use of the close-up, reliance on multiple cameras to capture, or construct, narrative action, and the origins of the medium in live, real-time production have become its defining features.[21] Consequently, the aesthetic elements of line, shape, and color predominate in television's visual impact.[22] Each of these features delineates television's capacity as an art form, which, Metallinos observes, is further affected by the small size of its display monitor,[23] its editing techniques, the fact that most viewing occurs in personal or domestic settings, and the fact that television is more of a visual than an auditory medium (industry insiders told us that a plot has to be understood with the sound off). In short, television's aesthetic properties, including the form and content of its on-screen action and as well as its production techniques, are consequential to the kinds of narratives that can be effectively told by the medium because they so profoundly affect *how* they are told.[24]

Finally, unlike with film, the experience of viewing television usually takes place in a domestic or a similar quotidian setting, as mentioned above, and these mundane aspects of viewing affect the kind of viewer-medium social bonds that form and shape the way it is experienced as an art form.[25] Because of television's embeddedness in domestic life, its inter-ruptability by those routines, and viewers' control over when, and how, they drop in and out or otherwise engage the medium, the aesthetic expe-rience of viewing television is on the one hand intimate and personal and on the other hand completely casual and undifferentiated from the ac-tivity surrounding its screening.[26] Thus, the continuous flow of television programming as its scheduled airing unfolds—a defining insight from es-tablished television scholar Raymond Williams[27]—furthers the indetermi-nacy of viewing by blurring the boundaries of its narratives, any acuteness of its visual or aural properties, and its separateness as a fictional illusion. Newer forms of distribution and the shift to video-on-demand (VOD) only heighten this fundamental indeterminacy. As television scholar Ruth Lorand succinctly put it, "TV reigns in a disordered territory,"[28] and its transcendence is hard won. However different the medium of television may be to that of film, it is nonetheless produced by creative workers and experienced as an art form in its own right with aesthetic properties that are both central and consequential to its purchase and sale.

Of particular relevance to our focus in this chapter is the way tele-vision's distinctive properties are recognized and managed—made acces-sible for product appraisal and valuation—in the export/import market for television. In our usage here, "aesthetic elements" refers to the unique features of series that industry personnel identify as enabling resonance with local audiences. It is well known that audiences derive pleasures and construct meanings through aesthetic valuation of television's attributes, and they form appraisals about the worthiness of programs as entertain-ment on the basis of prior experience. Industry participants understand this with varying degrees of insight and accountability, and they formulate a wide range of arrangements to retain creative control (and ownership) over products while simultaneously adapting them to attend to or tran-scend cultural differences. How, then, are television's aesthetic elements made accessible for global buyers so that they are able to assess a pro-gram's potential to engage local audiences, garner ratings, and generate revenue?

The Salience of Aesthetics to the Global Marketplace

We begin our discussion about aesthetic elements by considering their role in the global success of three syndicated series: the game show *Who Wants to Be a Millionaire?*, the reality series *Pop Stars*, and the adventure drama *Xena: Warrior Princess. Who Wants to Be a Millionaire?* was launched in the United States in the summer of 1999 and became the first highly successful game show on American prime-time television since the late 1960s. Although game shows were popular fare on prime-time during television's very earliest days, a series of quiz show scandals in the 1950s all but eliminated the genre from the evening schedule. Despite the successful revival of game shows in the 1960s, audience preferences changed and the genre disappeared once again, not resurfacing until *Millionaire* aired as a summer replacement program on ABC thirty years later.[29]

Millionaire is a program format imported from England. Originally developed by Great Britain's Celador Productions for airing on the ITV network in the U.K. in 1998, it was brought to the United States by Michael Davies, then an executive vice-president of alternative series and specials at ABC. Recalling his reaction to seeing the British version for the first time, Davies said, "I thought it was flat out the best television program that I had ever seen. No exaggeration."[30] Commenting on ABC's plans to add the program to its regular prime-time schedule in January 2000, Stu Bloomberg, ABC Entertainment Television Group's cochairman declared at the time, "This November *Millionaire* moved beyond the realm of hit program and became a cultural phenomenon."[31] By 2000, the format had been exported by Celador to at least thirty-one countries worldwide[32] and, by 2002, to more than eighty countries.[33]

In order to maintain creative control, the owners of *Millionaire* stipulated that certain aesthetic features must be "almost identical" wherever the format is produced. These features included use of the same music, set design, lighting, and action. Specifically, the *Millionaire* imagery included "dimmed lights, suspense-charged sound effects, and sleek pods where the choice of answers flashes before contestants' eyes."[34] The only variation allowed was the language and the host, who is always local.[35] In India, where the program was broadcast in Hindi, the show became so popular that it virtually emptied the nation's streets when it aired.[36] One explanation for its widespread appeal there, according to one local expert, was its " 'slick' factor—and the fact that it has normal people. Just regular, fairly unglamorous people who get the chance to win, and everyone loves winning."[37] But that alone does not account for its local success. According to Steve Askew, executive vice-president of programming for Hong Kong–based Star TV, "it's not about the money."[38] Crediting the format as a programming innovation for India, coupled with a lucrative advertising campaign, Askew attributed a great deal of the show's success to its host, Amitabh Bachan, who is one of India's leading film celebrities. For many viewers, the opportunity to see him in the intimate milieu of the television format was key to their interest in the show.

Who Wants to Be a Millionaire? was also a ratings hit in the Middle East. The aesthetic attributes that made it one of the most popular programs among Arab audiences in this region of the globe was its explicit use of politics as content for the show. The Arabic version of *Millionaire* was produced by the Saudi-owned MBC satellite station at a studio in Cairo, and it was hosted by former journalist George Kordahi, who covered the civil war in his native Lebanon. Kordahi made Arab politics a condition of his employment as host: "His show promotes pan-Arabism in its questions, asking contestants about politics and sports in the Arab word and about Islamic culture. Questions drawn from the Koran and Islamic history are commonplace. Though Kordahi is Christian, he peppers his patter with verses from the Muslim holy book."[39] This approach greatly endeared him to his Arab audience, which elevated him to celebrity status in large measure because of it. Known also for his designer suits (an aesthetic element of the show that replicates that of original U.S. host Regis Philbin) and for his culturally specific interactional style, he was able to cultivate "an immediate personal connection with his guests because of his warm manner and questions about their families and professions."[40] Clearly, Kordahi's style was instrumental to adapting the format to local customs and audience interests, which in turn contributed to his popularity. But it was his advocacy of the political ideology of the Palestinian cause that garnered him celebrity status within the region and made the show a hit there. In short, that ideology provided a meta-narrative that quickly turned a program permeated with Western values about winning money into a transcendent cultural experience. Viewing that achieves transcendence is consistent with Newcomb's observation that resonance with the audience's social and personal history is key to successful narrative aesthetics of television.[41]

A final *Millionaire* illustration is the adoption of its format by Mexico, with varying success. There were two such adaptations in that country, neither licensed from the U.K. format. One known as *A Millon* was an original production of the Hispanic TV network, Univision. The other—produced by Univision's competitor, Telemundo, and titled *Numeros Rojos* (meaning "In the Red")—strayed too far from the format concept (reportedly, it relied on contestants battling each other in competitive games) and did not last more than a few months. Both Univision and Telemundo tried to "graft the emotions of the Latin American soap opera, the telenovela, onto that North American favorite, the get-rich-quick game show, to create must-see TV for the 32 million Hispanics in the U.S."[42] Univision's more successful entry relies upon a set that reproduced the American version in features, quality, and design. To underscore that the goal is winning money (however melodramatically that goal is framed), the producers created a predominantly green color scheme, and contestants entered the stage over a bridge that spans an ocean of oversized dollar bills.[43] However, it was the casting of contestants and the visual representation of their reasons for participating that made the show a successful adaptation to Hispanic culture. Specifically, the show links contestants' dreams of winning cash to their aspirations for transforming their lives. This is noteworthy given that themes of bettering one's life socioeconomically and romantically are the most common narratives of telenovelas. In order to frame contestants' reasons for participating as culturally appropriate, the program would air a taped segment that illustrates the difficulties of their lives before the competitive portion of the show begins.[44] This touch of melodrama would be carefully balanced so that contestants' aspirations did not exceed what they might win in the game. Casting director Daniela Romo explains, "We don't want too much drama, like a woman that needs a million dollars for a heart transplant. What if she only wins $1000? People might think we are soulless."[45] To play it safe, financial needs would be frequently tied to culturally approved aspirations for families, including struggles to meet household expenses or to start a family business.

Of course not all attempts at format adaptation are successful. Japan's version, known as *Quiz $ Millionaire* and produced locally by Fuji TV, who acquired the rights, struggled despite the long-standing rule of thumb among Japanese programmers regarding imports for their country —that a program that is a hit in the United States is in all likelihood going to be a hit in Japan.[46] However, in this instance Japanese tastes and morals intervened. Although the look of the show was executed as prescribed, its premise and aesthetic elements were uninteresting to Japanese audiences. "It seems that watching ordinary people winning money isn't very enticing in Japan, a culture that has traditionally discouraged individuals from flaunting their wealth or achievements."[47] Adapting the format to Japanese game show conventions meant limiting cash winnings to token levels (which are curtailed by the country's antitrust laws) and utilizing celebrities who don't need the income and who know how to generate the kind of buffoonish antics and oddball events that register as game show humor in that country. Explaining its low ratings, the editor of Japan's TV monthly *Galac* said, "Americans may really identify with somebody winning big bucks on TV, but Japanese are more apt to think, 'What did he do to deserve that?' "[48]

Each of these case illustrations describes, to varying degrees and in varying ways, the contribution of aesthetic elements such as set design, lighting, and action (alongside content) to the success of a program format or concept. Moreover, they reveal how aesthetic elements interact with cultural preferences and expectations of local audiences—social customs, manners, norms, and practices—and just how consequential cultural milieu can be to local acceptance of them. In short, analysis of aesthetic elements per se, whether alone or in combination with others, can explain a great deal about the successful translation and adaptation of format concepts to other locales.

Emotional Resonance Generated through Aesthetics

While our study of the global marketplace underscores the importance of aesthetic elements to a format's success with audiences, our research also found that they are significant in less apparent ways. As we noted earlier, industry participants understand that programs have to resonate emotionally with local audiences in order to be accepted.[49] What is noteworthy, however, is the extent to which industry participants' *own* emotional resonance with a series' aesthetic properties plays into their decision making in buying and selling. We draw upon case materials from two international hits—*Pop Stars* and *Xena: Warrior Princess*—to illustrate this.

One of the most popular NATPE business panels in recent years focused on the international success of the reality/soap opera *Pop Stars*.[50] The concept for this series is simple: thousands of young women sign up for open auditions, which are conducted with brutal honesty on air, in the hopes of being selected as one of several finalists who then go on to form a new pop singing act. Once selected, the new group is signed to a recording contract and then is followed through professional training and career development en route to doing a concert tour and making an album, which hopefully (for the artists and producers) will be a financial hit. *Pop Stars* originated in New Zealand, became a hit in Australia, and has since been sold all over the world (the original U.S. version was broadcast on the WB network in January 2001, with imitators like *Making the Band* and *American Idol* appearing on other networks in the United States). Des Monaghan of Screentime Pty Limited in Australia is credited with picking up the worldwide rights to the series and pitching, commissioning, and further developing the concept that turned into a global phenomenon.[51] According to Monaghan, the series was conceived by an (unnamed) "guy watching his young teenage daughters aping what they saw on a top-ten show [and who thought that] there must people all over the world who share this fantasy of being pop stars." After the creator took the idea to Essential, a New Zealand production company, the series was launched there on a budget that Monaghan said could only be described as "minuscule or less."

By Monaghan's account, *Pop Stars* was probably the most successful show on the TV2 network in New Zealand in 1999. Toward the end of its run there, Monaghan's firm heard of it, and instantaneously "loved" (his word) the show, because "like all successful formats, it's essentially very simple. It allows the opportunity for fantasy to become reality." In accounting for its universal appeal, he explained, "what's extraordinary is so many people share this fantasy of being a pop star." After examining the New Zealand version and admiring the effective product they had produced on almost no resources, Monaghan determined that to take it to larger, more demanding markets his company needed to "expand the initial premise of the show and create an event." So, in large measure through his efforts, the concept turned into "a much more complex operation than merely the show itself" and is now "a genuinely multimedia event." Upon acquiring the distribution rights, Monaghan pitched the series to the Seven Network in Australia, who quickly picked it up. States Monaghan, "The interesting thing about *Pop Stars*, wherever it's been taken in the world, is everybody [understands] it."[52]

Following the involvement of key intermediaries in the global market, Scott Stone and David Stanley of (the now-defunct) Stone Stanley Entertainment, an independent production company in Los Angeles, became interested in acquiring rights for production in the United States. Prior to the sale of the *Pop Stars* format to Stone Stanley, the major Hollywood studios monopolized the business of licensing formats and acquiring broadcast rights from abroad for production in the United States. The sale to Stone Stanley was a first because it entailed a format owned by an independent producer and sold to a small U.S. producer/distributor that only then entered into a production agreement with a major studio/network, the WB.

What made this deal possible when prior industry practice favored large, established studios? In this instance, and in the case of *Xena: Warrior Princess* (see below), the emotional resonance generated through the aesthetics of production provided a convincing counter to the business uncertainty generated by the inability to predict a successful series. In short, industry participants also rely upon indicators of success that go beyond standardized "hard" measures such as proven ratings and projected revenues to include subjective perception of the emotional authenticity of a program as a key factor in the decision-making process of buying and selling television. That authenticity may originate from the characters, the narrative, or the quality of the writing, or may be identified in visual, action, or other formal aesthetic elements of the program. As a resource in decision making, it is variably articulated by industry participants. Indeed, we found that while these criteria are frequently mentioned by industry insiders, they are not systematically utilized or documented. Instead, they are conveyed through verbal interaction that emerges from a readily understood co-orientation for identifying potentially successful shows. Although not one of the so-called hard market considerations, it is nevertheless an essential component of the business of buying and selling television.

How did emotional resonance play a part in the selling of *Pop Stars*? After acquiring licensing rights, and in order to sell it to the WB Network, Stone Stanley Entertainment worked on revamping the show's production values to make it "more appealing" in look, feel, and sound while preserving its basic concept. Stated David Stanley about the considerations that went into adapting the concept for the U.S. market,

> I think the only thing that's really significant from my perspective is that we took a format that really worked, that's really about real stories of these people who show up, and make sure you don't lose any of that feel, of really feeling that you are participating in the process and understanding the emotion in telling the stories. But then we tried really hard to step up the production values. We added a lot more graphics . . . lots of color, lots of backgrounds, lots of depth of field to make sure things look the way

we wanted. When we got into post-production we made sure we added lots more music than existed in the original show. We [added] things that just made it look and feel more like an American television show than just a documentary. And the trick was to add all those things to the show without taking away from the essence of it.[53]

In short, Stone Stanley felt that while the format was effective, the Australian version lacked visual and narrative impact. Such comments reveal the extent to which the look and pacing of a show are part of the aesthetic elements that are central to acceptance by local audiences abroad (as we noted above). In the case of the U.S. version, the goal was clearly to intensify the representation of drama, and thus the emotional impact of the show.

In another example, the international success of *Xena* was attributed during a NATPE seminar to several aesthetic factors: quality of visual impact, good production standards, and the emotional resonance generated by authenticity of character.[54] A key consideration for Dan Filie, senior vice-president of first-run programming at Universal Television Group/ USA Networks, Inc., in acquiring the series was its ability to capture the natural beauty of New Zealand. With an eye to the bottom line, he stated, "You get a jillion dollars worth of special effects just from nature there." Expanding on this point, series creator and executive producer Robert Tapert explicitly linked aesthetics to emotional resonance: "The scenery and the look is something that we could not reduplicate anywhere else and that brings a whole texture to the show that gives it an inviting and appealing feeling." Another important aspect of the show's "look" is the period costumes worn by the characters, although the producers acknowledge that in this instance they do not strive for historical accuracy (and, presumably, whatever viewer interest this visual element generates) but only for "what works for the [camera] lens." These aesthetic elements contribute, in turn, to the emotional impact Tapert strives to achieve in each episode. Some episodes, according to Tapert, are "dark ones that bring a tear to the eye" while others are "comedy that makes [the audience] laugh." For him, the range of emotions as well as the unpredictability of the kind of story that appears from week to week are central to the way he engages the audience. To Ned Nalle, president of Universal Worldwide Television, Universal Television Group/USA Networks, Inc., *Xena's* international popularity is attributable to compelling characterization. "The stories come from the characters; that's what makes the show so relatable," he said. Finally, many people associated with the series believe its emotional resonance is directly related to its exportability. States Lucy Lawless, the actress who plays *Xena*,

> We do bring stories with heart. And whether people know it or not, the fact that they feel something when they watch our goofy shows keeps people coming back for more. . . . [T]he same things that make a French person feel make a Turkish person feel. [The show is] huge in the Philippines. And that's what matters. It's the same concept as sex appeal in advertising, that people feel something, they don't even know it. . . . We aim to make you feel every single episode. . . .[55]

Clearly, aesthetic elements and the emotional resonance they generate are recognized and understood to be central to the international success of this series. But in an interesting development, the panelists differed among themselves about the importance of aesthetics relative to genre in the series' success. Perhaps not unexpectedly, for writer/producer Robert Tapert, genre was key to the genesis of the series. Recounting how he wanted to do a female superhero show "for years and years and years," and needing an innovative spin for the American audience, he settled on giving "the hero a bad past [and putting her] on the road to redemption" as the way into the character. Senior vice-president Dan Filie essentially agreed with Tapert's view, stating, "TV is kind of like an x-ray and the audience kind of gets to know who the person is. . . . And part of the success of *Xena* is even though she has had this horrible past as a character, you can see goodness in her. . . ."

However, in the matter of whether genre or aesthetic properties matter more in the appeal of a show (whether domestic or international), industry opinion is divided, as we saw in Steve Rosenberg's view, which was quoted at the beginning of chapter 3. From his vantage point as president of domestic television distribution at Universal Television Group/USA Networks, Inc., aesthetic properties clearly carry more weight, at least in the syndication market:

> What makes [*Xena*] work is that it looks great, it has terrific writing, it cuts through the clutter. In first run syndication, you've got shows running in time periods all over the map. . . . You don't have the benefit

of national promotions so that people can find you. And so you need to have a show that cuts through the clutter. And it doesn't matter what genre it is, people are going to watch good programs.[56]

Michael Eigner, executive vice-president and general manager of WPIX-NY, the WB affiliate in New York that was instrumental in bringing *Xena* into production because of its agreement to air the series in such a major viewing market, agrees with Rosenberg: "In [the] fantasy [genre], the key is bringing fantasy to life . . . through the special effects and through the scripts, they have really brought these shows to believability and life."[57] The sharp difference of opinion captured here coincides in interesting ways with the social location of industry participants within the culture world of the television industry. To network executives like Eigner who are concerned with the bottom line, "quality" matters, however undefined its measurement may be. To creative personnel like Rosenberg, a series is a cultural object classified and managed according to given properties. The larger issue, given our interests, is to what extent these differences are significant to collaborative activity within the culture world of the international market for television.

Managing the Chaos of the Global Marketplace

Up to this point our discussion has relied upon case illustrations of discourse among industry participants to illustrate the relevance of television's aesthetic elements to its export/import and adaptation to other locales. In our analysis of the relevance of genre to the global market, discussed in chapter 3, we found that genre content and format are paramount in classifying syndicated series for industry participants. Undoubtedly, these criteria facilitate important business considerations as program buyers make determinations about the suitability of a series for a particular slot in their network's program schedule.[58] Our finding that genre is fluid as a classification device in the global syndication market does not, however, undercut the significance of aesthetic elements to the global marketplace. Rather, we argue that it is precisely *because* of genre's fluidity that the relevance of aesthetic elements moves to the foreground for classification purposes. At television marketplaces, where the allure of television programs is reduced to "just so much product" to wade through, as former *Los Angeles Times* television critic Brian Lowry made clear when writing about the 2000 NATPE convention,[59] aesthetic elements are engaged to represent a program's distinguishing features, its quality (for example, whether "the money is on the screen" technically, visually, aurally, or in the acting or production team), or the distinctiveness or uniqueness of a series within a well-defined genre like soap operas or telenovelas when other bases for product appraisals recede into the background. Among other things, aesthetic elements signal to potential buyers the audience demographics a program might appeal to, which ultimately assists in scheduling considerations associated with a purchase. Although scheduling is a matter sellers have very little control over, it is vitally important to both buyers and sellers alike because program placement is crucial to a show's ratings success, and thus the revenue it is able to generate.[60]

To investigate the importance of aesthetic elements of programs in the marketplace relative to genre, we examined their use in a key industry source—production company program brochures. As printed artifacts of the industry, these documents provide institutional traces that reveal how the import/export market draws upon television's less tangible, more subjective properties to manage the chaos of the marketplace. As tangible artifacts of this market, sellers' brochures encapsulate pertinent aspects of a series for ease of assimilation by buyers from diverse cultural backgrounds. These complex documents rely upon a combination of text and photos to describe creative as well as commercial considerations in a way that effectively captures the visual and textual features of the series, and sometimes even of the medium itself.

Promotional Brochures

As was mentioned in chapter 3, promotional materials at the annual NATPE Conference and Exhibition and the MIPCOM Conference include literally tens of thousands of glossy brochures describing programs to potential buyers. One of the most readily apparent ways in which television's aesthetic properties are represented for selling is through these high-quality, low-tech handouts, which are available at virtually every seller's convention booth. Effective brochures are ones that systematize representation of already-produced television programs along established conventions of production while at the same time indicating the uniqueness or distinctiveness of individual programs. Some are two-sided single sheets of glossy, expensive, quality cardstock, while others are very costly multipaged brochures. We sampled brochures from two conventions, the

1998 NATPE and 2004 MIPCOM conventions, that were provided by producers and distributors of telenovelas and, in addition, a subset of those from other genres that included dramas, sitcoms, reality, action-adventure, game shows, and miniseries.[61] We intentionally selected these genres for analysis in order to represent different geolinguistic regions of the globe—the vibrant Latin American market (Argentina, Brazil, Mexico), Eastern Europe's emerging one (Bulgaria), the Asian/South Asian arena (Japan, China, Australia), and the well-established Western European field (Spain)—among others. Because of our particular interest in the contribution of soap operas and telenovelas to the global market, our examination of these brochures distinguished between telenovelas and all other genres to isolate distinguishing features of the Spanish-language soap operas so as to see whether use of aesthetic elements differs within this well-defined genre. Table 4.1 summarizes the main details of the brochures themselves.

Brochures routinely identify a show's production and distribution companies and, to a lesser extent, its sales representative, and like expensive brochures included in the press kits that were once provided by the domestic U.S. industry for advertisers,[62] they also routinely identify key creative and production personnel, even characters. It is interesting to note, however, that while all brochures may include this kind of information, the telenovela brochures are *more* likely to provide it than those of all the other genres. Reputation of production personnel evidently matters in the import/export market, especially in the marketing of products within a well-defined and widely recognized genre like telenovelas, which are intended for a particular audience and where differentiation among individual products is a must. Interestingly, the *explicit* identification of genre among the *non*telenovela series, while still salient as a classifying device, becomes just one more element in an array of descriptors that lays out technical information for network programmers. In short, the fluidity of genre in the global marketplace affects the *extent* to which it is utilized as a classifying resource by production companies relative to other elements for distinguishing among offerings in the marketplace; moreover, we would argue that the relative importance of these aesthetic properties may also be relevant "downstream" at the level of local scheduling, something we explore in greater detail below.

Consistent with the visuality of the television medium, the pictorial aspects of promotional brochures are also very important to the process of

TABLE 4.1
Promotional Brochure Features $(N = 97)^a$

	Telenovelas[b]	Other Genres[c]
Production features		
Production company	100%	95%
Distribution company	100%	59%
Int'l sales representative	11%	22%
Actors	96%	66%
Director	89%	37%
Writer	88%	37%
Characters	75%	34%
Producer	52%	44%
Descriptive features		
Genre	57%	27%
Series length	54%	68%
Episode length[d]	54%	37%
Number of episodes	52%	46%
Brochure cover		
Photo dominates	80%	73%
Text dominates	9%	0%
Photo/text ratio even	11%	27%
Explicit int'l appeal	5%	7%
Description of series narrative: market factors		
Business appeal	18%	46%
Genre twist	20%	29%
Int'l/transnational appeal	16%	25%
Int'l reputation(s)	16%	39%
Program qualities	50%	71%

[a] We collected 59 brochures from the 1998 NATPE convention and 38 from the 2004 MIPCOM convention, for a total of 97. There are 56 telenovela brochures (44 from NATPE, 12 from MIPCOM), and 41 are other genres (all from MIPCOM). The number of pages in any given brochure ranged from 2 to 12, with the greatest number made up of 4 pages (n = 28).

[b] Telenovela brochures came from the following countries: Argentina (8), Brazil (28), Columbia (3), Mexico (10), Peru (1), United States (5), Venezuela (1). The following production companies are represented: Azul (1), Leda Films (1), Telearte (6), Globo (27), Caracol (4), TV Azteca (10), Aloma (1), Venevision (4), Tepuy (1).

[c] Other genres include action-adventure, animation, comedy, drama, dramedy, game show, mini-series, music, reality, serial, situation comedy, and soap opera. Brochures for the other genres came from the following countries: Argentina (9), Australia (9), Brazil (5), Bulgaria (2), China (1), Mexico (4), Spain (1), United States (10). The following production companies are represented: Azul (1), Beijing Yingshida TV Program Exchanging Center (1), Bell-Philip (1), Bulgarian National Television (2), Carsey Werner Mandabach (8), Divisa Home Video (1), Globo (5), Planet X Studios (1), Southern Star (9), Telearte (8), TV Azteca (4).

[d] Episode length for telenovelas ranged from 30 to 60 minutes; for other genres the length ranged from 30 to 60 minutes, with one at 14 minutes.

selling television because they not only represent but literally capture the aesthetic qualities of the programs themselves. Photos, not surprisingly, are the key feature of brochure covers, as we see in the examples provided. Text that is composed explicitly to describe the series is used far less extensively or not at all on the cover; neither is text in combination with a visual aspect much in favor for covers. Visuals feature actors in character (wardrobe, hair, setting, etc.) either singly or as an ensemble, actors in their "actor" personae, action shots from the series, actors posing with secondary actors/characters to depict genre-specific entertainment (e.g., a man surrounded by scantily clad women for a Mexican game show), and the like. Of particular interest, however, given our focus on the role brochures play in managing the export market, is that the explicit visual depiction of a series' international appeal is minimal. Although the absence of such visuals may be related to the expense of producing these brochures for this market, the upshot reaffirms what we found in our analysis of genre in chapter 3—that strategies for the *targeted* international marketing of existing programs are not extensively developed ahead of time, most series being, after all, just local programs. In short, the marketplace leaves the particulars of any possible appeal of a series in other regions or countries to resonance with buyers' instincts and intuition.

In contrast, aspects of transnational or international interest are far more likely to be mentioned explicitly in a brochure's *text*—in the description of the series' narrative or its production aspects (such as locations or soundtracks)—and these flag its distinctiveness, which could potentially attract international audiences and garner ratings. Some brochures feature information that is decidedly relevant to business considerations, as in the claims of these two:

> . . . the proven international bestselling action-adventure . . . family audiences around the world will delight. . . . (Australian Southern Star's action-adventure, *Bugs*)

> Produced with no limits on expenses, this delightful comedy will take viewers through an amusing story developed in the typical Northern Argentine landscapes and coloured by beautiful songs that will teach them daily lessons in love. (Argentina's Telearte comedy, *Flavia*)

Some hint at genre twists, as in this example from a telenovela brochure:

> An intimate story that none of us has had the opportunity to view "through the keyhole." *Mirada de Mujer* is different, of the present time, its [sic] unbearable as only a mirror can be. (Mexico's TV Azteca telenovela, *Mirada de Mujer*)

But somewhat surprisingly, on the whole, textual aspects that might explicitly appeal to international/transnational possibilities are not that heavily utilized, although when they are included in program descriptions, they tend to refer to series with already-proven global track records. Explicit reference to international reputations of personnel associated with a series, when they are mentioned, tend to highlight those of the actors in the cast instead of other behind-the-scenes production or creative personnel (see chapter 5). But of all the other marketplace-relevant indicators routinely included in program brochures, by far the most widely used are those that feature attributes that announce a show's distinctive and unique aesthetic elements:

> Fresh and innovative comedy, supported by a talented cast . . . unique blend of humor, music, and adventure makes for this story an entertainment like no other. (Argentina's Telearte comedy, *Maria Sol*)

> Music is "skillfully arranged" . . . everybody who discovers our land and our roots will be touched by our strength. . . . (Bulgaria's Bulgarian National Television music program, *Bulgarian Roads*)

Telenovela Brochures

Earlier in this chapter we described how the medium of television fosters an engagement by the viewer that is intimate, intense, and emotional. Our consideration of genre in chapter 3 revealed genre's malleability as a mechanism for selling programming, and our discussion to this point about the relevance of aesthetic elements indicates their centrality as a marketplace mechanism in the context of genre's fluidity. Telenovelas are a clearly delineated product genre, so clearly delineated, in fact, that they have become national brands; in addition, as a genre they are widely recognized as *the* staple of emotion and melodrama that many regard as the ultimate in intimate and intense viewing.[63] Thus, telenovela brochures can provide an interesting means for exploring in greater detail the relative importance of aesthetic elements compared to genre. When genre is a given, what is the role of product differentiation?

We separately analyzed the subsample of fifty-six telenovela brochures. By focusing specifically on the brochures for telenovelas, we are able to see more clearly how a series' particular aesthetic elements come into play in the marketplace. Telenovelas are well known for their high literary quality and reliance upon prominent writers, casting of established or highly regarded actors, emphasis on melodrama, and ability to appeal to all audience demographic groups.[64] Our analysis revealed that visual components of telenovela brochures prominently featured these aspects, and that these components comprised the following categories: stills of actors in character/costume (61 percent, n = 34), stills of dramatic scenes from the series (55 percent, n = 31), headshots of actors representing their character's persona (45 percent, n = 25), depictions of character dyads (30 percent, n = 17), stills of actors in character overlaying scenes from the series (20 percent, n = 11), and ensembles of the cast (13 percent, n = 7).[65] Each of these components, especially those used most frequently, conveyed crucial information about the type of story—including whether the narrative is historical or contemporary or whether the action is psychological or physical. The less frequently used category of characters overlaying scenes was, in fact, highly illustrative of the dramatic impact the audience could expect from the narrative; although used sparingly, these depictions signaled to buyers key scenes in the series. Visual components of the brochures also conveyed the social strata of the characters, the location of the story (e.g., a rural or urban setting; an affluent, middle-class, or impoverished household), whether the story focused primarily on female or male characters, whether it included religious, political, or cultural themes, or whether it emphasized the network of characters' interrelationships or focused instead on a few pivotal characters. In short, visually representing the characters' personae, the amount of dramatic action or other key events in the narrative, the characters' interrelationships, and locales or settings signals to buyers the audience the serial would be most likely to attract.[66]

In the international import/export market, where differences in language, pacing, story content, and other culturally specific elements must be surmounted for products to cross the borders of geolingistic regions, visual elements are crucial for conveying information, even for established genres like telenovelas. However, representation of aesthetic properties can prove necessary even *within* geolinguistic regions (for example, Asia or the Middle East) or in regions bound by a common language. For example, until recently there was little program exchange between Latin America and Spain, in either direction, due to colloquialisms and other linguistic differences. These extend to differences in cultural sensibilities that affect the content of programs in all aspects. Media journalist Lucy Davies explains:

> Brazil's involvement in the region is hampered by the Spanish-Portuguese language dissimilarity and a myriad of cultural disparities. Its more liberal attitude towards risqué and violent programming puts it at odds with its more conservative Spanish-language counterparts in the region. . . . Style and pacing also differ. According to [Horacio] Levin, [president of Buenos Aires–based Promofilms, a strategic partner of Madrid's Globo Media], Spanish programming tends to be slower in pace and delves deeper into its subject matter. Latino shows, on the other hand, are faster and lighter in content. They also tend to be shorter.[67]

Although telenovelas from Latin America once commanded a prominent place on Spain's prime-time schedule, according to Davies they eventually fell from programmers' favor and were relegated to less desirable early morning time slots throughout the 1990s—until recently, that is, when they experienced a resurgence in popularity that industry participants attribute to "improved aesthetics, marketing distribution platforms, and technical updates."[68] Perhaps this resurgence is due in part to solutions sought between Mexico and Spain that entailed efforts to develop coproductions between the two countries, a business strategy that would address cultural differences up front in order to assure programming that is acceptable to both. But, clearly, quality also matters, even in a well-established genre in high demand globally, and for individual series to catch the attention of buyers, that quality has to be adequately represented in the marketplace in order for buyers to differentiate among the myriad choices. A leading telenovela executive observed, "If you have a good telenovela, it will sell. If you don't it won't. Buyers are very sophisticated."[69] Short of that, the aesthetic representation of a series produced solely by one country or production company provides important indicators of the suitability of a program, even one within a well-defined genre.[70]

If visual and other aesthetic elements are crucial, even in a well-defined genre, how salient are they when genre is less clearly delineated? In short, very important. Consider, for example, the 2002 Columbia Tristar International Television insert in the convention publication *Television Europe*, which relied upon evocative descriptors as subject headings for groups of otherwise dissimilar series. "Always Proven" encompassed prime-time ratings leaders *Family Law, Dawson's Creek, The Guardian,* and *As If,* while

"Always Laughing" included the prime-time sitcoms *Just Shoot Me, The Tick, The Steve Harvey Show,* and *The Ellen Show.* "Always Sexy" listed the syndicated action-adventure *Sheena* and the Pamela Anderson vehicle, *V.I.P.,* as well as the daytime soap operas *The Young and the Restless* and *Days of Our Lives.* "Always Amazing" included several niche cable series —*Mysterious Ways, Strong Medicine, Ripley's Believe It or Not!,* and *Doc* —while the last category, "Always Daring," included the prime-time series *Rampart* and *Pasadena* and the daytime talk show *Ricki Lake.* These categories were genres (if one could call them that) devised on a very loose notion of similar program content. Format, the other genre element we found in chapter 3 to be important to framing television for export, appeared to be far less salient, with Columbia Tristar's shows seemingly grouped more by the imagination of the marketing department than by any established categories (to wit: a daytime talk show was included with canceled prime-time soaps, and daytime soap operas were included with provocative prime-time series that feature nearly naked female leads). More significant, however, was the importance of visual and other aesthetic elements for creating and representing similarities across these constructed categories. While "Always Proven" depicted the casts for the series in this category as ensembles, with the groups conveying a serious or somber tone, and "Always Laughing" showed the lead actor or actors in casual poses with warm smiles, "Always Sexy" (which included two daytime serials and two prime-time series) depicted the female leads of the series either in minimal attire or projecting a seductive gaze as they encircled their male partners. It is noteworthy that each series in this latter category has very different audience demographics in the United States; for example, daytime soaps draw predominantly female viewerships, while action-adventure series draw a predominantly male audience.

Aesthetic elements—however intangible or subjectively perceived—are a vital resource in the marketing of series for export abroad. When genre is fluid, aesthetic elements become important in marketing a show. When genres are well-defined and bounded, like telenovelas, aesthetic elements move to the foreground in differentiating among products. When genres are constructed just for the marketplace, aesthetic elements link disparate shows together. Like genre, such elements are carried through the process of transporting products across borders, providing important signals to buyers as they consider a program's placement on local schedules or how it can be locally publicized in order to draw in viewers.

Program Guides

As a final example of how the global industry relies upon programs' aesthetic elements as a resource to manage marketplace chaos, we observe an aspect of this culture world that occurs far from the trade floor and convention booths and close to the point of actual audience reception —the local television program guides. Program guides are considerably downstream from the marketplace, in many respects the last stop in the distribution flow of marketplace positioning. However, it is their position of being so close to the point of viewer/audience selection that makes them a compelling coda to our discussion of aesthetic elements. What form does the market's seemingly pervasive reliance on aesthetic elements take at the point of direct audience contact?

Program listings come in many forms. Increasingly, networks or their affiliates provide them online, but many still exist in weekly magazine form, either as independent publications or as regular inserts to local newspapers. Here, too, aesthetic elements of television are foregrounded. We purchased as many program guides as possible,[71] and while our opportunistically devised collection is hardly a random sampling of such publications globally (an all but impossible task to accomplish), the individual guides are remarkably consistent in what they emphasize. The covers, without exception, feature actors from selected television series. Film theorist Richard Dyer has identified the ways in which actors are themselves socially constructed cultural texts, their public personae being part reality, part fantasy, woven together from the cultivation of an actor's persona within the confines of the particular social and historical period in which he or she lives.[72] Historically, actors have figured centrally as commodities in the global marketing of Hollywood films,[73] and, pertinent to our interests here, that strategy was quickly adopted upon the emergence of the export market for television.[74] Celebrity appearances are standard fare at NATPE and MIPCOM, as was illustrated in the introduction, to attract interest from buyers, and that same aspect is heavily relied upon to draw in audiences through a hinted-at opportunity for proximity to the actor. As localized glimpses into the global market, these guides reveal how the very properties that make television the cultural product that it is—genre, narrative, dialogue, visual quality, and sound—are subordinated and reduced to this one representation—that of celebrity—in their final effort to attract an audience.[75] In that regard,

Fig. 4.4. Israeli television guide, with actors from *The Bold and the Beautiful*

the television industry borrows at least some of its practices from those reliably established in the film industry.

Managing Aesthetic Elements and Other Cultural Properties to Achieve Product Adequacy

In chapter 2 we discussed the relevance of trust among industry participants to facilitating the complex business interchanges of the chaotic global market. By observing how aesthetic elements of programs come into play we can see how the marketing (and advertising) process facilitates the initial alignment—or at least the identification—of cultural sensibilities *between* buyers, as well as also *for* buyers in their role as surrogates for audience tastes. Knowing what one is getting in a deal furthers trust and increases the likelihood of repeated transactions in the future, the backbone of sustaining a market. To be sure, aligning sensibilities matters in other key ways that transpire after a sale is made, and trust either underlies or resonates in each of these. In this section we touch on some of these important aspects that are characteristic of the international market.

To this point we have focused primarily on sellers and how they draw upon television's aesthetic elements to manage the process of marketing series to foreign buyers. Buyers play an equally important role as well in

Fig. 4.5. Japanese television guide, with actors from Japanese series

the marketplace, because as proxies for their audience, they are on the front lines of appraising products for cultural adequacy in the fullest sense. Technical quality, language, content, violence, sound tracks, commercial breaks, and the opening and closing program credits of a series —all of these attributes are subject to modification before a series is aired in another country. While we did fieldwork in Los Angeles, one senior project manager at Paramount who oversees distribution of programming to Europe recounted to us the high technical standards demanded by German broadcasters, who think nothing of returning copies of an about-to-air program for an improved replacement, on time, prior to scheduled airing. As his disclosure suggests, television's attributes are more than just resources that assist in managing the representation of television as it is sold. Long after the point of sale, they must be overtly managed in order for a program even to be shown. Here we discuss three examples pertinent to this: dubbing and translation, the attitude toward commercial breaks, and cultural standards for sex and violence.

Dubbing and the Art of Translation

Television exports were constrained by language from the very beginning of the international market.[76] In the case of the United States, for example, with the exception of Japan, U.S. exports went to other English-speaking countries. While language differences can be surmounted by subtitles or dubbing, a fundamental consideration for both buyers and sellers is literacy rates of purchasing countries. Specifically, literacy is a precondition for subtitling, but not for dubbing.[77] As a representative from China to the 1998 NATPE convention told us, imported programming is dubbed there because 25 percent of the country is illiterate. Translations and dubbing are done in China,[78] as is the case for Japan; such arrangements give considerable control over the management of cultural adequacy of a purchase. A related factor affecting the decision whether to subtitle or dub (and thus whether or not a program can be purchased) is economic cost. Dubbing, though necessary for some purchasing countries, typically costs much more than subtitling.[79]

In an extended example, we focus on Mexico, which has traditionally been the gatekeeper for translations of all products sold to Latin American countries. According to Antola and Rogers, Mexico inherited that role from Cuba, where nearly all dubbing for Latin America was conducted until the 1959 revolution.[80] Because of Mexico's established film industry,

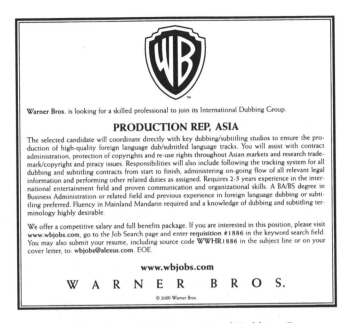

Fig. 4.6. Warner Bros. ad for International Dubbing Group

it possessed the organizational infrastructure and talent to take over the task. Mexico's role as gatekeeper eventually grew in importance because more often than not individual countries were unable to provide sufficient revenue to exporters that would also cover the cost of dubbing products into Spanish. One reason for the vested interest among Latin American buyers in maintaining the location of dubbing and translation in Mexico (Mexico City, to be exact) is that it facilitates censorship. At the time of Antola and Rogers's research, cultural policy was that certain types of stories were not allowed in imported products (for example, kidnapping, references to guerrillas, and depictions of certain types of sexual behavior); episodes with this program content were simply not aired. In addition, certain English words are censored in their Spanish translation. Indeed, a coordinator of acquisitions for Fox Latin America told us that to this day, buyers from Latin America are surprised ("shocked" was her term) at the vulgarity in American television and struggle with whether potential acquisitions can be made acceptable to their audiences. Dubbing and its supervision is a crucial and complex responsibility in the export market, as the Warner Brothers' "help wanted" ad for its international dubbing group attests.

To gain insight into what is actually involved in the process of translation, one of us visited a dubbing studio specializing in translation of programs into Spanish for Viacom, a major Hollywood production company.[81] Although its primary focus was dubbing television programs into Spanish, other languages such as German were done there as well. We were particularly interested in the way practical matters of translation were managed. Who translated the scripts? How was word selection arbitrated? What we found was interesting: the voice-over artists themselves not only did the actual dubbing; they simultaneously rendered judgment about cultural adequacy during the translation process itself.

The artists work in a cavernous, heavily soundproofed building of ten thousand square feet or more on a busy boulevard in Burbank, a San Fernando Valley suburb of Los Angeles.[82] Like so many other production facilities in Hollywood, it looked like a warehouse, with a small parking lot in front, and could have just as easily been a storage facility for a shipping company. There is nothing glamorous about this work other than, perhaps, that it is conducted indoors in comfortable, air-conditioned facilities that shield dubbers from the withering summer heat and glare of the San Fernando Valley. The facility's first floor consists of many large rooms with multiples of the very latest, most expensive technical equipment arrayed from floor to ceiling. A technical operator sits at a control booth, although many other booths were not occupied on this particular morning. The actual dubbing rooms were in well-equipped sound studios in the basement of the facility. Since most buildings in the Los Angeles area do not include basements, this seemed unusual, although in all likelihood it was a practical solution for circumventing the noise impacts from a busy airport nearby.

Voice-over artists work very hard at achieving aesthetic standards that present a seamless and flawless adaptation. Chief among the standards they strive for is to achieve the translation of a line of English that—in this instance—is spoken in Spanish for precisely the same length of time as the line is spoken on-screen in English. Thus, pacing, emphasis, inflection, and other paralinguistic details also have to be flawlessly incorporated. Even sound effects related to the dialogue have to be included. Another aesthetic standard entails the use of words in Spanish that in their pronunciation mimic the very movements of the mouths of the English-speaking actors on-screen. At the same time, all stock is placed in the voice-over artist's ability to select the most culturally appropriate words for translation. Often this decision making occurred on the spot and extended beyond to problematic dialogue that included slang, expletives, and sexual or other forms of innuendo. Offensive words were dropped altogether, and others were replaced with more acceptable alternatives, all based on the best judgment of the dubber. Dictionaries in English and Spanish were provided in the sound booths to assist in this effort and were consulted as needed to achieve clarity about semantic meaning. As if this did not require enough skill, all this occurs at the same time as the voice-over artists strive to replicate the distinctive voice of the actor or character they are dubbing.

As the above example illustrates, at some point the constraints on preparing an exported series for airing extend well beyond technological considerations and into matters of cultural adequacy in the broadest sense. One of us, while traveling in Italy in 1999, learned first-hand some of the more subtle ways in which a series is adapted to local cultural interests. In that instance, it was the prime-time sitcom *The Nanny* (which first aired in the United States on CBS and is distributed internationally by Columbia Tristar International Television). As an import it was dubbed; Fran Drescher's trademark "fingernails on a chalkboard" voice was closely mimicked (as was just about every other American actor's voice in television and films imported to Italy, including many former stars like James Cagney and Humphrey Bogart). What came as a surprise, however, was learning from Italian viewers that Drescher's character was not Jewish, as it is in the original American version; instead, she was "Sicilian" and her voice was dubbed into a distinctive Sicilian dialect. Indeed, local viewers informed us that Sicilian accents are dubbed for any character who is considered to be "gangster" or otherwise a foil for cultural propriety.

On occasion, though, cultural modification can go too far, as is the case in the adaptation of the satirical *The Simpsons* for airing in the culturally diverse Middle East. According to local viewers already familiar with Western fare in that region (who gain access though satellite or other forms of distribution), excision of offending content has left the series an unfunny variant of itself. Dialogue for *Al Shamshoon* has been fairly faithfully preserved in its translation into Arabic, and the series was dubbed into the distinctive Egyptian slang that is spoken on streets throughout the Middle East, making it accessible to the average viewer. However, episodes that clash with local sensibilities—such as those with Homer's gay roommate or visits to the local bar—are censored, and all references to drinking beer or the Christianity of Homer's neighbor, among other details, have been replaced, leaving in-the-know viewers feeling that the series as adapted for the region has lost its incisive critique of American society and politics and that it is now neither distinctively American nor distinctively Arabic.[83] In another example, an exile from the Middle East now living in the United States recounted to one of us how the sexual relationship between two characters living together in *Big Brother* was entirely eliminated, and in order to account for their sharing a household together the characters were completely rewritten as brother and sister and dubbed accordingly.[84]

Regardless of debates over genuineness of content, most dubbing is done by highly skilled talent. The Arabic version of *The Simpsons* is dubbed by some of Egypt's most successful actors, and Italian voice-over artists take pride in being among the most professional and expert in the world. Italy's 1,050 dubbers, representing eighty companies, are unionized, with the best becoming "stars in their own right" within Italy.[85] In their case, participation in the culture world of internationally syndicated programming contributes in crucial ways to the meaning of imported programming for Italian audiences. Dubber Mario Paolinelli explained, "For viewers, hearing our voices is like having close friends at home. If the characters speak a different language, they're not friends anymore."[86] When successful, this kind of intervention literally transforms the product into one that genuinely incorporates local cultural meaning. Indeed, while we were writing this book, a strike was underway among unionized Mexican dubbers for *The Simpsons*. The labor dispute, which was caused by the breach of an exclusivity contract by a privately owned dubbing company in Mexico City, started because in order to cut costs, the company hired nonunion dubbers to voice "Homero," "Señor Burns," and the other characters. The striking dubbers viewed this as a sign of disrespect for their contribution to the success of the series throughout Latin America. In speaking of the dubbers' dedication to their work and to underscore how essential they are to the success of an imported show, dubber Humberto Velez, who has given voice to Homer Simpson for the last fifteen years, stated, "Every one of us has given personality to the characters. . . ."[87] Clearly, the aesthetic experience of watching imported television is made up of many such elements that are not so readily known to audiences or easily achieved within the culture world of television.[88]

A melding of technical and cultural considerations that comprise television's aesthetic elements occurs in other ways as well. For example, audio dubbing is done "split track," which breaks out the voice track from the musical track. This is done because buyers in some countries wish to retain the source music as a feature of the imported production, which their audiences actively seek out as a reason for viewing. The program buyer from Lithuania, with whom one of us spoke at the 1998 NATPE convention, explained that Lithuania dubs its programming but preserves the original soundtrack and sound effects, "whose quality is valued and should not be sacrificed." Even this approach to music is complicated, as the senior project manager at Paramount who oversees distribution of programming to Europe pointed out to us. Because lyrics are the focal point of some songs, songs are often left untranslated and are heard in English.

Dealing with Commercial Breaks

In a related illustration we draw upon comments provided by the many viewers from other nations we encountered during the course of our research who have seen imported U.S. programs abroad. Some were Americans living or traveling abroad; others were visitors to the United States. Nearly all who were visiting the United States for the first time expressed outright surprise at the way American television series and their narrative structure are formatted by commercial breaks interspersed throughout an episode. Some countries limit by law the number of breaks for advertising in dramas and feature films,[89] and until privatization of national broadcast systems in other countries, most audiences abroad were completely unaware of this American convention and its effect on the aesthetic experience of viewing in the commercialized U.S. market. Because of television's commercial origins in the United States, Americans give little thought to the way program credits and commercial breaks are incorporated into a series or to their impact on how narrative structure unfolds around them, but they have a profound effect on the conventions of television storytelling. According to Swidler and her colleagues, television formats, which are "the units in which television programs are constructed and their continuity through time," constrain the possibilities of narrative closure in storytelling formulas—such as the melodrama of a love story.[90] Some of our informants were very disturbed by the disruption, likening it to a break in a film reel in a theater and adamant that Americans' aesthetic experience of television viewing is hardly typical, however natural it may seem to us. Of course this leaves unexplained to viewers in foreign locales the reason for the heightened emotional emphasis that characteristically appears just prior to a commercial break.[91] The disruption of a seamless aesthetic viewing experience, our informants also observed, extends to the way openings and closings of series are managed abroad. Several told us of being bothered by the presence of opening and closing credits, and our own anecdotal evidence indicates that closing credits are virtually meaningless in some countries. We were repeatedly struck by the truncation of credits at the end of imported American series (for example, *Perry Mason* in Germany, which simply ended with the fadeout of the last scene), the insertion of additional credits to acknowledge local technical contributors to the series' adaptation (for example, dubbing credits for *Colombo* and *Ally McBeal* in France), and sometimes even the re-creation of an opening segment, including the opening score, as is the case for the soap opera *The Bold and the Beautiful* in France. In short, as series are adapted to accommodate broadcast and viewing conventions elsewhere, thereby transforming the original form of the product into something other than what it was, they literally become different aesthetic experiences as they are made more familiar to audiences in other locales (see chapter 5). In sum, the very process of adapting a program to align with local broadcast conventions transforms the aesthetic experience of viewership in fundamental ways.

Censorship Practices

In the United States, there is widespread concern among some groups about explicit depictions of sex and violence,[92] and we expected to hear similar commentary readily voiced by those who buy and sell programming for the international marketplace. In fact, few brought up the topic in conversation unless we introduced it, although once we did, almost without exception, representatives from other countries found such aspects problematic, regardless of where programming originated. For example, the Lithuanian buyer we spoke with identified German programming as the most problematically explicit, and American programming as increasingly so, but felt that imports from both countries were manageable. In her country, all programming with sex or violence is scheduled to air after 11:00 P.M. Although the shows in question here were fictional, even documentary series that deal with nature are managed, as we discovered when viewing the U.K. version of Animal Planet's breakout hit, *Meerkat Manor*, which included graphic scenes of infanticide and mating not included in the U.S. version.

China manages the matter of violence differently. The representative of the government organization that handles imports of foreign programming told us at NATPE that action-adventure imports from Hong Kong are problematic for buyers from China because of frequency, not kind. Violence cannot exceed a certain number of occurrences within a given interval, and it "has to be justifiable." As the government representative explained, there are two levels of censorship, one prior to or at the time of purchase, and one after the acquisition, which can prevent the purchase from airing. If the series is rejected at that point, the supplier is obligated to supply another series in its place. How this is enforced is unclear, but it was represented to us as "a way around" problematic situations. The impact of China's policies on those who export programming to that country is illustrated by the following, which appeared in a *Wall Street Journal* article about Encore International, Inc., the China division of the International Channel cable network:

> To avoid alarming Chinese authorities, Encore's executives screen 1,200 hours of programming a year to select 500 hours they think CCTV will find acceptable. In the U.S., a broadcaster might buy a TV series after seeing one or two episodes; Encore screens every hour of every show, wary of a single episode on a homosexual affair or child molestation that would sink the whole series.[93]

As these examples illustrate, for exchanges to work, many different types of accommodations are made in response to the cultural context of the importing country.[94]

Foreign buyers new to the international marketplace sometimes find their assumptions about quality and popularity challenged. A producer in the satellite broadcast operation of the Korean Broadcasting System who was visiting the United States to learn more about American programming explained to us that as a legacy of her country's traditional practice of airing only acclaimed foreign documentaries and films from sources such as the BBC, PBS, or NHK, it was presumed that the increased presence of imported entertainment programming for Korea's two commercial networks could be of a similarly high (i.e., "educational") quality. Consequently, series sought for importation were also expected to impart culture and knowledge, and those, she explained, are identified and defined as ones that have achieved "high ratings" in a prime-time schedule. On her first visit to the United States she was learning about the U.S. syndication market as an additional potential source of popular programming, but to her surprise, she found that many of the series that did well in that market were unacceptable by Korean standards because of either their preoccupation with money or their questionable taste. To her, shows such as *Jerry Springer* (produced and distributed by Universal Television Group/USA Networks, Inc.) and *Change of Heart* (Telepictures Production/Warner Brothers Domestic Television Distribution) are "improper for a Korean audience."[95] Learning of these series' success in the global marketplace, she was confronted with the reality that concepts such as popularity, taste, and value, which in her view coincided in Korean culture, might not coincide elsewhere. Buyers and sellers adapt in numerous ways to regional and local needs and expectations, often according to informal understandings and arrangements that are the outcome of cultural practices.

Expanding the Culture World Approach to the Global Market for Television

We have sought in this chapter to address directly the way television's cultural attributes, its aesthetic elements and related cultural properties, figure into the business of the global marketplace. At a general level, sociological analysis of markets and market participants seldom focuses on the contributions that product attributes bring to managing the practical matters of business transactions. Only recently are sociologists who study culture industries attending to the ways in which the organizational production of cultural-product attributes are fundamental to understanding market mechanisms.[96] In that vein, Richard Peterson's study of country music focuses on how a singer's authenticity—that is, his or her creative voice[97]—is central to the ongoing construction and reconstruction of that genre. By directly examining the role such attributes play in the marketplace, we seek to expand understanding of the dynamics of the transnational context as a way to penetrate the apparent disorderliness of the global market and achieve greater understanding of it.

Prevailing sociological approaches to market embeddedness—the interconnections among its participants—attend to fundamental matters of trust in ongoing business relations. The global arena compounds such considerations in untold ways that are not easily reducible to formal organizational structures or processes. Participants may co-orient through trust developed over repeated exchanges, but there are an infinite number of arrangements through which such co-orientation transpires, as we have seen in this chapter, and they are under constant negotiation and renegotiation, even well beyond the conclusion of a transaction. While contract monitoring keeps the door open for sometimes unexpected and unwelcome interactions, our larger interest here is the way culture industries such as television, unlike most industries, must find a way to embrace the cultural attributes of its products as a central element of the business transaction.

There are two particularly interesting findings from our investigation of television's aesthetic elements to this culture industry that are worth commenting on. The first is that the cultural properties of television series are indeed central to television's import/export. As a facet of the business transaction, buyers and sellers both orient to television's ability to entertain by relying upon representations of its emotional resonance and by attending to their own overt emotional reactions. As *Grey's Anatomy's* executive producer Betsy Beers observed when speaking of her own series while attending the 2005 MIPCOM convention, exchanging information through meetings gives participants "an idea about where the show's *heart* is [emphasis added], to explain the characters and where the show is going."[98] The scholarly literature on organizations, in contrast, deals only in indirect ways with the significance of emotions to the conduct of business.[99] We were less interested in the complications that result from the inclusion of so-called personal business in workplaces, the one aspect of employee emotions that the literature does address, than in how products intended to elicit emotional engagement are represented in order for business to take place. And indeed, participants in the culture world of television freely engage their own and one another's affective resonance with a series as they vouch for its potential to entertain. This practice further personalizes the business relationship by foregrounding trust in a particular way, by building reliance on one another's taste or judgment when other properties lack a stable basis for interpretation.

This point in particular speaks to our central finding in this chapter, which is just how fluid cultural properties really are, especially when cultural products are transported from one locale to another. When genre shifts to the background as a classification device, aesthetic elements become relatively important to understanding what a cultural product *is*. Even the interrelationship among aesthetic elements can be shifted around to become more or less meaningful, as we saw when programming reaches the point of reception. Moreover, aesthetic elements *themselves* can become transformed when cultural products cross borders. This fluidity of cultural attributes, whether it is genre, aesthetic elements, or aspects of cultural adequacy, points to the highly socially constructed nature of such elements that inhere in cultural products. This hardly negates the importance of studying them, or of understanding them as formal properties. But it does point to the fundamentally sociological observation that such matters are themselves cultural products (or productions), however they may be made, even when that making is (only) through the process of interpretation.

Finally, we view our findings here as useful extensions to Diana Crane's conceptualization of culture worlds. Our focus on the attributes of cultural products invites further inquiry into the mechanisms operating in culture worlds—not just the interplay between participants but how that interplay is derived and enacted though the products themselves. Transnational interplay clearly compounds the complexity of these mechanisms, because reflective co-orientation among participants has to occur, and in ways that do not jeopardize the potential for ongoing transactions. Akaah has observed that attempts to standardize global marketing strategies are challenged by consumer characteristics, the nature of corporate ownership, and the orientation of corporate ownership.[100] Our analysis in this chapter indicates that in order to meet these challenges it is essential for global strategies not only to encompass product adaptation but also, perhaps more importantly, to appreciate the relevance of attending to product attributes themselves. Our exploration of the ways in which these attributes are utilized in global market transacting underscores the importance of attention to their inherently cultural nature.

In our quest to understand television's global marketplace, we have been able to ascertain how entertainment value is made into something tangible. We are reminded of Havens's observation that buyers are surrogate consumers, but they are more than that; they also act tangibly as cultural interpreters, adapters even, when they purchase and program television content.[101] Unlike art forms such as sculpture, painting, or classical music that are premised on distance, detachment, or decontextualization for analysis of an object's relation elements,[102] the aesthetic properties of television, which are experienced through the proximity, participation, and immediacy of the medium to the viewer, have to be closely "read" for their potential resonance with audiences.[103] Industry participants know this, and at some level their success in the marketplace depends on knowledge drawn from their own personal preferences and experience with the television medium. Thus, buyers and sellers are not only essential resources for gauging television's potential resonance elsewhere; they contribute to the very fluidity of the medium itself.

5

Discourses of Distribution
Circuit Models of Television

U.S. TV Shows Losing Potency Around World
—headline in *New York Times*[1]

Fans often forget that television shows are not just the place where they find cuddly characters with which they spend a little time each week. Rather, each series is an ongoing business concern, and how long they last has very little to do with art and a whole lot to do with commerce.
—television industry critic and analyst Brian Lowry[2]

"Ya gotta tell me these things buddy. That's why we're here."
—conversation overheard on the convention floor of NATPE 2002

In chapter 4 we examined among many pertinent matters the importance of discourse to the import/export market for constructing accounts of factors that explain a hit series. Such accounts are important as post hoc explanations of success because they convey to stake-holders that the business of the market is more rational and organized than it actually is. Because success in the import/export market is so difficult to predict in advance, as we have noted previously, anticipating a priori which aspects of organizational structure, conditions, or dynamics will lead to the creation of a hit is challenging, to say the least. As chapter 4 further revealed, individuals in key structural positions—those with penetrating insider knowledge and experience or a capacity for envisioning matters outside the prevailing frame (Hirsch's "boundary spanners" mentioned in chapter 2)—are better able to respond to unanticipated structural opportunities by virtue of their rich institutional knowledge. Insider cultural knowledge about how content might resonate in other locales is crucial to the social construction of this market, and equally important is the means by which that information is communicated—the discourse among industry participants about a hit.

In this chapter we consider the relevance of discourse and of discursive frames as formal mechanisms that bind and integrate the culture world of the global television marketplace. The first two seemingly unrelated quotations opening this chapter come from industry insiders who are speaking to outsiders, and while the content of the quotations may seem dissimilar, each speaks to important matters of commerce, one pertaining to the robustness of demand for U.S. products abroad and the other to considerations that underlie what is kept in production domestically for possible future export. The third quotation reflects why trade show conventions remain vital. We envision industry discourse such as this as flowing through circuits of communication that formulate recurring pathways of interaction, and we do so as follows. First, we discuss conceptually how we envision the function of discourse in the culture world of exported television. Second, we consider three sites in which industry discourse takes place and the ways in which it is consequential. These sites occur within industry trade publications, and they encompass discourse about industry trade conventions, including market trends in content and genre, and about national industries; discourse about evolving business models; and discourse about circulation of programming. By focusing specifically on the mechanism of discourse we are able to reveal its centrality to the conduct of this industry and to the discursive frames that define it as a market and a marketplace.

Cultural studies approaches to television have long been based on various versions of a circuit model, from Stuart Hall's path-breaking encoding/decoding model to D'Acci's more recent circuit-of-media-studies model. In these models, the cultural product, its discursive message, or the research question and its analysis are posited to travel some kind of circular path.[3] None of these models includes distribution as its own moment or site on the circuit, instead implicitly subsuming it under sites of production and/or regulation. For example, the Open University's circuit-of-culture model emphasizes five major processes at work, including representation, identity, production, consumption, and regulation.[4] In this model, distribution is implied most clearly under the site of regulation. In contrast, in the circuit-of-media-studies model distribution is subsumed under the site of production, which D'Acci conceptualizes as "encompassing all phases of the production moment or the industry or the overall institutional context from which programming emerges and is regulated."[5]

We have argued throughout this book that distribution is analytically distinct from other production/industry processes—involving different actors, practices, norms, expectations, and tensions—and thus needs to be interrogated explicitly by scholars interested in fully understanding the workings of global television. Analyses of distribution can help correct the productionist bias in the sociology of culture (e.g., the production-of-culture perspective) and the consumptionist bias of cultural studies, in part by showing how distribution serves to "articulate production with consumption, and draw consumption back into the process of production."[6] In the context of global television, subsuming distribution under other circuit processes mistakenly implies that it contributes nothing unique to television and its meanings.

Most of this chapter is devoted to exploring the various discourses, at times overlapping and at times competing, that frame our understanding of global TV distribution. We conceptualize these as *nested* discourses in that they are located at different distances or scales from actual trade show activities. All are relevant to the way scholars and/or industry members make sense of distribution, but they have different degrees of influence on the distribution process itself. At the outermost distance, we consider broad academic discourses about globalization that frame or precontextualize deal making but are rarely heard explicitly on the trade show floor. Moving a step "closer," we consider the discourses of regulation, policy, and protest that shape the kinds of transactions possible and help make visible cultural trade to the general public: recent protests in Chile and Hong Kong, for example. Moving yet another step closer to the trade show floor, we consider the discourses reflected in the "deep industrial texts" of the production industry; that is, the texts produced by and for trade show participants.[7] Deep industrial texts include various items produced prior to the fairs (e.g., promotional brochures) and others produced on-site (e.g., daily briefings on proceedings). Finally, we consider the discourses overheard at the trade fairs themselves: the banter among participants, the content of seminars, the discussions about programming content and the state of the industry, and so on. Our point

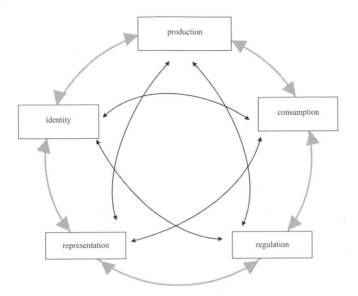

Fig. 5.1. The circuit of culture (du Gay et al., 1997)

is not to engage these discourses, theories, and debates directly. Rather, we are interested in their distance from, and relationship to, the trade show floor.

We analyze these discourses with the goal of making two larger conceptual points about circuit models of television. First, we aim to show how distribution helps connect production and consumption to one another and *transform* TV texts and their meanings in the process. In other words, following the quotation above, we argue that the site of distribution reveals the "residue" of production and the "anticipation" of consumption, as well as serving its own unique intermediary function on the circuit. Second, our analysis allows us to introduce a conceptual *depth* (or three-dimensionality) into circuit models. To put it another way, mapping discourses of globalization onto circuit models reveals *vertical* as well as *circular* motion on the circuit (picture the Octopus circus ride, if you will).[8] Below, we contextualize each of these goals in the scholarly literature and will return to them explicitly in the conclusion. For ease of presentation we rely on one circuit model throughout this chapter—the Open University's circuit of culture that emphasizes representation, identity, production, consumption, and regulation.[9]

Chapter Goals

Our first goal in this chapter, elucidating distribution's function on circuit models, begins with Dean and Jones's extension and refinement of the circuit of culture.[10] The authors observe that while du Gay and his colleagues caution against treating the divisions between sites too literally, since "in the real world they continually overlap and intertwine in complex and contingent ways,"[11] there is also "a danger inherent in the division of the cultural circuit into moments, in that the divisions themselves will be reified and, in the process, the interconnections between the moments will be lost."[12] Dean and Jones rely on prior scholarship that conceptualized subjects as "monads" that "have no windows, by which anything could come in or go out."[13] In a radical reading of this concept, Deleuze posits that

> [t]he fact that the monad "has no windows" is not because it is divided from the external world, but is rather because the world is not external to it. The monad is not separated from an external world by a hole or window through which it could access the world, but is always already *folded onto* the world, not through a simple line of separation (inside/outside, for example), but by one of mutual interrelation.[14]

Dean and Jones argue that this reading is useful in thinking through the relation among the five sites on the circuit of culture:

> In the model as it was proposed, we seem to have five distinct elements which are then linked to one another, looking out onto each other through "windows." But . . . we might want to suggest a Deleuzian monadism: each of the five moments does not simply look out on the other four, but *always already includes them in advance*. One will never find any of the elements not involving, in some way or another, the others. So we see each of the "moments"—which can no longer be seen as such—as directly implicated with the others.[15]

Scholars who study the movement of TV shows around the world focus almost exclusively on where texts start (production) and where they end up (consumption). In this research, the moment of distribution (to follow Dean and Jones's critique) is assumed to be merely a window or portal through which texts pass if the price is right and regulatory hurdles are overcome. This implies, as noted above, that nothing "happens" at the site of distribution but a sales transaction. Even scholars exploring the middle-range factors that enable or inhibit the success of imported programming tend to emphasize activities that occur *after* a TV program or format has been purchased for airing in a new market. Our first goal in this chapter is thus to explore the interrelation of distribution with other processes on the circuit—specifically, the way distribution "always already includes" both production and consumption.

Our second goal in this chapter is to introduce a new type of spatial consideration into circuit models of television. In their recent edited collection, Nick Couldry and Anna McCarthy discuss the influence of geographical theory on media studies and introduce the notion of "MediaSpace," which they conceptualize as "encompassing both the kinds of spaces created by media, and the effects that existing spatial arrangements have on media forms as they materialize in everyday life. Like cyberspace, the kind of space defined by this concept is a curious, multidimensional one."[16] There has been very little scholarly treatment of issues of space in relation to the social and cultural practices of TV distribution.[17] Indeed, our own interest here focuses more on conceptual space than geographic space. Specifically, our second goal in this chapter is to clarify how discourses of global television exist at different scales or distances from different sites, moments, or processes on the circuit-of-culture model, thus introducing depth and a new form of motion into cultural studies approaches to television. We turn below to an explication of the four levels of discourse that surround global television syndication.

Discourses of Global Television Trade

We offer a very simple diagram to guide the following discussion (see figure 5.2). This represents the distance of four major discourses of global television trade—academic discourses on cultural globalization, discourses of regulation, policy, and protest, discourses of deep industrial texts, and trade show discourses—from actual trade fair activities.

Level Four: Academic Discourses of Cultural Globalization

At the furthest distance from TV distribution practices are the myriad academic discourses on the circulation of cultural products across

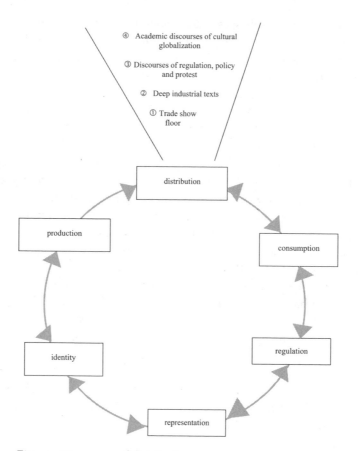

Fig. 5.2. Discourses of distribution

national borders and regional boundaries. These discourses, situated in a variety of academic niches and covering a seemingly infinite range of topics, have exploded since the 1974 UNESCO report.[18] There is a considerable distance or gap, however, between these discourses and what is actually heard on the trade show floor. Academics as individuals are largely unwelcome at trade fairs, as will be discussed below, and as is true in many corporate settings, research access is difficult for scholars to obtain.[19] In return, we find little evidence that industry participants take into account, or even seek out, academic knowledge on global television trade. As a result, scholarly discourses about cultural globalization and what industry members themselves find meaningful as they conduct business transactions are at times strikingly different.

In a recent analytic review, Diana Crane explores the dominant theoretical models used to explain or interpret cultural globalization: the cultural imperialism thesis, the cultural flows or network model, reception theory, and a model Crane proposes that captures various national and urban cultural policy strategies (see figure 5.3).[20] We discussed the most controversial model, cultural imperialism, in chapter two. We explore below theories of cultural flow and media reception, situating cultural policy strategies as a Level Three discourse—i.e., one step closer to the trade show floor.

CULTURAL FLOW

The term "flow" first emerged in the 1970s following the UNESCO report and is used by scholars to refer to the movement of TV programs and formats through different world markets.[21] In contrast to cultural imperialism models that propose a one-way transmission from center to periphery, the cultural-flows or network model suggests that cultural influences can move in many different directions and that their effect is likely to be cultural hybridization, not homogenization (see chapters 3 and 4). In this conceptualization, world television is less global than regional, with cultural-linguistic or geolinguistic markets strongly shaping audiovisual

Model	Process of Cultural Transmission	Principal Actors, Sites	Possible Consequences
Cultural imperialism Media imperialism	Center-periphery	Global media conglomerates	Homogenization of culture
Cultural flows/ Networks	Two-way flows	Regional and national conglomerates and corporations	Hybridization of culture
Reception theory	Center-periphery; multidirectional	Audiences, publics, cultural entrepreneurs, gatekeepers	Negotiation, resistance
Cultural policy strategies e.g., preservation, resistance, reframing, glocalization	Framing of national cultures	Global cities, museums, heritage sites, cultural memory, media, ministries of culture and trade	Competition, negotiation

Fig. 5.3. Models of cultural globalization (Crane, 2002)

trading patterns.[22] As White points out, scholarly emphasis on notions of flow ultimately situates television according to a kind of "traveling theory" that evokes certain logics to explain global television institutions, texts, and modes of reception.[23] From the concept of flow emerge discourses of tourism, migration, global trade, and diaspora, and the image of both TV programs and TV viewers as travelers, tourists, sojourners, exiles, vagabonds, pilgrims, or nomads.[24] One could argue that this discourse of flow is conceptually appropriate in that it metaphorically captures (through invoking dynamism or motion) the mutual interrelation of moments on the circuit of culture.[25] It has been criticized for any number of reasons, however, including its romanticization of mobility as intrinsically progressive and its concomitant denial of stratification mechanisms that shape one's ability to be mobile.[26] Our own critique rests on what traveling theory obscures—we suggest that while the discourse of flow may be metaphorically appropriate, it is to date an incomplete discourse. We illustrate the distance between academic writings on cultural flows and trade-fair practices by discussing what the former fails to capture. White notes that "the enterprise of television studies as a whole has been stymied because the implications for understanding the medium have been taken for granted, rather than interrogated."[27] To reiterate our point above, most global flow research examines the meaning(s) of TV programming before and after its arrival in a new cultural context, thus obscuring the actual process of "getting there" (i.e., the trap identified by Dean and Jones.)[28] To explore this conceptual blind spot, we briefly discuss factors that disappear in the process of distribution (i.e., they flow "in" to trade fairs but fail to flow "out"); those that are interrupted by distribution but reconstructed in receiving markets; and those that travel through the distribution process.[29]

What disappears at the site of distribution? As of this writing, there is at least one element that generally fails to flow through the distribution process—the reputation of an individual producer, director, or writer in the eyes of viewers. Television has never enjoyed the auteur status that film has, but certainly in some domestic contexts of production and reception, reputational identity matters in selling programming to viewers.[30] In the United States, for example, it matters whether J. J. Abrams is still writing for *Lost,* whether a new reality program is a Mark Burnett production, or whether the movie-of-the-week is part of the venerable Hallmark Hall of Fame series. We suggested in earlier chapters that the individual reputation of buyers, sellers, and the companies they represent matters at global trade fairs because it can make or break a deal. The same holds true, to varying extent, for the reputation of a show's producers, writers, and directors. To buyers, this type of reputation indicates a program's potential quality, popularity, or longevity and can help provide contextual information regarding a program's domestic ratings or target demographics. The U.S. market is more talent dependent than most other world markets, and sometimes having just one "name" associated with a project is enough to secure a deal.[31] But while this form of reputational identity flows into the site of distribution and is relevant to buyers and sellers on the trade show floor, programmers in new cultural markets are only just beginning to utilize it systematically to sell imported shows to local audiences.[32]

What is interrupted and reconstructed through distribution? Many other factors relevant at local sites of production and consumption fail to travel through the global distribution process. These factors do not disappear, per se, but rather are interrupted at the moment of distribution and reconstructed in receiving markets. The first will be discussed below in our examination of reception theory: the viewer. A second factor interrupted through the distribution process is genre. We emphasize two related points here from chapter 3. First, of all the ways in which genre might be conceptualized and understood (experienced) during processes of production and consumption, only two are relevant at the site of distribution: genre as content, and genre as format. Genre is thus experienced during distribution differently (e.g., more narrowly) than at other sites on the cultural circuit (such as the site of consumption, for example). Our second point from chapter 3 is that genre is not a program feature assigned at production to carry through the distribution process undisturbed and uncontested; rather, it is a fluid and negotiated designation. Recall the marketing of *The Bold and the Beautiful* as a series rather than a serial, allowing for different programming opportunities in import markets and thus different viewing experiences for new global audiences. So while genre may be experienced differently at the site of distribution than at that of production, it anticipates in advance new arenas of consumption. To refer again to the concept of the monad, "each of the five moments does not simply look out on the other four, but always already includes them in advance."[33]

A third factor interrupted through the distribution process and reconstructed in receiving markets is a program or format's *success* with viewers and professional critics. As noted earlier, sellers routinely marshal ratings indicators as part of their marketing and sales strategy, and buyers are clearly oriented toward whether an established program or format was successful in its country of origin. However, success in one cultural context does not guarantee success in another. Related is a program or format's success with professional critics. While a discourse of quality television permeates trade fairs, as was discussed in chapter 4 and will be discussed further below, no one really knows what that means, and critical acclaim in one market does not readily influence a show's reception with professional critics elsewhere. Finally, most elements of the TV *paratext*, the "semi-textual fragments that surround and position the work,"[34] are interrupted by the process of distribution and must be reconstructed in local markets of consumption: print and on-air advertisements, previews, product tie-ins, local newspaper and magazine coverage, and so on. Increasingly, however, conversations about that reconstruction are happening on the trade show floor.

What travels through the distribution process? In contrast to those elements that either fail to travel or whose traveling is interrupted, our research identifies at least three elements of global television that manage to flow fairly effectively through the distribution process, though they too are altered by the journey. First is the text itself, as buyers are obviously purchasing programs or formats produced in one cultural context for the purpose of airing them in another. Program content, discussed earlier, is subject to dubbing, subtitling, censorship, and a range of other practices designed to influence local reception. The sale of program formats is similarly predicated on the ability of buyers to reshape key elements to resonate more effectively with local tastes. Altering textual aesthetics (such as a program's theme music) means altering what it is that viewers and fans engage with, which ultimately means that viewing experiences are unique to local contexts of reception. On one hand, this is an overly obvious statement—decades of research have shown convincingly that viewers make sense of imported programming through local frames of reference. However, media scholars have not fully taken into account the extent to which those local meanings may reflect textual considerations as well as (or as opposed to) cultural considerations. To put it another way, different cultures respond differently to texts, but the texts themselves are also different—that is, the version of *America's Next Top Model* viewed in Bangladesh might be very different from that viewed in the United States.

How do we know local interpretations reflect the culture and not the text? This is an especially important consideration for scholars who study comparative fanship (rather than viewership), in that one of the hallmarks of media fandom is fans' intensely close textual readings.

A second element that travels fairly effectively through TV trade fairs is the *image of the nation* of production, though it too is altered in the process. While nations are not products, "the notion of the nation as brand has an instant and even populist resonance" even though "the image of a nation is so complex and fluid as to deny the clarity implicit in a term such as *brand image.*"[35] As discussed in chapter 3, in the context of global TV trade fairs the two main strategies for constructing brand identities are programming genre and national identity. National images are not used by all distributors as a marketing tool, in part because building a nation-based brand is expensive and not all sellers can afford to do so, and in part because "the extent to which television programs are an efficient mechanism for the promotion of national culture and identity is unclear."[36] Despite this uncertainty, national images are routinely used by buyers as another piece of data on which to make purchasing decisions,[37] as well as by local schedulers in promoting imported programming.[38]

Finally, the reputation or *celebrity* attached to actors, actresses, and other on-screen personalities flows fairly well through the distribution process. To most viewers in most parts of the world, the power of television rests on the faces and stories appearing on-screen rather than on the various other professionals involved in the production and dissemination of programming; hence, this form of celebrity travels much more easily than other forms of reputational identity discussed above. As more and more TV shows are viewed in multiple world markets, and as new media platforms celebrate media personalities in ways simultaneously accessible to users in diverse geographic locations, recognizable TV stars facilitate sales transactions for buyers and sellers and thus usher programs and formats through the distribution process into new viewing arenas.

To briefly summarize, we have suggested above that academic discourses of cultural television flows are incomplete due to their continued productionist/consumptionist biases. By focusing on where texts start (contexts of production) and where they end up (new contexts of consumption), these discourses obscure the ways in which distribution practices variably *transform* identities, texts, reception experiences, and so on as they travel the circuit. In the following discussion of reception theory, also situated at Level Four, we examine the disconnect between scholars' and industry insiders' understandings of the television "viewer" or "audience."

RECEPTION THEORY

Reception theory is the second model of cultural globalization we situate as part of Level Four discourses, relevant to our scholarly understanding of global TV trade but relatively distant from actual trade show practices. As summarized by Crane, "reception theory concentrates on the responses of audiences and publics. On the one hand, reception theory looks at people's responses to specific cultural products. On the other hand, it theorizes the long-term effects of cultural products on national and cultural identity."[39] Reception theory suggests that viewers are capable of making interpretations in many different ways (at times radically different from what the producers anticipated), and thus the meaning of TV imports is always subject to local contexts of reception. In terms of U.S. programming, for example, meta-level analyses find that "U.S. imports have a small but statistically significant impact on foreign audiences."[40] The highest correlations are with preference for U.S.-produced goods/programs and attitudes toward the United States, and the lowest correlation is with viewers' perceptions of their own country and perceptions of the United States and its citizens.[41] The authors conclude that "exposure to U.S. television programming alone will not automatically generate an adoption of U.S. values."[42] In addition to examining the effects of imported programming, a recent focus in global reception studies is the geographic mobility of viewers and the impact of their (dis)location on media reception. Raymond Williams's classic essay on watching U.S. television is the standard here. More recently, Milikowski analyzed Turkish immigrants' reception of Turkish television in Holland, Naficy explored Iranian television as experienced by Iranians in Los Angeles, and Barrera and Bielby and Mayer studied telenovelas aired on U.S. Spanish-language channels watched by Hispanics/Latinos living in the United States.[43] All of these studies share an analytic interest in questions of identity, geographic mobility and/or location, and reception experiences.

While reception theory continues to build a long and rich history, the notion of the audience has become one of the most hotly contested concepts in media and cultural studies.[44] Originally an industrial (marketing) term linked with the rise of commercial radio broadcasting, the concept of the audience quickly became one of the central ideas in mass communications research. As scholars moved beyond the transmission model of communication in the late 1980s, however, and began exploring the rich and complex ways media forms are culturally embedded, the notion of the audience gradually destabilized within the academy. Since various forms of media are now naturalized in everyday life, the audience is understood by scholars to be both "everywhere and nowhere."[45] "How do we draw the line in our data collection between audience research and the study of society, the family, the community?"[46] In short, if we cannot define an audience, "is it effectively possible to study it?"[47] This notion of "elusive audiences" has been critiqued, however, by scholars working in global media studies. In his work on Indian music television, for example, Juluri questions, "what does it mean for us as scholars to bow to postmodern recognition of the impossibility of total knowledge precisely at that moment when millions of people all across the non-Western world have only begun to become global television audiences?"[48] Acknowledging that the commercial construction of audiencehood (e.g., in terms of ratings indicators) is problematic for our understanding of global television, Juluri encourages scholars to rethink the relationship among globalization, television reception, and identities.[49]

Our aim, again, is not to engage Level Four discourses directly but to understand their inadequacies in capturing (or reflecting) trade show activities. In our own research, one of the most interesting features of NATPE, MIPCOM, and MIP-TV and (we presume) the by-invitation-only L.A. Screenings (we've never been invited) is the relative absence of the "everyday" viewer or audience, both discursively and physically. Articulated repetitively at trade fairs are discourses relating to textual properties such as genre, quality, popularity, innovation, and so on. There is obviously an implied readership or viewership inherent in some of these discourses, but viewers themselves are not treated as a relevant (or perhaps knowable) topic of conversation. Everyday viewers are also physically absent; NATPE, for example, has a promotional strategy that is largely internal, prohibitive registration fees, color-coded entry badges that restrict who can access the sales floor (and effectively advertise one's status to other trade fair participants), and a well-established pecking order to keep nonplayers and small-time players away from the main business of the fairs.[50]

The audience is not entirely absent from trade fairs, however, and can be said to participate in three indirect ways. First, viewers participate as a form of institutionally constructed data, represented most frequently through Nielsen ratings or other comparable ratings indicators and market research. While dismissed by most scholars as an inadequate representation of the meaning of global audiencehood, this form of data remains the industry's best guesstimate of the "knowability" of TV audiences and their viewing preferences. Ratings are, of course, an unsystematic form of viewer participation in that methodologically consistent ratings data have only recently been available from all regions of the world,[51] and (as discussed earlier) market research in other countries is extremely expensive. Some buyers simply cannot afford it, whereas for others there is little economic incentive to conduct research because imported shows typically draw lower ratings than domestically produced programming. Finally, of course, since even the most exhaustive audience research cannot guarantee a hit show, it is not necessarily a deal maker (or breaker) during sales transactions.

Second, recall that the audience participates indirectly in TV trade fairs through buyers who function as surrogates for the generalized audience:

> Buyers are the primary consumer in international television sales, but they ultimately serve a surrogate function because the success of an internationally syndicated program lies with viewers. Though independent, buyers' choices are never wholly their own. Instead, they receive their authority because they lay claim to being privileged interpreters of viewers' tastes, much like book reviewers.[52]

As noted earlier, buyers make purchasing decisions on the basis of a variety of factors, including the distributor's reputation, country of origin, word of mouth on the program or format, marketing and promotional materials, and the buyer's own preferences. Buyers' surrogate function helps to ease the potential challenges of conducting business transactions cross-culturally:

> Because buyers function as surrogate consumers in international television, distributors can focus their promotional efforts on courting their favor, rather than trying to create programming that appeals to viewers around the world with far-flung tastes. This practice rationalizes the process of international television trade and makes manageable the otherwise insurmountable task of trying to understand the cultural affinities and dislocations between national and sub-national groups and specific television series or films.[53]

Finally (see below), the audience is implicated in the industrial texts that circulate during the trade fairs, from promotional brochures and program pitches that feature plot points or characters that hypothetical viewers will hypothetically love, to seminars and daily news briefings on global TV consumption patterns.

In contrast to the slippery presence of television *viewers* at TV trade fairs, increasingly spotlighted are television *fans*. As the cost of production rises, competition increases, and profits decline, TV industries worldwide have shifted their focus from generalized ratings to target demographics; this is true in the context of global syndication as well. The shift from broadcasting to narrowcasting brings new niche markets, including those based on youth, gender, and racial-ethnic identities and histories, under increased scrutiny by global syndicators.[54] Fans are another niche market both actively sought and deliberately cultivated by producers and programmers.[55] Writes du Gay,

> With market-dependent consumption playing an enhanced role in the formation of consumer subjectivity and identity, the reproduction of the market requires the continual creation of new ways for consumers to be. In other words, as the economic folds seamlessly into the cultural, the battle for market share becomes articulated as a struggle for the *imagination of the consumer*; organizational success becomes increasingly dependent upon the ability to win over or more accurately to "make up" the consumer. While this is obviously still a matter of "numbers" . . . it is also a matter of "meaning," of interventions aimed at the expressive or symbolic dimensions of consumption practices.[56]

The question of consumers' imaginative capacity for fanship precontextualizes the reception of programming in new cultural markets, and thus the deals that are made at the site of distribution. Global TV sales transactions increasingly anticipate complex promotional efforts to construct a fan following in new cultural markets, often before a show hits the local airwaves, with the hope that word of mouth will then attract a broader audience. Says one distributor,

> You need to start changing people into *fans* of the brand. People who really want to engage in the brand, because this is no longer an atmosphere in which you can push yourself on the consumer, you're going to have to pull them in. . . .[57]

We emphasize that fans are now being actively courted not just at the level of production but again and *differently* at the level of global distribution—and not necessarily with programming that was consciously produced to be fan-friendly worldwide. For example, Rob Tapert, executive producer of *Xena: Warrior Princess* (which was definitely designed to be fan-friendly in the domestic market) was asked during a NATPE seminar whether the references to pop culture sprinkled throughout the series travels well to other countries. With a surprised look on his face he responded that he had no idea.[58]

What is the distance between these two reception theory discourses —one focusing on reception effects, the other on the conceptual disappearance of the audience—and trade show activities? In terms of the former, the distance is vast and disturbing. The media industry is famously secretive about its practices—its own audience research, its efforts to secure deals, its revenue from international sales, and so on. Scholars are obviously not that secretive, and we have at least thirty years of global reception studies that offer rich insight into viewers' experiences and preferences with imported television. Those research findings, and thus scholars' understandings of the myriad effects of TV reception, simply have no presence on the trade show floor. What do we make of this disconnect? In terms of academic discourses on the conceptually inaccessible audience, the distance between them is a bit closer. Industry members share scholars' perception that the TV audience today is increasingly difficult to identify—but while some scholars ultimately question the usefulness of the concept, industry members strategize about new methods of capturing and maintaining viewers. In short, for the industry, the audience is still out there no matter how narrow or niche; as the title of a recent conference seminar queried, "It's the Year 2004: Do You Know Where Your Audience Is?"[59,60]

To recap the above discussion, we have positioned two of the dominant academic discourses of cultural globalization—cultural flows and reception theory—at the furthest distance from actual trade show activities. While these discourses are central to the way scholars understand media in the context of globalization, they seem to hold little relevance to buyers and sellers as they conduct transactions. More relevant, however, are the various discourses (academic and otherwise) of regulation, policy, and protest that frame trade fair activities. We turn to these discourses below.

Level Three: Discourses of Regulation, Policy, and Protest

A wide range of cultural policy strategies—including preservation, resistance, reframing, and glocalization—serve as a fourth approach to studies of cultural globalization (see figure 5.3).[61] According to this model, globalization is "a disorderly process, fraught with tension, competition, and conflict" as companies and countries "attempt to preserve, position, or project their cultures in global space."[62] Cultural policy itself can be understood as

> the stage where power struggles are waged on national and international levels to set global policies and priorities for cultural globalization and to resist threats to the dissemination of national or regional media. Cultural policy is a political instrument that countries use in an attempt to control the types of channels and types of content that enter and leave their territory. A country's success in responding to the pressures of cultural globalization has major consequences for the future of the country's culture.[63,64]

Discourses of regulation, policy, and protest are more directly relevant to trade show activities than the Level Four discourses explored above, but while they define the parameters of trade *activities*, they are heard on the trade floor only indirectly. (Note: our discussion here engages with the microlevel—not macrolevel—implications of Crane's argument.)

Most audiovisual trade is governed by rules established by the World Trade Organization (WTO), created in 1995 out of the original General Agreement on Tariffs and Trade (GATT)[65] and including about 150 member nations. Since its establishment the WTO has been the target of sustained international protest for its efforts to facilitate the global circulation of goods and services, charged by critics with being purely an instrument of global capitalism in the service of exploiting poor nations and peoples. Recent WTO meetings in Chile (2004) and Hong Kong (2005) spawned violent multiday demonstrations. As noted above, media corporations have growing influence on policy decisions, often working closely with governments to establish, enforce, or curb regulations on media trade. As a result, "conflicts over cultural industries in free-trade agreements, whether in regional or international forums, often amount to little more than corporate wars via other means, namely, inter-governmental arbitration."[66] While some nations, most notably the United States, tend to approach trade as a purely economic transaction, other nations recognize it as both economic and cultural. In policy discussions both before and after the formation of the WTO, for example, the role of trade in cultural products has been central, manifested in vociferous debates about quotas, national identities, and the preservation of cultural heritage. These debates heavily target media forms like film and television since their consumption is "perhaps the most immediate, consistent and pervasive way in which 'globality' is experienced."[67] Interestingly, trade in TV *formats* is not nearly as controversial as trade in TV *programs*. Since format adaptations are geared toward local tastes, antitrade activists are perhaps less likely to realize the origin of the format.[68]

In his examination of the way trade agreements impact global television flows, Galperin[69] suggests that regional integration agreements such as the NAFTA (North American Free Trade Agreement),[70] the EU (European Union),[71] and the MERCOSUR (Mercado Común del Sur),[72] while sharing the goal of free-trade zones, represent three distinctly different ways to reconcile the tension between economics and culture that have resulted in three different policy outcomes. These outcomes reflect variations in industrial profile ("the distribution of economic and political resources among the trading partners' audiovisual industries"), domestic communication policies within each country, and cultural barriers that impede trade, such as language, viewing habits, and genre preferences.[73] The NAFTA thus features an exemption clause for cultural industries as well as a double standard reflecting the protectionist stance adopted by Canada but not shared by Mexico. In contrast, the EU has adopted "the 'Fortress Europe' formula: liberalization within and protectionism from outside."[74] Finally, the MERCOSUR has engaged in considerable debate over the coordination of cultural policies, but there are few references to cultural industries in MERCOSUR legislation.[75]

While formal trade agreements ultimately determine what types of transactions may occur and with whom (we are ignoring here the heavily trafficked black market of TV trade), there is little discussion of those agreements per se on the trade show floor at global TV syndication fairs. There is not, in other words, an explicit discourse of GATT or the WTO circulating among distributors at the annual fairs. Nor is there a visible activist presence at the fairs—the protests in Chile, Hong Kong, and elsewhere are not echoed by similar protests in Las Vegas (NATPE), Los Angeles (L.A. Screenings), or Cannes (MIPCOM, MIP-TV). The discourse that *is* present centers on the more symbolic aspects of trade policy: identity, community, and culture. Nowhere is this more present than in discussions of the EU, which has attempted to a much greater extent than the NAFTA or the MERCOSUR to construct a transcendent common culture, and thus a common audience, among member nations.[76,77] For example, the Television Without Frontiers directive refers to a series of EU policy initiatives aimed at constructing a pan-European media market.[78] Some critics argue that the pan-European model forces or assumes homogenization, and indeed TV producers and distributors (along with scholars, policy makers, and others) recognize the inherent irrationality in conceptualizing Europe as a single cultural market:

> [D]espite what it might say in the business plan, Europe is not a "region." It is many, many different countries . . . many linguistic centers, many religions, many political schemes, many different cultures with different views of themselves and of their position within Europe, indeed different views of what it is that television is there to do.[79]

In the following quotation, a buyer's representative explains the difficulties of implementing pan-regional advertising in Europe:

> [W]hen you're talking about a region like [Scandinavia], which has some sort of bona fide cultural contiguity, it's quite easy to do a regional arrangement there because you can get people to talk to each other, you can get them to sit around the same table, and you can make some fundamental decisions. There's some question as to the extent of the cultural contiguity in Europe as a continent. There are some countries that don't particularly like other countries, officially or unofficially, and it's sometimes difficult to get them to sit down and speak the same language, much less transact in the same currency. . . . Those are the principal hindrances to putting together pan-regional deals. . . . It's not the economics.[80]

This message is reiterated repeatedly at trade fairs, both in deep industrial texts and on the convention floor—France is not Finland is not Portugal is not Hungary; rather, these are different nations with different histories, cultures, and ways of doing business. As cultural industries shifted from broadcasting to narrowcasting, the EU's diversity was increasingly considered a strength rather than a liability.[81] In general, the discourse of cultural exemption in trade negotiations "has evolved from defending national modernities to commercializing local hybridities."[82] This is reflected on the trade show floor, where the effort is to spotlight cultural diversity rather than cultural sameness through practices such as nation branding, the decoration of booths, the goodies offered free to conventioneers, and so on.[83] Newcomers are instructed repeatedly in NATPE and MIPCOM seminars to do their cultural homework before entering into business transactions with other nations.

There is also, however, a recurrent message that "Europe" *means* something, both symbolically in terms of the way nations position themselves vis-à-vis the global market and in opposition to "American" ways of doing business. We were fascinated during our data gathering by the ways industry participants strategically position themselves, the corporations they represent, and their national origin vis-à-vis world geography. It is treated almost as a joke—for example, no one claims to be from Eastern Europe because of the connotations that presumably evokes. Countries widely understood to be part of Eastern Europe are marketed as Central European or simply European on the convention floor—a practice that symbolically rewrites contemporary cartography (among other things). Research in other contexts finds that no matter the extent to which their business has gone global, corporate executives continue to conduct business *as* Americans, *as* Germans, *as* Japanese, etc.; the presumed abandonment of national allegiances in the wake of transnational and multinational transactions is not borne out empirically.[84] We find this true in the global TV syndication market as well.

To summarize this section, discourses of policy and regulation are situated one level closer to the trade show floor than academic discourses of cultural globalization because (a) formal trade agreements fundamentally shape the types of transactions that can (legally) occur; and (b) issues of identity, community, and culture implied by those agreements are manifested in myriad ways on the trade show floor. In the following section we explore discourses situated at the closest levels to the trade show floor.

Levels Two and One: Deep Industrial Texts and the
Trade Show Floor

We discuss both levels of discourse here because, while analytically distinct, they are so close to one another in scale and so dialogic that it would be difficult to discuss them separately. Deep industrial texts are the material and nonmaterial artifacts that reflect the way the industry makes sense of itself to itself, and that serve as "institutional geography lessons" or "user guides and road maps" for trade show participants.[85] Made by practitioners for practitioners, deep texts are largely inaccessible to TV viewers and fans; indeed, they "precede and prefigure the kinds of film/television screen forms that scholars typically analyze."[86] Deep texts exist in a variety of forms. Below, we identify those that precede and precontextualize trade show activities and thus exist at Level Two, and those that unfold coterminously with verbal discourses on the trade show floor and are thus situated at Level One. Again, however, we collapse these levels in the following discussion.

Deep texts at Level Two (preceding the trade fairs) include

- promotional brochures;
- seminar schedule;
- online and print preshow newsletters, bulletins, and press releases.

Deep texts coterminous with Level One (produced onsite at the fairs) include

- seminar content (filmed and subsequently marketed to participants in audio- and videotapes);
- daily press releases posted on trade show websites and released to secondary sources;
- daily news briefings available in print form to conference participants and televised onsite during conference proceedings.

Global TV syndication fairs are the site of at least four related discourses on the meanings and functions of television: television as a *product*, television as an *industry*, television as an *employment ladder*, and television as a means of *communication*. While these are familiar discourses to any practitioner and/or scholar of television, the content of these discourses is less straightforward than one might think. Of particular interest to us are the value systems that underlie each discourse. These value systems serve as ongoing points of contestation among trade show participants and help construct the meaning(s) of this particular market.

The most prevalent discourse permeating TV trade shows relates to television as a *product*. Obviously, the most important purpose of the fairs is to facilitate sales transactions, and the primary value underlying these transactions is that of "quality" television (see chapter 4). A focus on quality is an interesting theme of the fairs. On one hand, the message is clear that economic profit matters the most—participants remind themselves and are reminded by others that whatever else it might aspire to, television is a business and must be understood as such. However, notions of quality are embedded in the everyday discourse and activities of the fair. Quality is a key element in product pitches, promotional materials, and debates about the future of the industry, and is (supposedly) indicated through such data as audience ratings, production standards, nation of origin, the reputational identities of the corporation and individuals involved, and any awards a particular program has won. Each of these sources of data is obviously problematic—popularity and quality are not the same thing, to begin with—but it matters in the current TV market that the products being bought and sold are "good" products.[87]

Ultimately, good television is in the eye of the beholder, and as discussed earlier, buyers routinely rely on their own aesthetic preferences to guide their purchases. Explains Ben Silverman, international packager for the William Morris Agency,

> [I] look for shows obviously that are good. I mean, just something that strikes my own personal interests is my biggest driving factor. . . . When I stick that tape in, if I like it [I go for it, even if my research tells me it isn't working].[88,89]

While Havens is accurate in pointing out that programming fairs "have few pretensions to art,"[90] the notion that television programming can be more than merely entertaining—it has the potential to be intellectually stimulating, emotionally moving, and artistically satisfying—is also relevant to global sales transactions.

There is also a discourse of television as an *industry* that fundamentally organizes trade show activities. Obviously, the four major fairs serve as temperature gauges for the economic robustness of the industry as a whole, and the fairs' internal communication systems as well as the TV trade press (e.g., *The Hollywood Reporter*) report almost breathlessly on attendees and no-shows, deals made and lost, celebrities present, hot new products, and the year's biggest bombs. Online press releases prior to MIPCOM 2004, for example, included "An Innovative and Exciting Programme for MIPCOM and MIPCOM Junior 2004" (released about three weeks before the conference opened), "Twentieth Century Fox Television

Distribution Stars to Shine at MIPCOM 2004" (released about two weeks before the opening date), and "MIPCOM 2004 Embraces Emerging Mobile Content Market" (released one week prior). The fairs function at least in part as a celebration of the industry and its participants, so the discourse tends relentlessly toward the optimistic, but there is a strong undercurrent of concern about the future of the industry in light of increasing fragmentation of the market, expanding entertainment options, new media technologies, rising production costs, and growing competition. Industry members repeatedly point out how difficult it is to launch a new show in the current market (the process is likened by one to a form of "trench warfare"), to attract and retain viewers, to interpret ratings data in order to predict future programming, and to know what will sell in particular cultural markets. This concern is reflected both in press reports and in the types of educational seminars hosted at the fairs. For example, seminars at both NATPE and MIPCOM regularly explore emerging opportunities as well as the general health of the industry. NATPE panels over the past decade include "The Future of Television" (1998), "Advertising in a Brave New World" (1998), "The Eastern European TV Market: New Developments, New Opportunities" (1999), "If You Speak Spanish, Your Time Has Come" (1999), "Outlook 2004: Boom, Doom, or Gloom?" (2004), and "Great Expectations: New Opportunities with VOD and HDTV" (2004). Similarly, recent MIPCOM seminars include "The Independent Production Industry: Survival Strategies," "Programming Choices for an Ever-Changing Market," and (at MIPDOC) "Programmers' Perspectives: A Q&A on the State of the Non-Fiction Programming Industry." The value promoted throughout this discourse is the inherent value of television itself as a dynamic cornerstone of the entertainment industry, even while insiders acknowledge that the industry needs to evolve to better meet the demands of its viewership.[91]

The third central discourse heard at Levels Two and One is that of television as a potential *ladder of employment* success. TV trade fairs attract a wide diversity of attendees, from independent producers and start-up companies struggling to make their first sale to major international corporations. Trade fairs and the deep texts that surround them function both explicitly and implicitly to socialize newcomers into the business culture.[92] For example, on-site seminars include formal sessions on the importance of networking (e.g., "How to Network: Schmooze or Lose," NATPE 2003), on developing effective pitches (e.g., "How to Pitch Your Pitch," NATPE 2001), on bringing those pitches to fruition (e.g., "From Womb to the

Living Room—the Development Process," NATPE 2004), and on selling to specific global markets (e.g., "Doing Business with the US—A Format For Success," NATPE 2001; "Programming, Co-Production and Producers in China," MIPTV 2004; "Conquering America: Case Studies for Selling into the US," MIPCOM Junior 2004). NATPE's Educational Foundation, which promotes educational activities on behalf of the association, also offers a series of instructional videotapes on topics such as "Inside TV: Careers in Broadcasting" that describe the basic workings of the television industry. Professional association websites offer additional instructional content, such as NATPE's three-paragraph feature "Pitch Tips" for newcomers. The three tips offered? Keep your pitch brief, get to meetings on time, and make sure to get people's business cards.[93]

"How-to" messages are also threaded informally throughout trade show proceedings and are manifested in interesting ways. For example, most seminars conclude with a question/answer period. We have attended numerous seminars at both NATPE and MIPCOM where what starts off sounding like a "real" question from an audience member devolves quickly into a product pitch—"I just produced a television show about blah blah blah." In most cases the panelists respond initially with nominal politeness but eventually lose their patience and instruct the questioner that he or she is pitching inappropriately. From the pitchers' perspective this might be the only time they ever have an interaction with some of the major industry players, so pitching might be in their best interests even though it violates the purpose of the gathering, but it ultimately functions as a moment in which industry norms are communicated and reinforced. It is not just audience members whose behavior must be monitored, however. The seminar schedules at NATPE and MIPCOM are developed months before the gatherings take place. Organizers report that it is an ongoing challenge to select panelists who won't try to transform a seminar into an extended advertisement for their own company and products. Such efforts sometimes fail; we have witnessed more than once the spectacle of experts seizing the floor for a lengthy (and often only tangentially relevant) description of personal or corporate success stories.

Relatedly, we find fascinating the extent to which professional educators are marginalized during seminar proceedings.[94] On numerous occasions we witnessed academics (or, at least, attendees wearing badges identifying them as educators) ask questions of panelists that seemed clearly oriented toward their own research projects and/or teaching interests, such as questions about how industry members conceptualize the viewing audience, about the representation of women and racial-ethnic minorities in TV production, about the amount of revenue generated from foreign sales, and so on. We perked up at those questions, knowing the answers would be useful to our own research, but the questions were routinely ignored (drawing blank faces and vague smiles) or answered in roundabout or generalized ways. For example, at one NATPE seminar an audience member queried, "What ideas do you have about the audience and how do you know them?" (clearly an academic-style question, in our view). The only panelist who answered at any length was the general manager of a TV station in Brownsville, Texas, who replied that since she lives in the community in which she works she regularly takes the pulse of that community in determining how best to serve local viewers. The other panelists, who included representatives from national and international firms such as DirecTV, Eyemark Entertainment, Hearst-Argyle, and Discovery, offered the collective (and unhelpful) insight that each market is different.[95] In instances such as this it is not clear to us whether panelists are responding to the color of the questioner's entry badge or the perceived banality (or complexity or irrelevancy) of the question being asked. The message, however, is clear—much as academic research tends to be marginalized in the industry (see discussion of Level Four discourses above), academics themselves are outsiders on the convention floor.

These "how-to" messages and interactional monitoring of industry norms are accompanied by a clearly expressed and emotionally volatile value system known in the United States as the American Dream. The employment-oriented educational sessions described above are typically followed by newcomers asking questions such as, "What do I do if the production company doesn't return my calls?" and "How do I arrange a meeting with the corporate head?" and "How am I supposed to finance my show if I have to *have* financing to *get* financing?" The invariable answer? If you want to make it in this business, keep knocking on doors, keep making phone calls, and don't take "no" for an answer. In the classic functionalist approach, both success and failure are understood as results of individual effort or lack thereof, and the question of whether struggling start-ups are "owed" anything by industry successes is debated repeatedly in trade show discourse. At times, the tension is palpable. For example, a NATPE session in 2002 was titled "Beyond the Telenovela: Program Opportunities in the U.S. Latino Market." Panelists talked enthusiastically about the explosion of the Latino/Hispanic market, implications of English-language versus Spanish-language programming, and NBC's acquisition of Telemundo. The dominant message of "great things are on the horizon" was not well received by everyone, however, and a low-level grumbling was audible in the auditorium. The small-time producer of a fishing show, who has apparently tried repeatedly and unsuccessfully to sell the show to one of the major distributors, finally stood up and complained loudly:

> [E]very year there's a panel like this and everybody tells us how beautiful it will be for Latin producers and nothing gets done. . . . I've heard this soap opera and been to the puppet show so many times. . . . They're always saying "[opportunities are] coming, they're coming," but they never come. . . .

He was angry, others chimed in to support his statements, the panelists were clearly uncomfortable, and their eventual response was simply a reiteration of the original theme: opportunities exist for those willing to work for them. Not all industry professionals share this view, however. For example, in a NATPE seminar on niche minority programming lead by Montel Williams, panelists acknowledged a sense of responsibility toward other racial-ethnic minorities working in the industry. In the U.S. context, the lack of diversity among TV writing, production, and directorial staffs is well known; these panelists believe they owe a helping hand to other persons of color trying to rise through the ranks. Ultimately, however, an individualistic orientation and a pull-yourselves-up-by-your-bootstraps mentality trumps collective responsibility on the trade show floor.

The final discourse heard at Levels One and Two includes two distinctly different themes that center on television as a *means and medium of communication.* One theme, based on the value of social responsibility, focuses on the long-standing issue of TV's varying obligation to educate, inform, and/or entertain its audience. For example, we attended a 2001 NATPE seminar titled "Muy Caliente! The US Latino TV Market." The panelists included Jim McNamara, the president and CEO of Telemundo Network, and Marco Camacho, president of Hispanic TV Network. The discussion was dominated by the revenue potential of Latino-oriented television and by the type(s) of programming that might best attract new viewers. At one point in the discussion, a self-identified Mexican producer in the audience stood up and asked somewhat incredulously, "Is this all about money for you guys?" After a considerable pause Camacho responded,

Well, personally, I feel that I have a social responsibility with my network. I feel that we do have to take into consideration the social impact that we have on the Hispanic community, and that's part of our focus. It's part of our mission statement . . . to provide relevant programming and to be socially responsible.

However, according to McNamara,

What Telemundo has become is a little bit of a mixed bag, but always governed by the principle that it's got to be good, because we're a business, and we live and die by the ratings, and so it really doesn't matter . . . in the long run . . . if you're satisfying a greater social good if you're going out of business in the short run.

Discussions about TV's social responsibility emerge most frequently, perhaps, surrounding children's programming. Trade show participants acknowledge that what constitutes "educational" programming for children is highly debatable. The U.S. network PBS, for example, has guidelines for children's educational television, but many networks do not, and the U.S. regulatory agency, the FCC, lacks official guidelines as of this writing.

The second, more central theme in this discourse of television as a means and medium of communication centers on new technologies and the value of technological change as perceived by the industry vis-à-vis viewers. In the past few years, trade fairs have been dominated by concerns about the transition from analog to digital television and the strategies needed to make digital as effortless as possible for consumers.[96] Indeed, NATPE 2004 launched a new day-long summit titled "NATPE Mobile++" to address the impact of new technologies for industry members who readily acknowledge that they have no way of predicting where the transition to wireless, mobile, and digital technologies will lead. As Lynn Spigel puts it, "at the present moment of transition, uncertainty is one of the only certainties in the television industry."[97] At the center of attention are technologies that allow viewers to bypass traditional advertising strategies, thus impacting the business model that underlies most commercial television.[98] Obviously 30- and 60-second ad spots are becoming a thing of the past in many parts of the world as advertisers move (back) toward product placement and integration and companies scramble to develop a valuation standard so that advertisers can calculate the return on their investments.[99] Corporate underwriting of TV show scripts is also rising;

here, the advertising message potentially truly "becomes" the program content. Overall, trade show participants freely admit that they do not understand what viewers want and need from television.

Thus far we have explored four nested discourses of global television distribution. Level Four discourses include academic theorizing on cultural globalization (network flows and media reception), which frame scholarly understanding of global TV syndication but are largely inaudible on the trade show floor. Level Three discourses center on issues of regulation, policy, and protest, which shape the parameters of (legal) distribution and are voiced at trade shows through discussions of identity, culture, and community. Levels One and Two incorporate competing and overlapping discourses of television as a product (with an underlying value of "quality" TV), television as an industry (with an underlying assumption of the inherent value of television as a form of entertainment), television as an employment ladder (American Dream-ish value system), and television as a means and medium of communication (with social responsibility and technological advancement serving as underlying values). In the concluding section below, we return to the larger goal(s) framing our analysis.

Conclusion

As noted earlier, our discussion in this chapter is oriented toward making two larger conceptual points about circuit models of television. First, we aim to clarify distribution's unique intermediary functions on the circuit-of-culture model, specifically its ability to implicate sites or moments on the circuit with one another and thus transform TV texts and their meanings in the process. Our discussion of cultural flows, in particular, focused on how the concept of flow in the context of global television mistakenly implies a fluid and uncontested journey from contexts of local production to new cultural contexts of consumption. In contrast to the ease of motion implied by the concept, our research finds that televisual elements vary considerably in their ability to travel undistorted through the site of distribution—from the TV text itself (routinely altered by dubbing, subtitling, and censorship) to its genre categorization to the reputational identities of the actors, actresses, producers, and creators attached to it, and so on. Each element is negotiated, contested, and reexamined during distribution, often by a different set of actors working in a different business culture than at other sites on the circuit. That which purports to flow, in other words, does not always do so (i.e., does not always travel the circuit).

As a second example of the way distribution connects sites on the circuit to one another, we point again to the educational seminars and panels that comprise much of the daily conference schedule at MIPCOM and NATPE. The topics are scheduled weeks if not months in advance, and panelists include not only buyers and sellers but also participants whose primary location is situated at other sites on the circuit: network executives, producers, actors, programmers, consumers, and so on. As indicated in numerous examples throughout this chapter, seminars are typically oriented toward the present and/or future status of the industry; as a result, the educational panels are very much about anticipating the moment(s) or site(s) *beyond* distribution. We emphasize that the activities and interactions that take place during distribution are not separate from those of other sites but rather are directly (and variably) implicated with them.[100]

Obviously, circuit models of television are not designed to capture every single action or operation involved in the process of studying, teaching, or constructing meanings out of television. In the context of *domestic* television industries, when programs are produced, distributed, promoted, consumed, and so on within the same general cultural context, models such as the Open University's (1997) circuit of culture do indeed provide a "common framework within which work [on television] may be conducted, understood and assessed."[101] But when the focus of analysis is *global* television syndication, the omission of distribution as a key site on the circuit significantly limits our ability to understand television in the context of cultural globalization. The TV text (and its meanings) that "exits" the United States is simply not the same thing as that which "enters" South Africa or elsewhere, and understanding what happens during distribution is one key to understanding the difference(s). Transformations that occur at the site of distribution must be explicitly interrogated by scholars studying global television.

The second goal of our analysis in this chapter is to insert a new conceptual depth or three dimensionality into circuit models. We have argued that discourses of cultural globalization as identified by Crane (2002; see figure 5.3), along with industry discourses reflected in deep industrial texts and in seminars and conversations on the trade show floor, hold relevance at different levels or distances from actual trade show activities. What academic and industry discourses are relevant at other points on the circuit, such as that of programming? Or advertising/promotion? Or consumption/reception? Which of the discourses we have discussed *remains* relevant and what other discourses *become* relevant to our understanding of global television? At what level or distance are they located from the particular site in question? We suggested in the introduction to this chapter that the circular motion implied by circuit models be expanded to include verticality, with the discourses or "chatter" surrounding each site moving in and out of position, in terms of both presence/absence and location (distance) from the site (the popular amusement park ride the Octopus demonstrates comparable motion). For example, the discourse of regulation, policy, and protest that we position at Level Three in our analysis has historically been absent from (or located at a considerable distance from) the site of production in the U.S. domestic context since, as discussed in chapter 3, U.S. producers long prioritized domestic audiences over global ones (a global orientation is a recent development in domestic production). This discourse is perhaps most relevant to the site of consumption in other parts of the world, in that formal regulation agreements fundamentally shape what TV programming many viewers are even permitted (legally) to consume. Since circuit models of television are designed in part to be "heuristic model[s] for scholarly analysis and teaching,"[102] taking account of the presence and location (distance) of the various discourses at play on the models is crucial.

It is a vast understatement to say that global television is a complicated topic of scholarly inquiry. Our introduction of depth/verticality into circuit models is aimed at providing a new conceptual framework to guide future analyses. We anticipate that our enriched model of distribution not only will bring conceptual depth to the circuit model of production and consumption but also set the stage for its investigation. Through the complex discursive interconnections we have observed, we anticipate, in particular, a fuller exploration of the concrete mechanisms that underlie the model and of the way those mechanisms might better be understood, and that both will assist in furthering understanding of the institutional logic of the global marketplace. Our elaboration also envisions the larger theoretical project of examining how the never-ending dynamics of the television industry are more than just artifact but are, in fact, a constituent of its institutional structure.

Conclusion

Television's Culture World

The fact is that in global terms, everybody is talking to everybody these days. The democratization process has definitely begun for the business on a worldwide scale.

— Rick Feldman, president and CEO of NATPE[1]

What is taking place within the inner workings of the global marketplace that would have the leader of the U.S.'s major trade show speaking of its democratization? How might the change Feldman refers to further our understanding of the television industry's culture world? In this conclusion we turn to these and other questions as we consider the sociological significance of our findings and their relationship to some of the predominant theoretical debates in the field.

Feldman has worked tirelessly, and successfully it seems, since his appointment as head in 2003 to expand NATPE's presence as a player on the global scene. A few years ago NATPE was struggling to sustain its position as a major trade site, and at that point it wasn't clear to many observers (including ourselves) that NATPE would survive as an important locus of commerce for the industry.[2] Long-standing, influential participants voiced extreme dissatisfaction with the expense associated with attending relative to the benefits of doing so and refused to rent space on the convention floor, opting to hold meetings in adjacent hotels instead, or refusing to send representatives altogether, arguing that NATPE no longer served their needs. Even as participating countries from other global regions formed exhibition pavilions to highlight their presence on the convention floor and create visibility for their national offerings, the association's focus, and indeed the primary tone of the convention, remained centered on sales and distribution of the domestic U.S. market. Integrating new technologies was pivotal to NATPE's eventual turnaround, pushing the association into a modern agenda. Although distributors have always relied upon multiple distribution windows—timed releases to different audience markets that include cable and syndication, the airlines, and videocassette and DVD rentals and purchases—the advent of multiple platforms (both mobile and broadband) significantly loosened the industry's tight control over distribution, and an inexorable need for content moved to the foreground in the marketplace. Nudging the industry along were stern admonitions by industry analysts such as Diane Mermigas, whose regular columns in *Television Week* and *The Hollywood Reporter* repeatedly observed that the business model of the entire industry needed to catch up with the opportunities new technologies were offering.[3]

Refocusing NATPE's founding, and, to a large extent, still relevant function as a domestic TV market, Feldman appears to have successfully incorporated an international perspective into the organization, bringing it in line with MIPCOM, the L.A. Screenings, and other major global trade sites as one that also actively highlights the programs, genres, and deal structures that are popular among buyers from leading networks in non-U.S. global territories, while realizing the contribution of new technologies. Hence Feldman's reference to democratization. What proved central to the industry's embrace of a more open marketplace was that viable business models began to emerge for generating revenue from new forms of distribution. By 2006, NATPE was back on track as programmers vigorously explored how to maximize a show's value via all emerging platforms.[4] This transformation is manifested in the schedules of recent conferences, which now regularly incorporate organized activities centered on topics of international relevance and feature speakers from recognized companies and established industries of other countries. But the international diversity now more apparent in NATPE's conference program goes beyond its embrace of a broader constituency; it also speaks to other transformations in NATPE's reorientation to the marketplace. One of the key ones from our perspective is that it illustrates the importance of the central reason for the creation of this market in the first place: content, and the never-ending challenge of managing its cultural properties. Branding may bring viewers to a show, but content is what sells a series to the audience. Referring to the challenges that the newer technology of mobile programming brings to distribution, industry leader Russ Kagan of Kagan Research, LLC, reaffirmed the centrality of content to reaching audiences: "Just like in the early days of HBO, it's about what's going to keep them subscribing. . . . It's just programming all over again."[5] Content has been central, indeed pivotal, to our study of the culture world of television's global marketplace. Industry participants co-orient to one another in order to build trust in the quality and reliability of each other's products and in the stability of one another's markets, and at the crux of this co-orientation is product content. As they trade in this content, participants' co-orientation is multifaceted, evolving at an interpersonal level out of personal preferences, experience, social contacts, social networks, and a strong and intuitive sense of the right entertainment for the right audience—underscoring not just the centrality of content to their business transacting but its very elements as the essential commodity of this industry. The marketplace still draws upon many of the business traditions that its founders brought to the then-fledgling market of the early 1950s, a good many of which entailed staking one's reputation on assurances of a program's value (whatever its quality). Although achieving acclaim in this marketplace often entails a heavy dose of trial and error and companies muddling through, it is still measured in sellers' finessing ways to make a sale work and buyers' sharpening their instincts for programming content that will attract viewers and turn profits.

In our quest to understand how the apparent messiness of this market is regularized, we opted for a middle-range view, one that bridges micro and macro approaches and targets meso-level conceptualization. Our conceptualization pinpointed the interaction between larger structural considerations that shape the social institutions of national economies and cultural policies, on the one hand, and, on the other, the organizational contexts and the ongoing, everyday business practices and other routines of the industry. With this focus in mind, we attended, in particular, to the mechanisms that make this market operational—hence, our concentration on the organization and function of industry trade sites, the accumulated knowledge residing in the history and development of the syndication end of the television industry, the marketing practices laid down as templates by influential founding figures, the management of the market's malleable products, and the integral discursive interconnections among the many levels of the marketplace. Expanding upon Crane's concept of the culture world as we have, we sought a deeper understanding of what makes this cultural industry not just operational but inherently *cultural*. With that goal in mind, we engaged evidence of culture writ large by moving it to the forefront as an aspect of the market's activities, bringing evidence of organizational, institutional, and economic issues into *cultural*

explanations. By attending to the organizational, material, and other practical mechanisms the media industry relies on, we directly linked the
particular contribution of the industry's cultural products themselves to
the organization and dynamics of this market. Focusing as we did on the
fluidity and malleability of the properties of television programs and on
the way those attributes are managed as a central business concern broad-
ened understanding of what makes the products of the television industry
distinctive among those of other cultural industries. By attending to the
industry's levels of discourse we drew attention to its institutional channels of distribution. But given all this, how do our findings contribute to
larger theoretical concerns such as media hegemony, cultural imperialism,
and related political-economy concerns that have occupied the attention
of sociologists and media scholars alike for so long, as well as the interests
of organizations scholars who are increasingly focused on the effects of
global capitalism on corporate structure?

Despite scholars' long-standing debates about media hegemony and
the cultural dominance of the United States in the global market, escalat-
ing global media concentration and its cultural effects, intensifying privatization of the industry, and, increasingly, the consequences of new technologies for intellectual property, to date there is surprisingly little sys-
tematical *empirical* research on the many serious concerns raised by these
debates. It would seem that this is the case because collecting and analyzing such evidence is a very complicated undertaking. Cultural geographer
Allan Scott's insightful study of the locationally interdependent economic
synergies that underlie Hollywood's global vitality concluded with just
this point by noting the urgent need for *empirical* evidence of the corporate organization of cultural production as well as of the wholesale com-
modification of culture on the global level.[6] Targeting *mechanisms* as we
have—the accounts of what brings about industry change and that reveal
how institutional components interrelate—is one useful place to start.
Mechanisms permit asking useful questions that probe the industry's institutional and production logics and begin to open up new avenues for
investigation that can concretely speak to the larger theoretical concerns
that dominate study of the media.

Understanding the institutional logics of, for example, mergers and acquisitions underlying global consolidation as business practice would be
one important line of investigation and would permit investigators to ask
informed questions that speak to anthropologist Mary Douglas's important
quest to penetrate "how institutions think."[7] It would allow researchers to

tie trends in bureaucratic hierarchy, such as the institutionalization of international divisions within major studios, with trends in the domestic market, such as the promotion of successful domestic industry leaders to head those international divisions. It would also challenge investigators to take into account recent trends in the disaggregation of global conglomerates that business practice dictates—from the fabled failed synergies of AOL-Time Warner (now back to "Time Warner" in name) to media giant Viacom's 2005 split that undid the 1999 merger of Viacom and CBS Corporation.

However, it is important not just to note trends such as these as evidence but also to seek understanding of the rationale for mechanisms underlying them, especially when studying the logics of international forms abroad and the cultural contexts that shape their effectiveness. For example, China may have been penetrated by News Corp.'s Star satellite distribution system, and it now seeks Western programming to fill its expanded broadcast system. But doing business in China without *guanxi*—business contacts that originated in lifelong school friends or in weathering the Cultural Revolution together—dooms to failure Hollywood's conventional practice of combining bonding and business over lunch.[8] Earlier plans of Rupert Murdoch's Sky Satellite services to establish a pan-Asian and/or pan-Chinese network were forced into adaptation and eventually abandoned in favor of establishing multiple smaller, more culturally specific channels. The plans were scuttled by key miscalculations regarding varying internal taste markets, language differences, logistical difficulties of competition with local broadcasters, and direct government intervention against these plans;[9] the guiding conventions that worked elsewhere for the company did not apply here. In this instance, the company's organizational mechanisms (business strategy for growth, organizational expansion/development) were disrupted fundamentally by China's culturally distinct expectation that markets be subordinated to political institutions and ideologies. Thus, conventions (shared understandings) about market/corporate growth were not shared and remained unaligned. In short, the cultural assumptions underlying the requisite co-orientation were absent, miscommunicated, out of reach, unknown, or unattainable, and the business plan could not proceed as Murdoch intended because it ran counter to China's practice of subordinating the business of its economy to government.

Attention to mechanisms of the television industry's vigorous profit-oriented logic that exist to manage uncertainty in the marketplace would be another fruitful avenue of inquiry. There are three broad areas of uncertainty in business transactions; these pertain to the search for business partners ("search/contact"), agreement among the parties to rely upon collective standards and norms governing membership in the industry and associated groupings ("agreement/contract"), and the extent to which contractual agreements are formalized to preempt opportunism and to structure business transactions.[10] More importantly, inquiry along these lines could highlight in locally specific ways that such mechanisms are culturally understood, practiced, and enacted (such as in China, as noted above, where socially based relational roles play a pivotal role in economic transactions).[11] Our particular sociological concerns pointed to the cultural frames that impinge upon the co-orientation of culture world participants, centering on participants' interactions around production of programs (creating new ones and transforming/adapting existing ones), and the considerations that affect the transformation/adaptation of the features or elements of the cultural products themselves in order to transact sales and to improve the penetrability of markets. But, there certainly are others. As we revealed in chapter 4, the culturally and symbolically laden programs are themselves a pivotal source of uncertainty in the industry, and although our focus in the book did not extend to include direct analysis of the audience, work by other media scholars points to the relevance of the industry's institutional-level logic for keeping the audience at arm's length and managing it through the mechanism of scientific ratings to measure a program's success and determine its value in the marketplace.[12] Whether audiences are similarly conceptualized and commodified by national industries in other locations is an open question.

Mechanisms in the television industry pertain to more than just commerce, however; they can also be applied to art. The television industry is well known for the complex interplay between commerce and creativity and its need to manage this publicly in order to sustain institutional legitimacy with its constituencies,[13] and some institutional mechanisms pertain exclusively to the creative process. Becker's seminal study of art worlds offers a useful illustration of the utility of one such mechanism for gaining insight into media industry institutional logics.[14] Becker's important insight is the notion of artistic *conventions*—shared understandings among art world participants that organize participants' contributions to a project. As a mechanism, artistic conventions align creative workers with disparate but interdependent skills, specialties, and backgrounds so that they can orient to the task at hand and so that the creation of an artistic product can be accomplished. However, attempts by U.S. industry participants to adapt particular creative practices that have evolved in the United States—such as the writing of scripts by committee or the input of network executives—are not always well received in other locales and complicate efforts to develop coproductions. In short, the way the mechanism of co-orientation works (or doesn't work) in the culture world of global television can tell us a lot about the consequences of its implementation on the ground in the context of television's vigorous profit-oriented logic.

We have described here ways to probe the logic of institutional structures, an important place from which to launch the undertaking of empirically penetrating the television industry's profit-oriented logic. However, we note that focusing exclusively on the organizational or institutional architecture of media industries, however fruitful this may be, neglects the important contribution of industry dynamics, yielding somewhat limited insight over the long term because television is such a cyclical industry (a matter we were confronted with as well). Program genres emerge, evolve, and disappear altogether: consider how TV movies-of-the-week and miniseries, among many other formats, are now seen only on pay cable networks or as imports airing on PBS, or how game shows and Westerns die out and then suddenly reappear. Participants come and go, and there is an almost constant turnover of personnel at firms, and of firms themselves, throughout the industry. Consider also how industry business models continuously evolve, sometimes in forms that threaten the very future of the industry, but then revive unexpectedly.[15] Observe, for example, how guardedly the television industry has approached ways to capitalize on distribution over the internet, largely because of the difficulty it has had in determining how to harness revenue from alternative technologies and scattered audiences. One solution, the ever-increasing reliance on product placement within the narrative of a series,[16] is on the one hand new, and on the other quite old. (Until the networks gained control of television production, product placement was common practice, as were commercials delivered by a show's host or actors.) As a final example, consider that a pattern exists by which national television industries evolve, as Sinclair has noted, from an initial stage of dependence to a mature national market indicated by growth of audience size and of domestic program production, with the latter usually meaning that long-standing import markets evaporate or relegate offerings from once-dominant exporters to the graveyard slots on the schedule.[17] Such was the

U.S. experience around the globe for at least the last decade until the re-surgence of the strong narratives and characters of shows like *Desperate Housewives, Lost,* and *Grey's Anatomy* appeared on the scene and restored demand for U.S. products.[18] Our point here is that the dynamic fluidity of this industry poses particular challenges for scholars intent on collecting empirical evidence for analysis of the industry. Even institutional and production logics are changeable and may themselves be variably, inconsistently, or unintentionally "strategic" in this industry, if the experience of other culture industries is any example.[19] Given these considerations, future research may do well to consider models of structure that simultaneously engage its construction, such as Giddens has done in devising his notion of structuration, which recognizes the constraining influence of structure on social agents and their agency even as that very structure is modified by its participants' agency.[20] Many aspects of the influential medium of television deserve fuller exploration—the historical importance of independents in its transformation;[21] the consequences of social structural constraints—such as law, technology, market, organizational structure, and occupational careers—on culture industries;[22] the impact of program and genre counterflows and (varying) boundary permeability across geolinguistic regions, including, increasingly, the United States;[23] and the fact that in an era of new technologies even the established logic of oligopoly over channels of distribution needs to be rethought,[24] even if these technologies end up being more like "add-ons" than outright replacements. Each of these aspects of the industry would have much to say about the influence of the embedded social networks and institutional transformations of a cultural market that so loosely couples yet so tightly binds so many nations around the globe.

Methodological Appendix

When we began the research for this book we had several goals in mind, being motivated by abiding scholarly interest in media, the ebb and flow of politics and social policy, a fascination with social structure, and a healthy dose of personal curiosity. We were intrigued by what we had discovered in our earlier work on domestic fans of U.S. soap operas. While doing the research for that project we could not help but be struck by how the accounts of fans in other countries about American television and the shows produced in their own countries began to open up for us the culture world of television abroad. The challenge we faced in venturing into the terrain of television in other countries was how to study such a complex subject that virtually every social science and cultural studies discipline has tackled in one way or another. Resonating in our minds as we contemplated taking on this endeavor and even throughout our investigation were the words of noted cultural sociologist Howard Becker, who as visiting professor at the University of California at Santa Barbara stated to us at an early stage in our undertaking that the biggest challenge we would face would be deciding what criteria to employ to study exported television. As it turned out, the problem was not one of finding evidence of all that could be observed and understood—indeed there was often too much of it—but rather of how to most efficiently and effectively delineate the topic in order to contain it conceptually and empirically so that the industry's and market's social organization and the product's development and use—its social construction—would be best revealed in ways that met our substantive goals. As social scientists, we knew in advance that such decisions are crucial, rooted as they are in more than seemingly obvious, even mundane, organizing decisions. They are, in fact, instrumental to what we would be able to uncover and illustrate about a very complex topic. Should we track a single program as it traversed the globe? If so, which one? Or, instead, should we track a genre, such as action-adventure, which is noted for its ability to transcend borders, or one such as comedy, which has far greater difficulty doing so? Or, should we focus on an industry notable, famed for innovation, or a group or organization well known for the way it moved the industry in its development? Or, on the other hand, would the study of the global television industry benefit from focused attention to a particular cultural context? If that were our aim, would seeking insight into the established industry of a particular nation or global region be more enlightening, or would tracing an emergent one? Would it be beneficial to focus on the constraints the industry faces, such as impact of policy upon its history and development, or take on its almost dizzying momentum for growth? In considering each, we had to ask ourselves which would bring fresh insight to the field.

As cultural sociologists who read across the humanities and social sciences and engage with colleagues across a variety of disciplines, we were advised at one time or another to consider every one of these approaches as potentially the most interesting and revelatory. Given the abundance of possibilities, we finally opted to follow our instincts as sociologists of media who keep an eye on the horizons of the field to pursue an approach that drew upon evidence that was transdisciplinary and thus could potentially integrate what was most intriguing to the multiple audiences who follow television as a medium and an industry: the way its marketplace dynamics socially construct it as an industry. Our approach enabled us to ground our understanding in concepts pertinent to the operation of markets and thus its foundation as a commercial enterprise while simultaneously attending to the institutional- and individual-level mechanisms and dynamics that construct it through social practices around the very feature that sustains it—the television programs themselves. Although a great deal has been written about this particular industry, as we noted earlier in this book, the relative absence of sociological work that attends to television's workings as a culture world on the international front stood out to us, and with that in mind we felt our expertise in cultural sociology could bring novel insights to the subject.

We carried out the project by relying on data generated from a range of qualitative and quantitative approaches to study global television syndication. Since the mid-1980s we have followed press coverage of the entertainment industry. We had been reading industry trade publications (*The Hollywood Reporter, Variety*) for many years and following media coverage of the business of the industry within these publications as well as in several newspapers of record, in particular, the *Los Angeles Times,* the *New York Times,* and the *Wall Street Journal.* We added industry sources to our list that significantly expanded our archive—*Broadcasting & Cable* (both the print and electronic forms), *Electronic Media, Television Week, Television Business International,* specialty publications such as *Soap Opera Digest*—and we also monitored online reports (e.g., *C21 Media, Multichannel News, World Screen Weekly, World Screen Newsflash, B&C Today, Mediaweek, Hispanic TV, Eurodata TV,* among others, some of which have since come and gone). In combination, these venues provided overlapping coverage of all layers and segments of the domestic and international industry and its global market.

To learn more about the industry, we simultaneously launched participant-observation fieldwork to become more familiar with the way this segment of the industry was structured and conducted organizationally, and the way its members actually framed it to themselves in talk and action. We accomplished this in two primary ways. During a sabbatical the first author enrolled in the semester-long UCLA Extension course "Television Syndication: A Worldwide Phenomenon," taught by industry expert Dick Block, president of the television consulting firm Block Communications Group of Santa Monica. The students in the class were already employed in the industry and had enrolled in the course to further their careers. As a long-time participant in the syndication market, the course instructor, Dick Block, drew upon his experience as former president of Kaiser Broadcasting, executive vice-president of Metromedia's television station division, and consultant to NATPE to bring notable industry figures to speak to the class, including Dick Robertson, then of Warner Brothers Domestic TV Distribution, David Mumford of Columbia TriStar TV Distribution, Tony Cassara of Paramount Television Stations, Judy Girard of Scripps Cable Networks, and Steven Mosko of Sony Pictures Television, among others.

Simultaneously, we began fieldwork on the industry by attending several NATPE conventions, beginning in 1998, some of which were held in New Orleans and others in Las Vegas, and one MIPCOM convention in Cannes, France, in 2004. We registered as professional educators each time, which gave us access to the convention floor (though not to the interior sections of all booths), as well as to seminar proceedings and other industry events. We spent hours walking the convention floor, observing interactional dynamics among potential buyers and sellers, chatting informally with vendors, and collecting hundreds of brochures and other material artifacts on various companies and their products. We attended numerous seminars on a range of topics, which were educational not only in terms of actual content but also in terms of our ability to observe the way panelists interacted with one another and with audience members. We took field notes on seminar proceedings as they unfolded and purchased videotapes of the seminar series after the convention ended. Quotations used in our book are verbatim. Registration also gave us access to an entire range of pre- and postconference publications and other artifacts. In short, the industry's trade sites were crucial for our observations about the presentation and conduct of the marketplace for syndication—its social organization and stratification, social networks, cultural tone and sensibilities, vocabulary and discourse, interpersonal tensions, industry issues, and institutional hurdles and goals, as it oriented to the product it markets.

Through our participation in these multiple field sites we developed contacts, conducted interviews, and established connections for further fieldwork. We visited a dubbing studio where international voice-over production takes place, attended a Television Critics Association press tour, spoke to soap opera industry journalist-critics, toured the studio where a soap opera is produced, attended the taping of two different soap opera programs for the syndication market (one a prime-time special for the national market and another a daily program for a Seattle television station, which included a guest appearance by the first author), and attended a soap opera industry award show, *The Soap Opera Digest Awards*, whose audience is limited solely to industry members. We conducted in-depth interviews with numerous industry participants ranging from producers and project managers to company directors of international sales/acquisitions and of development to deputy sales managers of national trade groups, marketing executives, heads of foreign relations, and coordinators of acquisitions. We spoke to actors and others involved in program production at several of these field sites to gain insight into their understandings of the industry. We were interested in speaking to individuals at all levels, but were particularly interested in contact with manager- or director-level industry participants because it was at this tier that the actual practices of the industry's culture world became most apparent. The entertainment industry, like other culture-industry markets,[1] is notoriously guarded about its strategic business plans, impending deals, and detailed aspects of its production partnerships, and despite these constraints those with whom we spoke were generous with their time and showed considerable interest in our work. As our research goals increasingly focused, we came to realize that to have limited ourselves strictly to ethnographically driven research would have occluded the broader view-point that was needed to elaborate the many mechanisms, features, and properties of the culture world of the global marketplace.

The industry trade sites—the conventions—and the attendant public-ity and media coverage surrounding them provided us with the industry's institutional traces and artifacts, including promotional materials, con-vention issues of publications, and the like. We compiled these materi-als during the years 1998 through 2007, and we supplemented them with data from the online product information of participating companies. The global market for exported television relies upon a variety of approaches to advertise its products—promotional tapes, billboards, product brand-ing, inserts in conference editions of industry trade publications, celebrity appearances, word of mouth, and so forth. At NATPE and other trade conventions, product brochures on display at company booths on the ex-hibition floor are one of the most established means of conveying infor-mation about television programs. From these archival materials we were able to select samples of distributors by relevant analytical categories, de-vise coding schemes, and conduct textual analyses of brochure content. In short, by analyzing these qualitative materials, we were able to inductively develop a classification of conceptual categories to demonstrate, for exam-ple, how genre is used as a framing device in the marketing of television series for export. The content analysis of industry documents and presen-tations generated textual material that we analyzed substantively for the presence of, for example, aesthetic elements of internationally successful licensed program concepts and exported series.

We supplemented our personal archive of media coverage of the televi-sion industry with archived materials in our university libraries and online topic searches to track substantive issues of relevance to the syndication market, such as station consolidation, trade site participation, emerging markets, the world economy, and activities of key industry members. Ad-ditionally, we identified relevant coverage by searching for selected articles that included direct quotations of statements made by industry producers, agents, actors, and journalists. Transcriptions of industry seminars held at NATPE conventions between 1998 and 2004 were analyzed for discus-sion by attendees about the industry. From that collection of seminars we selected direct quotations by industry participants and inductively devel-oped a classification of substantive categories. Finally, whenever traveling abroad, we acquired ancillary materials wherever we could that included local television guides and popular media periodicals.

Out of this evidence we developed sociological and media-relevant categories of data for analysis that became the basis for our substantive chapters. The history of this segment of the industry, including national policies that played a role in its shaping, was crucial to understanding its legacy. The consolidation of the domestic syndication market and the explosion of the international one coincided as notable ripples in the industry's transformation. The substance of its cultural product, and the way that substance interlinks the orientation and practices of this industry's business, proved relevant to making sense of the industry's commerce. This, in particular, guided us to close study of its classificatory schemes of genre and aesthetic elements, and of its organizational discourse in our effort to understand the industry's multiple sites of production, distribution, and consumption. In order to understand and illustrate the particulars of conceptual categories, we formulated case studies of individual series and tracked them across settings, assembled multiple observations of single sites, aggregated data within and across settings, and relied upon conceptual "snapshots" of occasions to capture their essence.

This has been a rewarding and challenging project, the challenges being due to the multiplicity of potentially fascinating research questions (and the need to isolate a specific approach), the speed at which the industry transforms, the guardedness of industry insiders, the sheer volume of potential data sources, and the changing role of the industry in broader patterns of cultural globalization. Throughout the course of the project, we had to remain vigilant about our own cultural expectations and blinders, which we did by continuously cross-checking information across the multiple sources of data in our archives, conferring with industry members about our impressions, and discussing our emerging understandings with locals and other insiders here and abroad. We have been attentive to the feedback we've received and have incorporated suggestions along the way as well as we could. We are deeply grateful to all those who have been so forthcoming and enriched our effort.

Notes

NOTES TO THE PREFACE

1. Keith Negus, "Cultural Production and the Corporation: Musical Genres and the Strategic Management of Creativity in the U.S. Recording Industry," *Media, Culture & Society* 20 (1998): 359.

2. Ibid., 360.

3. Patricia H. Thornton, *Markets from Culture: Institutional Logics and Organizational Decisions in Higher Education Publishing* (Stanford, CA: Stanford University Press, 2004).

4. Timothy J. Dowd, "Structural Power and the Construction of Markets: The Case of Rhythm and Blues," *Comparative Social Research* 21, no. 1 (2003): 47. Timothy J. Dowd and Maureen Blyler, "Charting Race: The Success of Black Performers in the Mainstream Recording Market, 1940 to 1990," *Poetics* 30 (2002): 87.

5. Mary Douglas, *How Institutions Think* (Syracuse, NY: Syracuse University Press, 1986).

6. Steve Brennan and Mimi Turner, "Going Mobile," *Hollywood Reporter*, March 28–April 3, 2006: S-1, S-19.

NOTES TO THE INTRODUCTION

1. Faye Fiore, 2000, "Show Biz Icons with Little to Show for It," *Los Angeles Times*, May 17: A1.

2. Quoted in Steve Hockensmith, "Gold Rush," *Hollywood Reporter*, September 11–17, 2001: 13.

3. For a history of the industry, see Barnouw (1975); for discussion of founders and innovators, see Auletta (1991) and Anderson (1994). Cantor (1971, 1980) and Bielby and Bielby (1994, 1999) studied the industry's organizational form, and Gitlin (1983) considered its social values within that context. Press (1991) and Gray (1991) studied its reception within specific audience groups.

4. By the late 1950s Americans no longer considered television a luxury but a necessity or an entitlement, a key component by which citizens were to be connected to the national culture (Sterne, 1999, p. 518). A 2005 study by the Con-

sumer Electronics Association indicates that the average U.S. home now has 3.1 television sets, up from an average of 2.4 sets in 2004, and almost 10 percent now own digital video recorders (DVRs) (http://www.ce.org/press_room/press_release _detail.asp?id=10753).

5. In the 1970s, the three major networks' share of prime-time viewership stood at over 90 percent. By May of 1997, that percentage was down to 62.1 percent, according to Nielsen ratings (Pope, 1997), and to around 47 percent by August 1998 (Lowry, 1998). Expected to drop to 28 percent by 2005 (Blumenthal and Goodenough, 1998, p. 13), the broadcast networks combined actually captured 43.1 percent of the viewing audience in 2005, according to Nielsen Media Research (Becker, 2005), down from 47.2 percent in 2004 (Andreeva and Littleton, 2004, p. 14). The broadcast share for summer 2005 was reported to be an all-time low of 32 percent (Collins, 2005).

6. MIP-TV is the acronym for Marche International de Programmes Television. The Reed Midem Organization, founded in 1965, has various spin-offs of MIP-TV that include MIPDOC, which focuses on the documentary market, MIPCOM Jr., covering the children's and youth program screenings, and MILIA, which as part of MIPCOM attends to interactive content.

7. Reported in Scott Roxborough and Charles Masters "MIPCOM Defies Dire Forecast," *Hollywood Reporter*, October 12–14, 2001: 4, 120.

8. NATPE conventions have taken place in other locations since the organization's founding, including San Francisco, Miami Beach, and Las Vegas (see http:// www.natpe.org/about/conference history/).

9. Reported in *NATPE Facts*, February 28, 2000.

10. Statistics compiled from Brennan, 2004a, *Variety Market Central*, 2005, and Roxborough and Masters, 2001.

11. Reported in NATPE Brochure, 2000a. At NATPE's high point, a brochure for the 2001 convention in Las Vegas anticipated more than eighteen thousand executives involved in the creation, production, distribution, financing, sponsorship, marketing, leveraging, and management of content. Of the eighteen thousand individuals who attended the 1999 NATPE convention, 32 percent were content distributors, 29 percent were content buyers, 25 percent were content developers, 7 percent were advertisers, and 4 percent were involved in new technologies (NATPE Brochure, 2000b).

12. Steve Brennan, "Sharper Picture: NATPE's Feldman Has Passport to Open Doors," *Hollywood Reporter*, January 3–9, 2006: 14.

13. Chris Lancey, president and chief operating officer, Western International Syndication (NATPE Brochure, 2000b).

14. Reporting on the 2007 roast marking the career of domestic syndication leader Dick Robertson, *Broadcasting & Cable.com* wasn't shy about its history, declaring "NATPE Has a Sordid Past" (online January 21, 2007).

15. Quoted in Brian Lowry, "So Not Fun, It's Not Funny," *Los Angeles Times*,

January 16, 2002: F1, F5 (http://www.latimes.com/entertainment/printedition/calendar/la-000003937jan16.story).

16. According to the *Wall Street Journal*, "between building booths and renting space on the convention floor as well as flying in talent and staff, expenses at NATPE can easily top $2 million for a couple of days' work" (Flint, 2000, p. B10). The cost of just the booth is considerable, with the largest ones running more than $1 million (McClelland, 2002a, p. 31).

17. See page 26 of Timothy J. Havens, "Exhibiting Global Television: On the Business and Cultural Functions of Global Television Fairs," *Journal of Broadcasting & Electronic Media* 47 (2003): 18–35.

18. Ibid., p. 19.

19. For example, in 1998, Disney, which owns ABC, generated $3.8 billion, or 17 percent of the company's overall revenues, through its international business (McClelland, 1999). In contrast, in 1957, foreign distribution for the entire U.S. industry grossed a mere estimated $14 million (Seagrave, 1998, p. 36). In 1999, according to Paul Kagan Associates, international licensing of U.S.-produced programming generated $6.6 billion, up 10 percent from a year earlier (Lowry, 2000a).

20. Charles Slocum, "More Than Ever," *Written By*, September 1997: 34–35.

21. See Diana Crane, *The Production of Culture: Media and the Urban Arts* (Newbury Park, CA: Sage, 1992). In selecting Crane's concept as an organizing schema for our research, we considered approaches by other sociologists to the analysis of cultural production. Foremost among our considerations was Howard Becker's concept of art worlds (1982). Becker's approach emphasizes networks of cooperating individuals who, through collective action, produce works of art. Underlying collective action are the conventional understandings that members draw upon in order to assure cooperation, regardless of who participates. Becker's perspective was of considerable appeal because, indeed, the medium of television relies heavily on shared conventions by all those involved in aspects of its production. His focus is, however, the production of the plastic arts—sculpture, paintings, and the like, rather than commercial industries and markets like television. Moreover, while Becker's approach includes gatekeepers such as critics and gallery owners, it does not explicitly incorporate coparticipants such as audiences who are integral to the success and longevity of television as a cultural product.

We also gave serious consideration to Griswold's concept of the "fiction complex" (2000). This concept grew out of her study of the Nigerian novel, in which she identifies the globally dispersed authors, editors, booksellers, and readers as key participants who shape that genre. Griswold's fiction complex was designed explicitly to accommodate the loosely coupled, globally dispersed set of interacting participants who are involved in the production and consumption of the Nigerian novel, and to take into account the permeability of cultural borders through which participants pass. In developing the notion of fiction complex, Griswold sought a concept that neither implied boundaries that classified or delineated global regions or groups nor assumed an integrated market or organization when there was none (2000, p. 29). The fact that Griswold's concept encompassed a global arena made it intuitively appealing to us, as did her inclusion of readers, critics, and other gatekeepers who are participants in the fiction complex. Moreover, her focus on the ways in which participants actively contribute to shaping the properties of the Nigerian novel was of interest to us. However, there are features of the global market of television programming that would be difficult to subsume under the fiction complex conceptualization. Television programming is produced and distributed within a highly sophisticated and complex technological infrastructure requiring enormous cash outlays upfront. In addition, it is heavily regulated by governments. These features call for a more expansive conceptual approach to address these distinctive features of television and its production, sale, distribution, and consumption.

22. See, for example, the *TV International Sourcebook 1997*, Baskerville Communications Corporation, Torrance, CA, 1997.

23. Michele Hilmes, *Hollywood and Broadcasting* (Urbana: University of Illinois Press, 1990).

24. Scott Roxborough, "Austria Ready for Primetime," *Hollywood Reporter*, January 4–6, 2002: 75.

25. See, for example, Craig S. Smith and Geraldine Fabrikant, "Hungry TV Giants Poised to Win Only a Slice of China's Audience," *International Herald Tribune*, September 11, 2001: 11; and Michael Curtin, "Murdoch's Dilemma, Or 'What's the Price of TV in China?'" *Media, Culture and Society* 27, no. 2 (2005): 155–75.

26. Crane, 1992, p. 112.

27. See Wendy Griswold, "A Methodological Framework for the Sociology of Culture," pp. 1–35 in Clifford Clogg (ed.), *Sociological Methodology* (Washington, DC: American Sociological Association, 1987).

28. Crane, 1992, p. 113.

29. See R. P. Snow, *Creating Media Culture* (Beverly Hills, CA: Sage, 1983).

30. See Shyon Baumann, "Intellectualization and Art World Development: Film in the United States," *American Sociological Review* 66 (2001): 404–26; and, Denise D. Bielby, Molly Moloney, and Bob Q. Ngo, "Aesthetics of Television Criticism: Mapping Critics' Reviews in an Era of Industry Transformation," pp. 1–43 in Candace Jones and Patricia Thornton (eds.), *Research in the Sociology of Organizations: Transformations in Cultural Industries* (Greenwich, CT: JAI Press, 2005).

31. Kurt Lang, "Mass, Class, and the Reviewer," *Social Problems* 6 (1958): 11–21.

32. Denise D. Bielby, C. Lee Harrington, and William Bielby, "Whose Stories Are They? Fan Engagement with Soap Opera Narratives in Three Sites of Fan Activity" *Journal of Broadcasting & Electronic Media* 43, no. 1 (1999): 35–51.

33. See page 283 of Robert R. Faulkner and Wayne E. Baker, "Role as Resource in the Hollywood Film Industry," *American Journal of Sociology* 97 (1991): 279–309.

34. Richard S. Belous, "How Human Resource Systems Adjust to the Shift toward Contingent Workers," *Monthly Labor Review* 112, no. 3 (1989): 7–12.

35. See William T. Bielby and Denise D. Bielby, "Controlling Primetime: Organizational Concentration and Network Television Programming Strategies," *Journal of Broadcasting & Electronic Media* 47, no. 4 (2003).

36. Bielby and Bielby, 1994; Bielby and Bielby, 2003.

37. Blumenthal and Goodenough, 1998.

38. Havens, 2003a, p. 22.

39. Ibid., p. 25.

40. Muriel G. Cantor and Joel M. Cantor, "American Television in the International Marketplace," *Communication Research* 13, no. 3 (1986): 509–20; and Muriel Cantor and Joel Cantor, *Prime-Time Television: Content and Control* (2nd edition) (Newbury Park, CA: Sage Publications, 1992).

41. Cantor and Cantor, 1992.

42. Richard Caves, *Creative Industries: Contracts Between Art and Commerce* (Cambridge, MA: Harvard University Press, 2000).

43. Havens, 2003a, p. 20.

NOTES TO CHAPTER 1

1. Brian Lowry, "Court Shows Continuing to Rule Syndication Television," *Los Angeles Times*, January 28, 2000: F2, F37.

2. Quoted in NATPE Educational Foundation, "From A to Ziv: Legends of TV Syndication," 2000.

3. Personal interview conducted May 10, 2002, Santa Barbara, California.

4. The original third network, DuMont, ceased to exist in 1955 (Anderson, 1994, p. 256). DuMont, whose failure was due in part to its lack of a radio network and ties to Hollywood and the FCC, aired the first television soap opera and daytime television game show (Gough, 2006, p. 14). ABC, which became a network in 1951 upon purchase by Leonard Goldenson, did not become major competition for CBS and NBC until 1955 (Lowry, 1999).

5. William Boddy, 1998.

6. As Sterne reminds us, the inherently social process that leads to television as we currently experience it includes the development of the necessary infrastructure, an aspect of the U.S. industry that most scholars take for granted. He observes, "In the project of American television, the creation of a national infrastructure was a problem and a project, not a given. . . . Television infrastructure was a physical, technological and institutional development; it was also a set of ideas circulating among technicians, industry executives, programmers,

congresspeople and audience members" (1999, p. 505). While he is referring to
TV distribution through 1962, these issues have obviously returned to the industry's agenda in recent years.

7. See, for example, Tim Brooks and Earle Marsh, *The Complete Directory to
Prime Time Network and Cable TV Shows 1946–Present* (New York: Ballantine
Books, 2003).

8. According to industry conventions, "daytime" programming is television
fare airing from 10:00 A.M. to 4:00 P.M. (EST) Mondays through Fridays. There
is no daytime on Saturday or Sunday. Primetime runs from 8:00 p.m. to 11:00
p.m. Mondays through Saturdays, and 7:00 P.M. to 11:00 P.M. on Sundays. The
term "late night" is used to refer to programming airing from 11:00 P.M. to 1:00
A.M. every day, including Sundays ("Television Talk," *New York Times*, May 13,
2003, p. Z10).

9. Hilmes, 1990.

10. In the early 1950s, independent companies included Ziv, Hal Roach, Jr.,
and Desilu. By 1952, there were twelve substantial independents whose productions were made in leased studio space. By 1955, the former studios that had
moved into telefilm production included Columbia (through its subsidiary,
Screen Gems), Republic (Hollywood Telefilms), Warner Brothers (through Sunset
Productions), MGM, Fox, Paramount, Monogram, and Universal.

11. Anderson, 1994, pp. 66–67, 259.

12. Wesley Hyatt, *The Encyclopedia of Daytime Television* (New York: Billboard Books, 1997).

13. Hilmes, 1990.

14. There are now far fewer independent stations that do their own program
buying. Most stations are owned by vast station groups, such as Hearst-Argyle
Television or Tribune Broadcasting Company, each with outlets in twenty or thirty
cities, as a result of massive consolidation following removal of station ownership
caps and an increase in coverage limits. These vast station groups buy most of
their programs collectively. Because of economies of scale, costs for the acquisition of syndicated programming by station groups are relatively low (Lafayette,
1998; Lowry, 2000b).

15. The networks quickly realized the importance of the affiliated stations
to their survival, not only as systems of distribution but as lucrative sources of
advertising revenue and of talent and creativity for future programming. See
Marilyn J. Matelski, *Daytime Television Programming* (Boston, MA: Butterworth-
Heinemann, 1991).

16. Until the mid-1990s, the three original major networks were permitted
seven owned-and-operated affiliated stations. Following changes related to the
1996 Communications Act, those limits were dropped, although a single company
could not own two stations within a single market, and a station group could not
reach more than 35 percent of the U.S. population (see, for example, Blumenthal

and Goodenough, 1998, p. 17). In the spring and summer of 2003, the FCC was poised to implement one of the most significant overhauls of media ownership policy in a generation. The changes—since struck down by the courts—relaxed or eliminated a wide-ranging set of media ownership rules that are profoundly altering many long-standing, distinguishing features of the media landscape—significantly expanding the number of local television stations networks could own, allowing for more cross-ownership of newspapers and television stations, and generally facilitating the growth of major media conglomerates.

17. Matelski, 1991.

18. In those early years all programs carried by the networks were developed, owned, and controlled by the advertising agencies whose clients underwrote their sponsorship; this system of commercial underwriting did not change until 1957 when NBC pioneered control of program ownership.

19. Anderson, 1994, p. 60.

20. Boddy (1998) reports that in 1961, CBS's telefilm division shifted from the production of original programming to syndicating network-licensed independently produced programs. "That year, CBS Films, Inc. sold 1,500 half-hours in fifty-five foreign countries; two years later, CBS Films Inc. became the world's largest exporter of telefilm" (p. 36).

21. Bielby and Bielby, 2003.

22. Matelski, 1991, p. 8.

23. Frederic W. Ziv, founder of Ziv-TV in 1948 and known as "the father of syndication," died at age ninety-six on October 13, 2001. His company became a major programming supplier to stations by creating, producing, and distributing the 1950s hit series *Highway Patrol*, *Sea Hunt*, and *Bat Masterson*, as well as *Boston Blackie* and *The Cisco Kid* (see "Briefly Noted," *Electronic Media*, October 23, 2001, p. 4).

24. See Hilmes, 1990, for a history of radio.

25. Ziv's account of the early days of television syndication is from the speech he delivered at the 1992 NATPE President's Award Ceremony (see "From A to Ziv: Legends of TV Syndication," produced by the NATPE Educational Foundation in 2000). Ziv TV was sold in 1960 to United Artists (see "Briefly Noted," *Electronic Media*, October 22, 2001, p. 4).

26. Quote by Dick Block, president of Dick Block Entertainment and UCLA instructor, September 26, 1998, UCLA, Los Angeles, California.

27. NATPE Educational Foundation, "From A to Ziv: Legends of TV Syndication," 2000.

28. UCLA seminar, "Television Syndication: A Worldwide Phenomenon," Los Angeles, California, September 26, 1998.

29. Quote from Greg Meidel, president and COO, Massive Media Group, NATPE Educational Foundation, "From A to Ziv: Legends of TV Syndication," 2000.

30. UCLA seminar, Los Angeles, California, September 26, 1998.

31. NATPE Educational Foundation, "From A to Ziv: Legends of TV Syndication," 2000.

32. Greg Meidel, NATPE Educational Foundation, "From A to Ziv: Legends of TV Syndication," 2000.

33. By the 1980s and 1990s, the domestic syndication industry had evolved to include calls by company representatives to potential station clients to ascertain what could be developed to meet scheduling or market demands (Brennan, 2006b, p. 18). The relevance of tailoring programming to schedules and demographics in the international market is something we discuss in greater detail in chapter 4.

34. UCLA seminar, September 26, 1998.

35. See Betsy Frank, 1991, p. 1.

36. See Bielby and Bielby, 1994, 2003.

37. Gitlin, 1983.

38. In today's market, typically the concept for a new series is announced two years in advance of a planned premiere. A pilot or demo tape is produced, advertised, and talked up the first year while individual stations or station groups are solicited. Once an adequate revenue stream is assured, a series then goes into full production. Occasionally, even highly touted series with well-known celebrities as attached stars fail to ever reach the marketplace.

39. Interestingly, many of the early practices of the business persist despite the industry's efforts to professionalize. The continued extravagance of NATPE conventions, described earlier, contrasts with its more conventional approach to business. The notion that a show is characterized as something "to attract eyeballs," which is the same imagery used in reference to carnival sideshows, underscores the basis of the industry in salesmanship and of a "hawking" mentality. Interestingly, in its earliest incarnation, "booths" at NATPE conventions were hotel rooms, which, perhaps unintentionally, democratically cast all buyers and all sellers, big or small, on the same terms (see Havens, 2003a).

40. Brian Lowry, "Court Shows Continuing to Rule Syndication," *Los Angeles Times*, January 28, 2000: F37.

41. Their growth was fueled by passage by the FCC of the 1996 Telecommunications Act, which allowed, for the first time, a single company to own more than twelve stations. It also allowed companies to own stations that reach as much as 35 percent of American television viewers (Project for Excellence in Journalism, 2007, "The State of the News Media 2007," Annual Report on American Journalism [Washington, DC: Pew Research Center], available at http://www.stateofthe-newsmedia.org/narrative_localtv_ownership.asp?cat=5&media=6).

42. See Greg Spring, 1998, p. 32.

43. Although typically the broadcasters in these local markets decide where to place a program on their schedule to best suit their programming needs (Lowry,

2000c, pp. F1, F20), some syndicators with highly rated shows (like *Oprah*) are able to insist on particular time slots.

44. Quoted in Spring, 1998, p. 32.

45. Spring, 1998, p. 32.

46. Ibid.

47. Some leaders in the syndication business, such as Columbia TriStar Domestic Television's Steve Mosko, consider it to be undermarketed and have allocated company resources to institutionalize their division, with departments for promotion, research, programming, advertising, affiliate relations, etc., much like a network (McClellan, 2002b).

48. Quoted in Steve Brennan, "A Room with a World View," *Hollywood Reporter*, January 16, 1998a: S-34.

49. Brennan, 1998a, p. S-34.

50. How NATPE will continue to serve its original constituents remains to be seen (see chapter 6). In 2001 and 2002, several of the industry's major domestic syndicators opted out of formal participation in the annual convention. NATPE then-president Bruce Johansen stated, "What we're seeing is the absolute collapse of the domestic syndication marketplace. . . . This is a reaction to that" (quoted in Littleton, 2001, p. 30). However, "while domestic syndication 'implodes,' international sales are a booming business. . . . The developments at NATPE . . . demonstrate that international trade is an increasingly independent and lucrative sector of the syndication industry that responds to quite different economic realities than domestic sales" (Havens, 2003a, p. 24). As of the 2005 convention, NATPE had revived as a trade association by emphasizing the importance of business relationships. Stated Roger King, CEO of CBS Enterprises and King World, "NATPE is a very productive place to network, to see station reps that we don't ordinarily see and to thank them for all the business they've done for us . . . we'll do business too . . . but it's also about networking with producers, advertisers, stations and other syndicators" (Speight, 2005, p. 44). As an indicator of vitality, in 2006, NATPE announced acquisition of the content market DISCOP, which serves Central and Eastern Europe television markets (Speight, 2006).

NOTES TO CHAPTER 2

1. Quoted in Lowry, 2000b, p. F-37.

2. Steve Brennan, *Hollywood Reporter*, January 22, 1998: 1.

3. UCLA seminar, 1998.

4. Cantor and Cantor, 1986, p. 514.

5. Quoted in Brown, 1996, p. F-1.

6. See Havens, 2003a and Mohammadi, 1997. The first international exchange of television programming took place between the United Kingdom and France in 1950 (see Nordenstreng and Varis, 1974).

7. Statistics refer to the number of hours of airtime filled in the destination markets. That is, if twenty episodes of a one-hour series are sold in one hundred markets, that series accounts for two thousand hours.

8. We discuss the 1974 UNESCO report in some length because, while now over thirty years old, it quickly became a primary source in subsequent scholarly, policy, and cultural critiques of the preeminent presence of American programming abroad. We also believe that many of its key findings have been overlooked by scholars. The 1974 UNESCO report drew attention, in part, because of ongoing international debate over trade in cultural products. According to Hoskins, McFadyen, and Finn (1997), that debate was renewed following the 1947 General Agreement on Tariffs and Trade (GATT), which was primarily concerned with trade in goods but also contained an article allowing nations to impose quotas on feature film imports. Restrictions on television program trade began thereafter. The central reason for the attention garnered by the 1974 UNESCO report was due to the post-WWII New World Information and Communication Order (NWICO) debate within UNESCO among aligned and nonaligned nations over the consequences of the flow of information across borders. According to Gerbner, Mowlana, and Nordenstreng (1993), debate over the democratization of that flow, initially limited to the flow of news but expanded to include entertainment programming, broadcast technologies, and advertising, centered on whether it should be a "free flow" or a "free and balanced flow" among nations. As telecommunications technology and the development of transnational corporations became integral to the "modernization" model of development, which was based largely on U.S. capital investment, development assistance, and political support, concerns about a new form of cultural dependency emerged, along with concerns about cultural imperialism.

9. In a study published two years later, Read (1976) revealed that two-thirds of the foreign sales of U.S.-produced programs at that time went to countries with the most receivers and the largest audiences, in particular Canada, Australia, Japan, and the United Kingdom. Read's study reconfirmed that the principal direction of programming flow was from the United States to the other seven countries. Although it is uncertain whether all countries had an equal opportunity of being included in Read's study, given that its focus was on information from dominant countries, it was, nevertheless, revealing of the regional domination of countries with strong export programs.

10. A variety of factors prevent developing nations from producing their own programming, thus rendering them dependent on imports. Those factors include "low income resources, lack of industrial infrastructure, lack of support by weak governments, inappropriate models for production and lack of trained personnel" (Straubhaar, 1991, p. 45; see also Hoskins and Mirus, 1988).

11. (Varis, 1984, 1986a, 1986b).

12. Sales of Brazilian telenovelas, for example, are very successful in Eastern

Europe, Russia, and, increasingly, the Middle East. Television exports comprise a growing share of the revenues of television production companies across Latin America, with the United States (with its growing Spanish-speaking population) increasingly importing these shows. Top Mexican broadcaster Televisa, for instance, gets about a quarter of its annual revenue (around $160 million) from exports, with about half of this from licensing to U.S. network Univision and the other half from sales to Eastern Europe, Asia, the Middle East, and Latin America.

13. Iwabuchi, 2002.

14. See Sinclair, Jacka, and Cunningham, 1996b, and Straubhaar, 1991.

15. Statistics are from the 1999 DCMS report, cited in Freedman, 2003.

16. Colitt, Fifield, Johnson, Marcelo, and Larsen, 2003.

17. De la Garde, 1993, p. 27.

18. Schiller, 1991, p. 17. According to Schiller, the primary assumptions of the original 1960s version of the cultural imperialist theory were, first, that media/cultural imperialism was but one subset of a larger system of imperialism; second, that "what is regarded as cultural output also is ideological and profit-serving to the system at large"; and, third, that in the late twentieth century, the corporate economy is increasingly dependent on the media/cultural sector (1991, p. 14). Schiller argued that the cultural domination that exists today, while still heavily focused on the United States, "is better understood as transnational corporate cultural domination" (1991, p. 15; italics deleted).

19. Gramsci, 1991. Straubhaar, 1991, p. 40; see also the discussion in Croteau and Hoynes, 2000.

20. Garnham, 1990; McChesney, 1999; and Herman and McChesney, 1997.

21. Miller, Govil, McMurria, and Maxwell, 2001.

22. Miller et al.'s perspective intervenes directly in the humanistically based cultural analyses of "screen studies tradition" (i.e., film and television studies), which they regard as an overly textualist orientation of the field. In their view, that tradition romanticizes audiences, overstates agency, and ignores power (see 2001, p. 14). Other work, such as that represented by Jesus Martin-Barbero's (1993) engagement with debates about modernity and postmodernity, foregrounds the potential of culturally specific modes of communication, such as oral traditions, for contextualizing the presumed impact of imported media. Elsewhere, Daniel Mato's (2002) analysis of Miami as the geographic site that houses the extension of the telenovela industry into the U.S. questions the presumption that the production of globalized media necessarily deterritorializes consumers' sense of cultural place, as is argued by many postmodernists who monitor such trends. Nestor Garcia-Canclini (1995) argues that global media has diminished television's traditional role in creating and sustaining culturally important dimensions of national identity, yet he also sees transnational media reconstituting citizenship, albeit in a newer form, that is no longer based solely on a single nation or state affiliation

(thus his notion of hybridization). Ien Ang's (1991) long-standing interest in the relationship of audiences to the media industry attempts to problematize the dichotomy of political economic power *or* cultural analysis that marks scholarship in this field; instead she argues that global media are better understood by engaging power and political economy perspectives while also placing investigation of active audiences at the center of media analysis.

23. See Fiske, 1987.

24. See, for example, the work by Ron Lembo (2000) on viewers' "mindfulness" and Elizabeth Bird's audience ethnography that offers a "contextualized, nuanced reading of the role of media" (2003, p. 188). Other research has shown how gender (Press, 1991), social class (Hall, 1982), and institutional settings and subcultures (Morley, 1980) affect viewers' readings, revealing the extent to which audiences are composed of differentiated groups rather than the undifferentiated masses presumed by the cultural imperialist view.

25. Kang and Morgan, 1988.

26. See, for example, Frith, 1991, and Elasmar, 2003.

27. Tomlinson, 1997, p. 137; see also Thompson, 1997.

28. Sinclair, Jacka, and Cunningham, 1996a.

29. Antola and Rogers, 1984.

30. Davis, 1997.

31. Hoskins and Mirus, 1988, p. 500; see also Straubhaar, 1991.

32. Liebes and Katz, 1990.

33. Allen, 1997.

34. Cunningham and Jacka, 1994.

35. This strategy is followed even among newly emerging commercial networks. When asked specifically about soap operas, the head of programming acquisition at a Lithuanian network whom we interviewed at the 1998 NATPE convention explained how her network was airing some popular imported soap operas during daytime and others in the evening, depending on the intended audiences.

36. Writing about the ABC network's programming success under Fred Silverman in the 1970s, Hirsch observed that scheduling (and promotion) of programs, as well as forms and genres within which programs are based, proved very important in attracting audiences. Content mattered but was not the crucial factor, in Hirsch's view (1980, pp. 88–89).

37. Crofts, 1995, p. 112.

38. Cantor and Cantor, 1986, p. 518.

39. The model developed by Schement, et al. (1984) to explain the international flow of television programs consists of two sets of elements: structural conditions, which establish the potential for media flow, and catalytic actions, which consist of the efforts taken by individuals or organizations to enable the transfer.

40. See, for example, Parks and Kumar, 2003.

41. Mowlana, 1997, p. 34.

42. Brennan, 2003a, p. 14.

43. See, for example, Owen and Wildman, 1992.

44. "The value is not intrinsic to the good or service but is rather imparted to the good or service by consumers' perceptions of the degree to which their wants and needs are satisfied by it" (Picard, 1989, p. 36).

45. Hall, 1980, p. 128. See also DuGay, Hall, Janes, Mackay, and Negus, 1997, p. 85.

46. But see for example, Levine, 2001, and Parks and Kumar, 2003, who call for a shift in attention to production.

47. Of course, as noted earlier, empirical research has effectively demonstrated the various ways in which aspects of social location (e.g., gender, class, ethnicity) may influence interpretation. We do not mean to suggest otherwise here.

48. Griswold, 1987, p. 4.

49. See Harrington and Bielby, 2001.

50. See, for example, Newcomb, 1974; Swidler, Rapp, and Soysal, 1986.

51. Gans, 1974, p. 14.

52. See Matelski, 1999, pp. 45–46. *Santa Barbara* was an enormous hit in Russia, and we experienced the strength of its following first-hand. In 1995, one of us was approached in our capacity as a soaps researcher by a Russian scholar on sabbatical at a southern California university, who had made a point of visiting Santa Barbara in order to find out the resolution of the relationship of one of the show's leading romantic couples so that he could phone his wife in Russia to tell her the outcome. In addition, he wanted to learn the geographic sites for all the show's location shoots so he could photograph them for his fellow viewers back home. As thanks, he provided photos of himself posing in formal attire with his favorite actors from the show at the Russian Emmys.

53. Galetto, 1997, p. 8; also see Sutter, 1997.

54. *Soap Opera Now!* 1996.

55. Barker, 1997, p. 93; see also Borchers, 1989; Liebes and Katz, 1990; Lopez, 1991.

56. Brooks, 1976; Gledhill, 1992.

57. See Allen, 1996; Lopez, 1995; Matelski, 1999; O'Donnell, 1999.

58. McAnany and La Pastina, 1994, p. 831.

59. Geraghty, 1995.

60. In another interesting illustration of this phenomenon, Miller (1995) describes the unexpected success of the U.S. soap opera *The Young and the Restless* in Trinidad. In this instance, the soap was literally a ratings success; Miller reports that even before total national viewership reached its highest levels, at least 70 percent of those with a television watched the show, and that this exceeded all other programming then on the air, including the news. Buried in the early afternoon portion of the schedule known as the "housewives' slot," and following the

lunch-hour soaps, it was not expected to be as successful in terms of audience interest as the other imported, more expensively produced, faster-paced prime-time ratings hits in the United States, *Dynasty* and *Dallas*, which aired at more opportune viewing times. Another factor that was presumed to work against widespread audience interest in *The Young and the Restless* was that as a daytime soap, it emphasized dialogue over action; action is often presumed to be more easily understood abroad because of its more elemental quality.

Miller identified two factors that were central to the unexpected popularity of this particular soap. One was that technology facilitated access to the program, either through use of battery-operated miniature televisions at work or over the lunch hour, reliance upon video cassette recorders for time shifted viewing, or the opportunity to see the week's episodes through weekend reruns. While these solutions to accessing the show are not unique to this program, they do underscore a point we raised earlier—the importance of access for potential impact upon a local culture. But by far the more important factor central to the popularity of this particular show was the way in which the narratives themselves and the ways in which they were told resonated with Trinidadians' preference for "the bacchanal." In Trinidad, observes Miller, the bacchanal refers to the impact of scandal and confusion on the stability of the social order, but most importantly, it also refers to truth, and to the moral value of scandal to reveal hidden truths. According to Miller, the popularity of the show was in large measure due to its "metacommentary on the nature of truth itself" within Trinidadian society (1995, p. 218).

61. Gu, 2002.

62. Chu, 2002; Rofel, 1995.

63. Lewes, 2002, p. 38.

64. Marc, 1997, p. 20 and pp. 22–23.

65. Covington, 1997, p. 13.

66. NATPE Educational Foundation seminar, "How to Turn a Homegrown Idea into an International Success," 1999.

67. Lewes, 2002, p. 38.

68. Gordon, 2001, p. 14.

69. Brennan, 2001a, p. S-32.

70. Spano, 2000.

71. Woods, 1999.

72. Channels, 1990; EIDC, 2005; James, 2006.

73. Quoted in Lowry, 1997, p. F-1.

74. Covington, 1997, p. 13.

75. Freeman, 1995, p. 14.

76. Jensen, 2000, p. F23.

77. Quoted in Sofley, 2000.

78. Ibid.

79. *Hollywood Reporter*, 2005, p. 56.

80. Quote from O'Regan, 2000, p. 312. O'Regan notes further that the advent of concept sales, often regarded as having emerged in the late 1970s and 1980s, in fact began in the 1950s and 1960s through the formalized exchange of scripts among broadcasters.

81. So vigorous are current U.K. efforts in the United States that one industry observer stated, "If you go to [Los Angeles Airport] at three in the afternoon on any given day, there is a new British company coming in with program [formats] to sell" (Antony Root, cochair of the British Academy of Film and Television Academy in Los Angeles, quoted in Brennan, 2004b, p. 18).

82. Australia's Grundy Organization eventually became a foreign company, and then in 1995 a subsidiary of the large British media company, Pearson (Bonner, 1997).

83. See Cunningham, 1997, p. 109. Nevertheless, these complex arrangements do not guarantee success in the American market. Australian media scholar Frances Bonner writes, "Such companies may have become necessary but their involvement does not guarantee success. *Paradise Beach* was not a success in the US market and it is notable that the subsequent program from this same production group, *Paradise Drive*, was sold overseas to European and South American countries, but not to the US" (1997, p. 252).

84. Brennan, 1998c.

85. Brennan, 1998d, p. 21.

86. Stuart McFadyen, Colin Hoskins, and Adam Finn, 1998, p. 523.

87. Quoted in Brennan, 1998e, p. 6.

88. Quoted in Brennan, 2002a, p. 12.

89. Ibid.

90. NATPE Educational Foundation seminar, "The Living Curriculum: Formats: The New Reality," 2001.

91. Owen and Wildman, 1992, p. 181.

92. Elizabeth Hirschman, 1983, p. 50.

93. Michael Schudson, 1989, p. 170.

94. Barrera and Bielby, 2001, p. 6.

95. Granovetter, 1985. See Powell and Smith-Doerr, 1994, and Uzzi, 1997, for applications of Granovetter's concept to relational contracting; and Hamilton and Biggart, 1988, and Biggart and Orru, 1997, for extensions to international commerce.

96. DiMaggio and Louch, 1998, p. 634.

97. Quoted in Brennan, 2002b, p. 38.

98. Hirsch, 2000. Hirsch's early thinking on this subject appeared in his 1972 publication (see Hirsch, 1991).

99. Havens, 2003a, p. 35.

100. Hirsch, 2000, p. 356; see also Havens, 2003a.

101. See for example, Curtin, 2005.

102. Gulati and Di Maria, 2000.

103. See Dacin, Ventresca, and Beal, 1999.

NOTES TO CHAPTER 3

1. Quote from the NATPE seminar, "*Xena Warrior Princess*: Warrior Princess and Worldwide Phenomenon," 1998.

2. Quote from the NATPE seminar, "Muy Caliente! The U.S. Latino Market," 2001.

3. However, Fox's abandonment of the traditional fall launch in favor of three separate launch periods in June, November, and January did not sit well with buyers outside the United States. According to Richard Sattler, CEO of RSP International (which represents foreign TV buyers), "the international buyers are very confused by Fox announcing so many schedules with summer, fall and midseason launches. It makes it all very confusing, especially when we have spent time convincing the industry that time slots are everything" (Brennan, 2004c). Starting with the 2005–2006 season, Fox scaled back to a two-part schedule (Wallenstein, 2005).

4. The debate about product placement is growing as brands have shifted from storyline props to front-and-center story elements; as to date, however, no set pricing or valuation standards are in place, leaving advertisers unsure of branding's economic value and companies racing each other to develop a standard measurement formula (Howard, 2004; Parkes, 2004; Roberts, 2005; Schiller, 2004). In early 2006 the Screen Actors Guild and Writers Guild of America West staged their first joint protest over product placement, demanding a code of conduct be established addressing issues of creative rights, consultation, and compensation (Hielstand, 2006).

5. Lowry, 2003.

6. Carter, 2003.

7. Goldsmith, Nelson and Karnitschnig, 2003.

8. Andreeva, 2007.

9. Our interest here is on genre as manifested primarily through programs and/or program formats. Clearly, the import/export of genre-specific channels raises a different set of social and cultural considerations. MTV Networks is the leader in this regard. Airing in 164 countries and territories and broadcast in eighteen different languages, about 80 percent of MTV's viewership now lies outside the United States (Roberts, 2005, p. 34).

10. Feuer (1992) explores the different meanings of the term "genre" for literature, film, and television. In literature, the term refers to broad categories that are generally not treated in a historical or cultural context, whereas film and television genres are "culturally specific and temporally limited" (1992, p. 139). As such, film

and television genres tend to be historically defined while literary genres tend to be theoretically defined.

11. Crane, 1992, p. 112.

12. Havens, 2003a, p. 18.

13. While not a primary focus of this chapter, classification by genre also retains significance as a model for cultural creators, an organizer of audience expectations, and a means of evaluation for both viewers and critics (Bowles, 2000; Cunningham and Jacka, 1994; Cunningham and Miller, 1994; Feuer, 1992; Frith, 1996; Gledhill, 1997, 2000).

14. Bowles, 2000, p. 128.

15. See Frith, 1996, p. 93.

16. The role of serials in these debates has been well documented elsewhere and is beyond the scope of the current project; see Abu-Lughod (1993), Allen (1995, 1996), Ang (1985), Barker (1997), Biltereyst and Meers (2000), Gutierrez and Schement (1984), Liebes and Katz (1990), Liebes and Livingstone (1998), Lopez (1991, 1995), Lutgendorf (1995), Matelski (1999), Miller (1995), Morley (1992), Rofel (1995), and Rogers and Antola (1985).

17. Allen, 1996, p. 124. Oltean (1993) explains the distinction between series and serials as follows, "'Series' means structure and transformation of the narrative material. Structure means interdependence of all the narrative constituents, transformation refers to the possibility of change in the functioning of narrative in order to realize the chain construction. Series as such is a network of relations. While having an internal organization of their own, the episodes have hierarchical relations with the whole they comprise (the series) and which they represent (the episodes execute a 'decomposition' of series). The purpose of the serial transformation is to bind the audience to a narrative sequential process, maintaining its involvement as a receiver of successive episodes, and attempting to seduce it as a co-author of the whole" (1993, pp. 10–11).

18. Allen, 1995; Hagedorn, 1995; O'Donnell, 1999; Oltean, 1993.

19. O'Donnell, 1999, p. 2.

20. Allen, 1996, p. 116.

21. Livingstone, 1998, p. 80.

22. Ibid., pp. 53–54.

23. O'Donnell, 1999.

24. Matelski, 1999.

25. Liebes and Livingston, 1998, p. 153.

26. Ibid., pp. 159, 172.

27. Ibid., p. 175.

28. A potential drawback to the exportability of continuing serials is delineating the boundaries of the narrative. This is especially problematic in the U.S. and British context due to the long history of the serial tradition. While providing a

large pool of episodes for buyer selection, some domestically successful programs make unwieldy export products. NBC's *Days of Our Lives*, for example, is in its forty-second year on the air as of this writing, while Britain's *Coronation Street* is in its forty-seventh year and CBS's *Guiding Light* remains the grande dame of serial programming with seventy years of storytelling on radio and television. With cultural products like these, how many episodes constitute "the story"? How much of the text are buyers willing and able to purchase?

29. Edmunds, 2004, p. 78.

30. See O'Donnell (1999) for an analysis of domestic soaps and telenovelas appearing in Europe in the 1990s. See Matelski (1999) for a region-by-region account of serial industries worldwide. See Liebes and Livingstone (1998) for an examination of domestically produced serials in Europe.

31. Bielby and Bielby, 1994, p. 1293.

32. Cohen, 2002, p. 205; see also Gledhill, 1997; Turner, 2001.

33. Allen, 1985, p. 47.

34. Liebes and Katz, 1990, p. 5.

35. Matelski, 1999, p. 46.

36. Antola and Rogers, 1984; McAnany and La Pastina, 1994; Straubhaar, 1991.

37. Allen, 1996; Martin-Barbero, 1995; Straubhaar, 1991.

38. Biltereyst and Meers, 2000, p. 395.

39. Ibid., p. 400.

40. Ibid., p. 407.

41. Allen, 1996, p. 117.

42. Ibid., p. 123.

43. See "Fremantle Soaps Flot [sic] Overseas: 'AMC' Now in 14 Countries," press release by the Fremantle Corporation dated August 27, 2001, available at http://www.c21media.net/resources/detail.asp?area=78&article=32427; accessed online February 15, 2003.

44. See Brennan, 2001b, and *Soap Opera Digest* 2002, p. 5.

45. Some of the biggest global success stories for the U.S. soap industry have involved programs that no longer air domestically. For example, *Sunset Beach*, (NBC), which aired in the United States for only two years (1997–1999), was broadcast in more than sixty different countries worldwide (Dawn, 1999, p. 36). The half-hour serial *Loving* aired for twelve years on ABC (1983–1995) before morphing into *The City*, which continued to air for two additional years. Despite its 1997 cancellation in the domestic market, as of 2003 *The City* aired in seventeen different countries and *Loving* in twenty-six (www.fremantlecorp.com, accessed February 15, 2003). *Loving/The City* was an international favorite in part because it was the only soap that could offer "an entire package of shows to countries in one neat package" (*Soap Opera Now!*, 1995).

46. Biltereyst and Meers, 2000.

47. Allen, 1997; Barker, 1997.

48. According to the 2000 U.S. Census, the Hispanic or Latino/a population grew by nearly 60 percent in the 1990s and there are now more than forty million people of Hispanic origin living in the United States. In total numbers, the Hispanic population is now the largest racial-ethnic minority group in the United States. The five U.S. markets with the largest Hispanic viewing audiences are New York (with seven million households), Los Angeles (five million), Chicago (three million), San Francisco (2.5 million) and Dallas (two million) (*New York Times*, May 13, 2003, p. Z6; *Video Age International*, October 2004, p. 46).

49. Allen, 1996, p. 125.

50. *New York Times*, May 13, 2003, p. Z6.

51. Edmunds, 2004.

52. The median age of U.S.-born Hispanics is eighteen, while that of Latino immigrants is thirty-five. Industry insiders argue that while traditionally programming to Hispanic viewers was based on assumptions about language (i.e., Spanish or English as viewers' language of origin), it is actually more important to know whether viewers are U.S. born or non-U.S. born. Statistics show that "second and third generation Hispanics watch both English and Spanish language TV stations, even though they primarily speak Spanish at home" (*Video Age International*, 2004, p. 46).

53. Whoriskey, 2006.

54. Acevedo's observations were made in his capacity as a panelist at the NATPE seminar, "Beyond the Telenovela: Program Opportunities in the U.S. Latino Market" (2002).

55. Bowles, 2000, p. 128.

56. This is how a journalist described *Quest USA*, a bilingual reality show that aired in fall 2004 (Anthony, 2004).

57. Havens, 2003a, pp. 29, 30.

58. Ibid., p. 32.

59. These genre categories are not necessarily standard in the industry, even within Fremantle. For example, Bibnet, the online market for program buyers and sellers, lists forty-four broad genre categories available for browsing that range from "Art" and "Fine Arts" to "Religious" and "Erotic" (http://www.bibnet.com/serieszone/, accessed June 10, 2004). In contrast, Breakthrough Entertainment markets only eight genres at international trade fairs, including Animation, Kids/Youth, Documentary, Drama, Factual Entertainment, Factual Entertainment/Medical Series, Lifestyle, and Variety (promotional brochure obtained at MIP-COM 2004). Fremantle's own print brochure, also obtained at MIPCOM 2004, represents genre categories differently than it does online. In print, programs are categorized as Action/Adventure, Animated Series and Specials, Comedy Series, Daytime Drama, Primetime Drama, Documentaries, Event Programming, Family Programming, Game Shows, How To Series, Infotainment, Music Series, Reality Programs, Science Fiction, Specials, and TV Movies. These differences speak to

the fluidity of genre classifications in the global distribution process; see concluding section of this chapter.

60. www.fremantlecorp.com, accessed February 15, 2003.

61. In Fremantle's print brochure (obtained at MIPCOM 2004), *All My Children's* program description is slightly different:

> *All My Children's* popularity is due largely to it's [sic] unique ability to capture viewers with a blend of social issues, satire and realism. Over the years, the program has undertaken story lines on abortion, drug abuse, incest and interracial romance, always in a well-informed and sensitive manner. The program has won over thirty Emmy Awards, two for Outstanding Drama Series and in 1997 it won its fourth for Best Writing, as well as seventeen 1998 Daytime Emmy nominations including Best Daytime Drama. After being nominated for 19 consecutive years, in 1999 *All My Children* star, Susan Lucci, won a Daytime Emmy for Best Actress and *All My Children* continues to receive Daytime Emmy nominations each year.

Interestingly, in the brochure Fremantle designates *All My Children* as a "Daytime Drama" rather than a soap opera. These are interchangeable designations in the U.S. domestic context but it is unclear whether that holds true internationally.

62. Fremantle's 2004 print brochure offers, again, a slightly different description:

> New racy daily soap opera produced by MTV, aimed at the teen crowd, which pokes fun at the sudsy storylines, as it remains faithful to the genre's conventions. Centered on the Carlisle family, owners of the Spyder video game empire, it has the requisite soap attractions: a murder mystery, sibling rivalry, a hot love triangle, an unspoken crush, a torrid top secret fling, bare abs and closeted gay action.

Of interest here is the reference to comedy/camp, absent from the online description but potentially attracting new and different kinds of viewers. More importantly, *Spyder Games* is explicitly marketed as a "soap opera" in the print brochure description rather than a "totally new genre of television" as it is online (even as it is subsumed in the Fiction/Drama/Soap Opera category online). Again, this points to the fluidity of genre classifications throughout the distribution process.

63. Cantor and Cantor, 1986, 1992.

64. Caldwell, 2004a, pp. 47, 48.

65. Barnes, 2005.

66. Dawn, 2002, p. 56.

67. Barnes, 2005.

68. Bauder, 2001.

69. Anger, 1998.

70. Davison, 1997.

71. See Dawn, 2000; Flores, 2001.

72. Staneley, 2000.

73. Barnes, 2005.

74. Mayberry, 2007.

75. See Ford (2007) for additional examples of transmedia and multiplatform storytelling as well as ideas for further economic revitalization of U.S. soaps. See Alvarado (2007) for similar ancillary businesses in the telenovela market.

76. See Barnes, 2005.

77. "SoapNet Launches GH Spin-Off," *Soap Opera Digest*, March 6, 2007, p. 6.

78. NATPE Educational Foundation video, "Coffee with Dick Wolf," 1998.

79. Quoted in Sloane, 2001, p. 43.

80. Martin-Barbero, 1995, p. 283.

81. Juneau, 1993, p. 19.

82. Quoted in Museum of Television and Radio, *Worlds without End: The Art and the History of the Soap Opera* (New York: Abrams, 1997), p. 161.

83. Quoted in Museum of Television and Radio, *Worlds without End: The Art and History of the Soap Opera* (New York: Abrams, 1997, 118.

84. Liebes and Livingstone, 1998, p. 175.

85. Olson, 2004, p. 114.

86. Ibid., p. 120; emphasis deleted.

87. Skuse, 2002.

88. See, however, Sandvoss (2005) on fandom and neutrosemy.

89. As Olson argues in his critique of cultural imperialism approaches, "There is an effect to the American media, but it is not to project American values; quite to the contrary, American media are now cleverly designed so as to reinforce existing values. This results in interstitial readings and polyglot cultures, but not monoculture" (2004, p. 126).

90. Bitereyst and Meers, 2000, p. 397; see also Lopez, 1995; Mayer, 2003.

91. Quoted in Whoriskey, 2006.

92. For example, Greg Haddrick, a writer for Australia's hit youth-oriented serial *Home and Away* (first airing domestically in 1988 and targeted toward 8–15-year-olds), says he pays no attention at all to the program's substantial foreign market in developing story content (informal communication, Telenovelas and Soap Operas Conference, Australian National University, Canberra, Australia, March 2002).

93. Barker, 1997, pp. 95–96.

94. Coons, 1996, p. 5.

95. Owens, 2004, pp. 36, 38.

96. MacFarquhar, 2002, p. 68.

97. *Soap Opera Digest*, 2001b, p. 6.

98. Bielby and Harrington, 2005.

99. Kinsey, 2000, p. 41.

100. Matelski, 1999, p. 47; as noted earlier, however, *All My Children* is currently selling well abroad.

101. Flores, 2004, p. 49.

102. *Soap Opera Digest*, 2001a, p. 14.

103. Calvo, 2001.

104. Quoted in "CBS Woos Hispanic Viewers," *Soap Opera Digest*, April 13, 1999, p. 13; see also Matelski, 1999, pp. 49–50.

105. Ordonez, 2006.

106. Bulkley, 2004; Friedman, 2004.

107. *Soap Opera Weekly*, November 12, 2006.

108. Garvin, 2007.

109. Quoted in Garvin, 2007.

110. Hornik, 1996; Matelski, 1999.

111. See Scardaville, 2005.

112. *Soap Opera Weekly*, 2002.

113. See Jensen, 2000.

114. Bowles, 2000; Cunningham and Jacka, 1994; Cunningham and Miller, 1994.

115. Bowles, 2000, pp. 124–25.

116. Cunningham and Miller, 1994, p. 10.

117. Bowles, 2000, p. 125.

118. Cohen, 2002, p. 205.

119. For example, Crofts, 1995; Cunningham and Jacka, 1994; but see Miller, 1995.

120. Cohen, 2002, p. 206.

121. Ibid., p. 207.

122. Levy, 2005, p. 55.

123. See Gledhill, 2000.

124. Turner, 2001, p. 5.

125. Ellis, 2000, pp. 26–27.

126. See Cunningham and Jacka, 1994.

127. Mittel, 2004, p. 172.

128. Ibid., p. 173; see also Gledhill, 2000.

NOTES TO CHAPTER 4

1. Brennan and Turner, 2005, p. 31.

2. Sidhva, 2005.

3. The complexity and differentiation that can exist within popular cultural forms is considerable. For example, in a recent study of the emergence of the rhythm and blues and country and western music markets, Dowd (2003) demonstrated how diversity in musical style, aided by technology and sustained by a demand created by underserved audiences with particular tastes, brought heterogeneity in musical forms to the recording industry despite resistance by the

mainstream market of the time. This, in turn, worked against the emergence of "race" and "hillbilly" music markets. Griswold's (2000; Griswold and Bastian, 1987) study of Nigerian novels identified appreciable product differentiation within fiction genres, some of which are themselves adaptations (or in Griswold's terminology, "reconstructions") of established Western genres such as romance novels. These adaptations arose because of cultural differences in gender relations and in reliance upon oral traditions between the United States and Africa. In an examination of racial representations in a diverse set of American children's literature from the 1930s to the 1990s, Pescosolido and her colleagues (1997) identified shifting representations in both frequency and kind that coincided with societal-level transformations in Black-White race relations in the United States.

4. Bielby, Moloney, and Ngo, 2005.

5. In an article about innovation in television, Newcomb and Hirsch (1983, p. 51) explain, "The goal of every producer is to create the difference that makes a difference, to maintain an audience with sufficient reference to the known and recognized, but to move ahead into something that distinguishes his show for the program buyer, the scheduler, and most importantly, for the mass audience." This process of "recombination" is typical as a market strategy for artistic products (see discussion in Crane [2000, p. 153] in another context, and in Gitlin [1983, pp. 75–85] as it pertains to television). Recombination "is not random but is always based on what was done immediately before" and consists of "the variation and rearrangement of elements that had been used successfully in the past" (Crane, 2000, p. 153).

6. See Caves, 2000. See also Heilbrun and Gray (1993) and Throsby (2001) for a general discussion of cultural economics.

7. Source: Hornik, 1998, p. S14.

8. Source: Hollinger, 2003, 2005.

9. Brennan and Turner, 2005, p. 31.

10. See Littlejohn, 1972; Caughie, 1984; Lang, 1958.

11. Newcomb, 1974.

12. Toogood, 1978; see also Harrington and Bielby, 1995a, 1995b.

13. McCarthy, 2001.

14. Hills, 2001, p. 154.

15. Prall, 1964 [1936], pp. 30–31.

16. Place, 1978, p. 42.

17. Ibid.

18. Cantor, 1971.

19. Metallinos, 1996, p. 223.

20. Drawing from the field of philosophy, television studies scholar Nikos Metallinos elaborates that the television medium operates on the idea of a continuous flow of time and motion, whereas film is based on the idea of finite motion (1996, pp. 272–73).

21. Lorand, 2002.

22. Like film, the rules of art composition regarding sight, sound, and motion comprise the essential elements of television aesthetics, but Metallinos (1996) concludes that television's distinctive formal visual elements are more consistent with modernist approaches to viewing works of art than traditional ones.

23. The size and shape of the television screen—its picture field—affects the shape and form of its compositional elements on-screen.

24. Lorand offers an interesting analysis of experiencing the magnificence of Greta Garbo's portrayal of Tolstoy's tragic heroine, Anna Karenina, in a film theater but finding it disappointing to watch on television. She observes, "the greatness of Garbo, projected onto a small frame, was transformed into a ridiculous, over-dramatized story" (2002, p. 11). In a contrasting example of how the technical aspects of the television medium better lend themselves to stories about emotional detail and nuance, Newcomb (1974) describes his positive experience viewing the BBC adaptation of Henry James's *The Golden Bowl,* a novel about personal intimacy that was effectively captured by virtue of the definitive visual intimacy of television.

25. Bielby and Harrington, 1992.

26. See Lembo, 2000, for example.

27. Williams, 1992 [1974].

28. Lorand, 2002, p. 16.

29. See Williams-Rude, 1999.

30. Quoted in Schlosser, 1999a, p. 24. Indeed, Davies was so enamored with the show and convinced it would be a hit that he subsequently quit his position at ABC to become co-executive producer of the U.S. production with Paul Smith, creator of the *Millionaire* format.

31. Schlosser, 1999b, p. 9.

32. Sutel, 2000.

33. *Television Europe,* 2002. By 2002, the format had been licensed to twenty-seven nations throughout the European region alone, with several additional Eastern European countries scheduled to begin production (*Television Europe,* 2002, p. 40).

34. Porter, 2000, p. 1.

35. Daswani, 2000.

36. One journalist reported, "Come 9 p.m., Mondays to Thursdays, big cities and small townships across India look as if they have fallen under some sort of military curfew." India's version is known as *Kaun Banega Crorepathi?* (or *KBC*), which translates literally to *Who Wants to Be a Crorepathi?* A crorepathi is "someone who has in excess of one crore, which works out to around $222,000" (Daswani, 2000, F12).

37. Delhi hotel chain president Priya Paul, quoted in Daswani, 2000, p. F12.

38. Quoted in Daswani, 2000, p. F13.

39. El-Magd, 2002, p. F12.

40. Ibid.

41. Newcomb, 1974.

42. Porter, 2000, p. A1.

43. Ibid., p. A6.

44. Ibid., p. A1.

45. Quoted in Porter, 2000, p. A6.

46. Schaefer, 2000.

47. Ibid., p. B6.

48. Ibid. There are, of course, numerous interesting examples of series or formats that do not successfully adapt because of local tastes. The quiz show *Weakest Link* (a British format) failed in Thailand because its "finger-pointing and the tension produced between contestants would raise some eyebrows in a society that abhors embarrassing people" (Elmore, 2002, p. 58). Public disapproval was expressed by Thai government representatives, who observed that it "encourages selfishness and overlooks the importance of friendship" (Elmore, 2002, p. 58).

49. Bielby and Bielby, 2004.

50. NATPE Seminar, "Doing Business with the U.S.: A Format for Success," 2001.

51. Ibid.

52. Indeed, the success of *Pop Stars* in India spawned an interesting development in that country, the success of the *adapted* imported format (in this case, the program *Indian Idol*, which locals regard as an "individual-driven" show that appeals to urban audiences). Prior to this, for an imported format to succeed it had to satisfy the widespread traditional cultural practice in which viewing was done by entire families (Brennan and Bhushan, 2005), which of course prescribed content as well. In another adaptation for Indian culture, the caustic equivalent of panel judge (and format creator) Simon Cowell has been eliminated. "We realized early on that this was an element of the show that would not play well in this country . . . where people are by nature very polite" (Andy Kaplan, senior executive vice-president, international networks, Sony Entertainment Television, quoted in Brennan, 2004d, p. 14).

53. NATPE Seminar, "Doing Business with the U.S.: A Format for Success," 2001.

54. NATPE Seminar, "*Xena: Warrior Princess*: Warrior Princess and Worldwide Phenomenon," 1998. Panel moderator, *New York Daily News* television critic and acknowledged *Xena* fan David Bianculli shared at the outset of the discussion that while initially he favorably evaluated the show for his readership as a "guilty pleasure," not long thereafter he changed his assessment by dropping "guilty" and elevating his evaluation to the more respectable "pleasure." The global and domestic U.S. audience agreed; it was a ratings leader in numerous countries, and in the United States in 1998 it was the top-rated series in syndication.

55. Quoted in NATPE Seminar, "*Xena: Warrior Princess*: Warrior Princess and Worldwide Phenomenon," 1998.

56. NATPE Seminar, "Doing Business with the U.S.: A Format for Success," 2001.

57. Ibid.

58. Ellis, 2000.

59. Lowry, 2000d, p. F1.

60. When a seller has leverage over the market, concessions concerning scheduling can be extracted from buyers. One such instance involves the selling of *Dr. Phil* abroad by its current owner CBS Broadcast International, the same company that handles the very popular, internationally successful *Oprah*. Because *Oprah* has been one of the best-selling U.S. exports for the last two decades, when the time came to license *Dr. Phil* abroad, CBS International was able to negotiate with buyers that the two shows would not compete with one another within a given market (Brennan, 2003b, p. 14).

61. Because the shipment of the brochures from one telenovela production company, Caracol, failed to arrive at the 2004 MIPCOM convention, our sample was unable to include them for that year.

62. Bielby and Bielby, 1994.

63. Hecht, 2005a.

64. Barrera and Bielby, 2001.

65. A subsample of forty-one of the 1998 NATPE promotional brochures from Latin American telenovelas—Columbia's Caracol, GloboTV from Brazil, TV Azteca from Mexico, and TeleArte from Argentina—revealed that of the two types of information (visual and textual) on the brochures, by far the greatest amount of space was allocated to visual representation of the series.

66. Textual elements of the brochures consisted of the following categories: cast lists of actors (n = 41), plot descriptions (n=41), and lists of writers, directors, and producers (n = 39). The production company was always mentioned. As noted in chapter 3, the text was in Spanish, but a description of the plot was also usually provided in English. The prevalence of these particular textual components is consistent with the tradition of telenovelas being well financed, prestigious productions that attract the best creative talent. Sellers/distributors would want to advertise the quality of their production to potential buyers.

67. Davies, 1999, p. 36.

68. Rolfe, 2005.

69. Palti, cited in Rolfe, 2005, p. 63.

70. A further illustration of the importance of visual elements to marketing in the global export market appeared on the cover of the 2002 NATPE convention edition of *Television Latin America*. The cover reproduced the brochure for TV Globo's telenovela, *El Clone* (The Clone*)*. This popular export was the story of a Brazilian woman living in the Middle East, in love with a local who dies. But

before he passes away, his godfather clones him, and years later the woman falls in love with his clone. Just how similar the clone's persona is to his "source" is the focus of the plot, which explores the limits and possibilities of cultural boundaries and identities. The cover of *Television Latin America* shows the three characters; the Latin woman is in Middle Eastern garb, while the different wardrobe of the two men suggests opposing lifestyles. As a backdrop to the three actors pictured in character is the silhouette of a man in Arab dress riding a camel in a desert. Across the silhouette is text in Spanish that reads, "The first telenovela that speaks about the Islamic world and human cloning." However, the story is already apparent by the visual composition of the cover and the title of the series.

71. Our collection includes publications from Wales, London, Turin, Naples, Paris, Kyoto, Ankara, Beijing, Sydney, Milan, Morocco, Rome, Jerusalem, soap opera magazines from Australia, and the telenovela magazine *TV y Novelas* that is sold in many U.S. regions.

72. Dyer, 1979, 1986.

73. Miller et al., 2001; and in the domestic origins of the industry, see for example, Scott, 2005.

74. There is an interesting history to how Hollywood arrived at its reliance upon actors to sell a film to potential audiences (see Scott, 2005, for example). At first, the studios suppressed such credits, and after much trial and error discovered that the best marketing strategy for film relied upon advertising actors, with whom audiences could identify. This approach became an especially important strategy for engaging international audiences, upon whom all other production aspects were lost (see chapter 5).

75. A study of the syndicated programming audience underscores the significance of our finding: U.S. viewers have more trust in stars of syndicated programming than in those on network shows (Purcell, 2007a).

76. See Nordenstreng and Varis, 1974.

77. Van der Weel, 1990, p. 24.

78. Deputy manager, sales, from the China International TV Corporation, Beijing, China.

79. Even economically prosperous countries make cost-efficient decisions. Sweden does not dub English-language programs but instead applies subtitles in Swedish (personal communication with Elizabeth Thomson, August, 2002, Chicago, IL). Other countries, like Russia, bypass dubbing altogether, opting to rely upon a commentator to narrate the action over the voices of the actors (Brennan, 2002c, pp. 6, 57).

80. Antola and Rogers, 1984.

81. Since the publication of Antola and Rogers's research, translation work is now also done in other locales and can be provided by the selling production company, as we found in our fieldwork.

82. Although the pay is good, employment can be intermittent, and while

the studio owner cultivates ties to its artists, many freelance at other locations or work in other occupations.

83. Khalil and Zayan, 2005.

84. Private communication, July 14, 2006.

85. Boudreaux, 1998.

86. Ibid.

87. Hecht, 2005b, p. 40.

88. It is perhaps worth noting that video games undergo customizing as well, largely due to the increase in script length, elaborate artwork, and complex characters that evolve over time (Pham and Sandell, 2003).

89. Bawol, 1998.

90. Swidler, Rapp, and Soysal, 1986, p. 325.

91. Countries that forego commercial breaks still advertise. Many insert extended commercial breaks with multiple advertisers prior to the beginning of an episode; others incorporate extended breaks at the top of the hour and at its midpoint. Still others, such as some channels in Turkey, stream advertising at the bottom of the screen while a program is airing or insert pop-ups at regular intervals, much like one would see on a computer screen.

92. Montgomery, 1989.

93. Chang, 2000, p. B-4.

94. Censorship issues are not limited just to existing programming; licensed formats that produce localized versions of programming also face adaptation to get on the air. *Fear Factor* in Asia avoids certain foods that would offend Malaysian, Indonesian, and Indian teams, and skin-bearing and body-contact stunts are performed by covered-up players (Stein, 2006). Audience access to China's *Super Girl*, its adaptation of *American Idol*, has been curtailed because it promoted instant-celebrity culture and allowed viewers to vote in a democratic fashion (Fowler and Qin, 2006).

95. *Change of Heart*, a hit show about relationships that was in syndication in 2000, featured young couples uncertain about staying together putting their relationship to the test through blind dates with others. The program's producer, Scott St. John, attributed its popularity to its ability to show "humanity," which he regards as the medium's "most basic level" of coverage (Shamas, 2000, p. F3).

96. See for example, Jones, Anand, and Alvarez, 2005.

97. Peterson (1997) defines this as the vocal artist's ability to resolve problems in unique and distinctive ways, often described as self-expression.

98. Turner, 2005, p. 75.

99. For example, Joanne Martin and her colleagues focused on how the practice of "bounded emotionality" at The Body Shop allows for discussion of intimate, personal issues among employees (Martin, Knopoff, and Beckman, 1998).

100. Akaah, 1991.

101. Newcomb and Hirsch, 1983, p. 53.

102. See Bourdieu, 1984.

103. Stigel, 2001.

1. Kapner, 2003.

2. Lowry, 2000e.

3. For example, in Hall's (1980) encoding/decoding model, it is the discursive message that "is transformed from social relations, practices, and economic means of production (encoding) into a moment of signification (program/discourse) and back again to forms of social relations and practices (decoding)" (D'Acci, 2004, p. 426). In contrast, Richard Johnson's (1986) model of a circuit of production, circulation, and consumption suggests that the cultural product itself is the circulant. On the Open University's (du Gay et al., 1997) circuit-of-culture model, the scholarly analysis of the cultural text is what travels the circuit (D'Acci, 2004, p. 429). Finally, D'Acci's (2004) circuit-of-media-studies model follows the Open University model in suggesting that the research question and its analysis is the model's main circulant, but differs by including fewer sites and by suggesting that the analysis traveling the circuit is not limited to that of a cultural text. See D'Acci (2004) for an extended discussion of circuit models and cultural studies.

4. du Gay, 1997.

5. D'Acci, 2004.

6. Nixon, 1997, p. 10.

7. Caldwell, 2004a, p. 185.

8. See Champ (2007) for a different approach to incorporating verticality into the circuit of culture.

9. du Gay et al., 1997.

10. Dean and Jones, 2003.

11. du Gay, 1997, p. 4.

12. Dean and Jones, 2003, p. 534.

13. Leibniz, cited in Deleuze, 1993, p. 27.

14. Deleuze (1993), cited in Dean and Jones, 2003, p. 535; emphasis in original.

15. Dean and Jones, 2003, pp. 536–37; emphasis in original.

16. Couldry and McCarthy, 2004, p. 2. To understand the processes through which MediaSpace is constructed, the authors outline five ways it has (or might be) analyzed by scholars: (1) "studying media representation"; (2) "the study of how media images, texts and data flow across space and, in doing so, reconfigure social space"; (3) "the study of the specific spaces at either end of the media process, the space of consumption and the space of production"; (4) "the study of the scale-effects, or complex entanglements of scale, which result from the operation of media in space"; and (5) "studying how media-based entanglements of

scale are variously experienced and understood in particular places" (Couldry and McCarthy, 2004, pp. 5–8).

17. In an important exception, Caldwell (2004a) explores how the ritual spaces of trade fairs function to create an illusion of community and cohesion among industry participants.

18. Nordenstreng and Varis, 1974.

19. See Abolafia, 1998.

20. Crane, 2002.

21. The term also refers to programming strategy or the planned sequence in which segments or strips of TV programming unfold on-screen (Williams, 1992 [1974]). Scholars have recently argued that the rapidly changing television environment marked by emergent interactivity and increased program access, among other factors, calls for a reconceptualization of this notion of flow. For example, Brooker (2003) proposes the term "overflow" to describe the tendency for media producers

> to construct a lifestyle experience around a core text, using the Internet to extend audience engagement and encourage a two-way interaction.... The contemporary phenomenon of overflow ... transforms the audience relationship with the text from a limited, largely one-way engagement based around a proscribed [sic] time slot and single medium into a far more fluid and flexible affair which crosses media platforms—Internet, mobile phone, stereo system, shopping mall—in a process of convergence.... Five years from now, this fluid, participatory engagement with the online intertexts around a television series may well be the norm, rather than the exception. (Brooker, 2003, pp. 323, 325, 333)

22. Sinclair, 2004; Straubhaar, Campbell, and Cahoon, 2003. As alluded to in earlier chapters, cultural-linguistic markets can be unified by language, history, religion, ethnicity, and culture broadly defined: "shared identity, gestures and non-verbal communication; what is considered funny or serious or even sacred; clothing styles; living patterns; climate influences and other relationships with the environment.... These cultural similarities and common histories come together to define cultural markets to which television responds" (Straubhaar, Campbell, and Cahoon, 2003). Current cultural-linguistic markets include an Anglophone market (United States, United Kingdom, Australia, Anglophone Canada, English-speaking Caribbean), Western Europe, Latin America (which also includes language markets in Italy and France), a Francophone market (France and its former colonies), an Arabic market, a Chinese market, and a South Asian market (Straubhaar, Campbell, and Cahoon, 2003). Formal integration agreements often contain a number of cultural-linguistic areas; the North American Free Trade Association (NAFTA), for example, includes Anglophone, Francophone, and Latin American markets. The Anglophone market dominates, in part, because English speakers around the world can generally understand one another (Sinclair, 2004, p. 132).

For an analysis of TV flow patterns within five regional markets in NAFTA since the 1960s, see Straubhaar, Campbell, and Cahoon (2003).

23. White, 2003, p. 99.

24. Sinclair and Cunningham, 2000; White, 2003.

25. Dean and Jones, 2003, p. 535.

26. Morley, 2000, 2001.

27. White, 2003, p. 108.

28. Dean and Jones, 2003.

29. This is a truncated version of an argument first presented in Harrington and Bielby (2005).

30. See Bielby, Moloney, and Ngo, 2005.

31. NATPE Seminar, "How to Turn a Homegrown Idea into an International Success," 1998.

32. The fact that TV texts are altered by distribution practices functions, in part, to effectively limit the ability of a producer's, director's, or writer's identity to travel through the site of distribution. To revisit an earlier example, in the U.S. domestic context there are established policies that regulate how often (and at what duration) production credits roll on-screen. Credit rolls are not necessarily preserved in import markets, which might have very different regulations (or none at all). As a result, an Aaron Sorkin production might not be presented as such to viewers in other countries or regions (at least not on-screen), thus restricting the flow of Sorkin's reputational identity.

33. Dean and Jones, 2003, pp. 536–37; emphasis deleted.

34. Gray 2003, p. 72.

35. O'Shaughnessy and O'Shaughnessy, 2000, pp. 56, 58; italics in original.

36. Papandrea, 1998, p. 4.

37. Havens, 2003a, p. 31.

38. We realize that our discussion here implies that nation branding is a banal or uncontroversial practice. Obviously it is a point of contestation in ongoing debates about global media exchanges. See discussion below of Level Three discourses.

39. Quote from Crane, 2002, pp. 9–10. See Alasuutari (1999) and Bird (2003) for a discussion of the history of reception studies. A full discussion of the long-term effects of media reception on national and cultural identities is beyond the scope of our analysis (see Hall, 1992; Iwabuchi, 2002; Morley, 2001; Sreberny-Mohammadi, 1991). According to Crane, reception theory

> requires modification to be useful in today's complex global environment. Understanding the public's responses to global culture in different countries and in different settings within those countries necessitates a broader conceptualization of reception theory, one that goes beyond focusing entirely on the audience itself and instead examines the relationships between the imported culture and the national culture, as well as the roles of cultural

entrepreneurs. (2002, pp. 18–19)
Recent efforts to address these and other concerns include Sandvoss (2003), Juluri (2003a, 2003b), and Murphy and Kraidy (2003).

40. Ware and Dupagne, 1995, p. 951.

41. Ibid., p. 952.

42. Ibid., p. 955.

43. Milikowski, 2000; Naficy, 1999; Barrera and Bielby, 2001; and Mayer,
2003.

44. Bird, 2003; Bratich, 2005; Hartley, 1992; Mosco and Kaye, 2000.

45. Bird, 2003, p. 3.

46. Seiter, 1999, p. 9.

47. Bird, 2003, p. 4.

48. Juluri, 2003a, p. 218.

49. Juluri, 2003b.

50. Caldwell, 2004a; Havens, 2003a.

51. For example, a buyer who focuses on the African market explains,
You've got to remember in Africa there's very little research. . . . It's a very
difficult market to predict audience share, even what audience you're reaching. If you go into . . . Uganda and ask "how many TV sets are there in
Uganda?," from three different people you'll get three different answers
because there are so many illegally brought into the country. If you travel
into Uganda on a plane, half the people seem to be bringing a TV set with
them, so there's lots of TV sets in Uganda but nobody knows how many.
(Mike Fenwick, African Barter Company; NATPE seminar titled, "Advertising in a Brave New World," 1998)

52. Havens, 2003a, p. 22.

53. Ibid., p. 29.

54. Havens, 2003b.

55. Jancovich and Lyons, 2003; Jenkins, 2001; Willis, 2003.

56. du Gay, 2000, p. 71; emphasis in original.

57. Bob Kuperman of TBWA Worldwide; NATPE Educational Foundation
seminar, "When the Advertiser Turns Producer," 2001.

58. NATPE Educational Foundation Seminar, "*Xena: Warrior Princess*: Warrior Princess and Worldwide Phenomenon," 1998. For a discussion of the implications of this shift in business practices for our understanding of the relationship
among TV audiences, viewers, and fans, see Harrington and Bielby (2005).

59. NATPE Educational Foundation, 2004.

60. See Mosco and Kaye (2000) for a discussion of the relationship between
academic and industry conceptions of the audience.

61. Crane, 2002.

62. Ibid., p. 4.

63. Ibid., p. 12.

64. Crane (2002) points to three goals of cultural policy at the international level: "(1) Protecting the country's culture from domination by the cultural achievements of other countries and from encroachments by the media industries of other countries; (2) Creating and maintaining international images of the country or of a region or city within the country; and (3) Developing and protecting international markets and venues for the country's international 'exports'" (2002, p. 13; emphasis deleted). Cultural policy indicates how a country's leader(s) perceives and values its culture. Countries, companies, and cities might preserve, protect, and enhance their cultural resources through preserving and protecting national local cultures, resisting global culture through protectionist strategies, and globalizing national or local cultures for export markets (glocalization) (Crane, 2002, pp. 13–17).

65. The original GATT (now termed GATT 1947) provided the basic rules for international trade from its establishment in 1948 to the founding of the WTO in 1995. GATT 1947 is no longer in force. While the GATT established in 1994 (termed GATT 1994) includes many of key elements from GATT 1947 (such as the most-favored-nation rule), they are legally distinct instruments.

66. Galperin, 1999, p. 630.

67. Murphy and Kraidy, 2003, p. 7.

68. Moran, 2004, p. 265.

69. Galperin, 1999.

70. The NAFTA was launched in 1994, creating a free trade zone among Mexico, Canada, and the United States.

71. The EU was founded in 1993 to enhance political, economic, and social cooperation among member states, now numbering twenty-seven: Austria, Belgium, Denmark, Finland, France, Germany, Greece, Ireland, Italy, Luxembourg, the Netherlands, Portugal, Spain, Sweden, United Kingdom, Greek Cyprus, Czech Republic, Estonia, Hungary, Latvia, Lithuania, Malta, Poland, Slovakia, Slovenia, Romania, and Bulgaria. Not surprisingly, there has been considerable discussion in the trade press about the implications of the EU's expansion, including increased flow of pirated material, delocalization of production, spiraling labor costs, the implications of border-crossing signals given broadcast quotas, and so on (Cendrowicz, 2004; Masters, 2004).

72. The MERCOSUR was created by Argentina, Brazil, Paraguay, and Uruguay in 1986 and was fully consolidated by 1991, with the goal of creating a common market among participating nations. The EU and MERCOSUR signed an interregional agreement in 1995 consisting of three main elements: political dialogue, cooperation, and trade issues.

73. Galperin, 1999, p. 627.

74. Ibid., p. 635.

75. Galperin, 1999. This is obviously an incomplete examination of formal trade agreements and cultural policy; for recent discussions, see Beale, 2002; Galperin, 1999; Schlesinger, 1997.

76. Morley, 2000; Schlesinger, 1997.

77. As noted earlier, audiences do not necessarily coincide with national borders but are increasingly constructed through cultural and linguistic regions.

78. Curtin, 2004, fn. 56.

79. Chris Haws, Discovery Networks Europe; NATPE seminar, "International Session: Francly Factual!," 1998.

80. Irwin Gottleib, TeleVest; NATPE seminar, "Advertising in a Brave New World," 1998.

81. Galperin, 1999, p. 638.

82. Beale, 2002, p. 85; see also Schlesinger, 1997; van Elteren, 1996.

83. Havens, 2003a; Sinclair, 2004.

84. See Kerbo, 2006.

85. Caldwell, 2004a, pp. 164, 185.

86. Ibid., p. 165.

87. See Spigel, 2004.

88. NATPE seminar, "How to Turn a Homegrown Idea into an International Success," 1998.

89. The legendary Brandon Tartikoff explains the importance of gut reactions in television production: "I've generally found that breakout shows fly in the face of research, break the rules. They usually come from one or two people's passionate hunch that something farfetched would actually work. I'm all for feedback, consultation and dialogue between networks and affiliates, stations and studios, but ultimately this is a game of gutsball, not everybody sitting around polling each other" (keynote address at the 1993 NATPE meetings, included in 1998 NATPE Living Curriculum video, "The Future of Television").

90. Havens, 2003a, p. 18.

91. Levy, 2005; Ryan, 2005.

92. Caldwell, 2004a; Havens, 2003a; Penaloza, 2001.

93. Source: http://www.natpe.org/industry/pitchtips.html, accessed June 10, 2004.

94. Professional educators are not wholly marginalized from the business of global TV syndication. For example, NATPE offers a special membership rate to educators and the NATPE Educational Foundation, founded in 1978, aims to promote "better understanding and working relationships between the university faculty who teach television and the electronic media practitioners who ultimately employ their graduates" (http://www.natpe.org/about/educational/, accessed June 10, 2004). Programming sponsored by NATPE's Educational Foundation includes Student Film & Video Production Awards, Faculty Development Grants that offer internship opportunities at leading industry companies, and the Faculty

Fellowship Program that provides access to the NATPE convention and a special seminar series as the convention unfolds.

95. NATPE seminar, "How We Do It: A U.S. Television Market Primer," NATPE 1999.

96. In 1997 the U.S. Congress called for analog signals to be switched off by the end of 2006 or when 85 percent of households obtained a digital TV. That deadline has now passed; as of this writing, legislation is being considered that would shut off analog TV signals at the beginning of 2009 (Boliek, 2005). In contrast, the Netherlands switched to digital in December 2006, the first step in a five-year process to transform broadcasting throughout the European Union by 2012 (Cendrowicz, 2006a).

97. Spigel, 2004, p. 4; see also Caldwell, 2004b. As Spigel goes on to suggest,

As images multiply on a variety of delivery systems and platforms, who knows what audiences are seeing—much less thinking—anymore? . . . Television—once the most familiar of everyday objects—is now transforming at such rapid speeds that we no longer really know what "TV" is at all. . . . [W]e are now entering a new phase of television—the phase that comes after "TV." (2004, pp. 6, 2)

Adds Caldwell, "The rhetorical shift from talking about productions as 'programs' to talking about them as 'content' underscores the centrality of repurposing in industrial practice. The term 'content' frees programs from a year-long series and network-hosted logic and suggests that programs are quantities to be drawn and quartered, deliverable on cable, shippable internationally, and streamable on the Net" (2004b, p. 49).

98. See Caldwell, 2004b; Schiller, 2004. The development and use patterns of new technologies raise important regulatory questions as well. For example, in early 2005 the Dutch cable operator Mediakabel contested the EU's rules on broadcasting quotas, arguing that technologies such as pay-per-view should be exempt. The EU's quota-setting Television Without Frontiers directive requires that European productions account for at least 50 percent of broadcasts where appropriate and that at least 10 percent of broadcast time be allocated to independent European producers. According to Mediakabel, "the minimum quotas for European-made productions are simply impractical to impose for pay-per-view, whose services are entirely consumer-driven" (Cendrowicz, 2005).

99. Laws surrounding product placement differ worldwide. Many Latin American countries, for example, have relied heavily for years on the types of product placement only recently reintroduced into U.S. network television. In contrast, product placement was severely restricted throughout the European Union until revisions of broadcast regulations in late 2006 (Cendrowicz, 2006b).

100. Dean and Jones, 2003; du Gay et al., 1997.

101. D'Acci, 2004, p. 424.

102. Ibid.

NOTES TO THE CONCLUSION

1. Quoted in Brennan, 2006a, p. 14.

2. Indeed, had we completed our research for this book then, NATPE's demise would have been part of the story. Participation has fallen from its peak of around twenty thousand individual participants and high number of exhibition booths to a low in 2004 of a little over six thousand, but it is once again rising, with around eight thousand participating in 2007. An economic downturn that affected advertising revenue, the 9/11 attacks in 2001, and massive domestic industry consolidation motivated exhibitors to cut costs, which led to NATPE's precipitous erosion (see, for example, Pursell, 2001a, 2001b, 2002). Among the contingents who benefit from the convention, however, are the international members who favor the meeting for the access it provides to the latest ratings successes within the United States and midseason replacements (Pursell, 2007b).

3. For example: "NBC Taking TV's Future by the Reins with On-Demand Content, Delivery," "Television Ad Model under Pressure on Two Fronts," "New Media's Effect on the Value of a Viewer," and "Social Network Sites Can Be a Tangled Web" (Mermigas, 2003a, 2003b, 2006a, 2006b).

4. Albiniak, 2006, p. 16.

5. *NATPE News*, 2005.

6. Scott, 2005.

7. Douglas, 1986.

8. Brennan, 2003c.

9. Curtain, 2005.

10. Whitley, 2001.

11. Chung and Hamilton, 2001.

12. Ang's *Desperately Seeking the Audience* insightfully observes,
[I]f television institutions need to know the audience in order to establish and maintain a relationship with it, they are generally not interested in getting to know what real people think and feel and do in their everyday dealings with television. Indeed, institutional knowledge about the television audience inevitably abstracts from the messy and confusing social world of actual audiences because their work is irritating for the institutions, whose first and foremost concern is to seize control over their own conditions of existence. . . . Institutional knowledge is driven toward making the audience visible in such a way that it helps the institutions to increase their power to get their relationship with the audience under control, and this can only be done by symbolically constructing "television audience" as an objectified category of others than can be controlled, that is, contained in the interest of a predetermined institutional goal. (1991, p. 7)
See also Ang, 1996.

13. Bielby and Bielby, 1994.

14. Becker, 1982.

15. For example, the international team at Reveille LLC has been very success-ful on the global scene by using a business plan right out of the old U.S. domestic syndication business—working directly with potential station clients, including broadcasters and producers, to meet specific time-period and ratings needs. In this instance, the company not only licenses programming but markets format-development agreements as well (Brennan, 2006b, p. 18).

16. See Dorsey, 2007; Cendrowicz, 2006b.

17. Sinclair, 2004, p. 133.

18. Kapner, 2003; Brennan, 2005a, 2005b.

19. Nokia's pivotal role in the transposition of fashion style to the technologi-cally driven field of mobile telephony was not strategic. Instead, Nokia was an accidental carrier of cell phone style, blundering into a fashion logic that trans-formed the entire industry (Djelic and Ainamo, 2005).

20. Giddens, 1984.

21. Scott, 2005.

22. Peterson, 1982.

23. Bielby and Harrington, 2005.

24. Curtain, 1996.

NOTES TO THE METHODOLOGICAL APPENDIX

1. Abolafia, 1998.

References

Abolafia, Mitchel Y. 1998. Markets as Cultures: An Ethnographic Approach. Pp. 69–85 in Michael Callon (ed.), *The Sociological Review*. Oxford, UK: Blackwell.

Abu-Lughod, Lila. 1993. Finding a Place for Islam: Egyptian Television Serials and the National Interest. *Public Culture* 5: 493–513.

Akaah, Ishmael. 1991. Strategy Standardization in International Marketing: An Empirical Investigation of Its Degree of Use and Correlates. *Journal of Global Marketing* 4 (2): 39–62.

Alasuutari, Pertti. 1999. Introduction: Three Phases of Reception Studies. Pp. 1–21 in P. Alasuutari (ed.), *Rethinking the Media Audience*. London: Sage.

Albiniak, Paige. 2006. A Different NATPE World. *Broadcasting and Cable*, January 16: 16.

Allen, Robert C. 1985. *Speaking of Soap Operas*. Chapel Hill: University of North Carolina Press.

Allen, Robert C. 1995. Introduction. Pp. 1–26 in R. C. Allen (ed.), *To Be Continued: Soap Operas around the World*. New York: Routledge.

Allen, Robert C. 1996. As the World Turns: Television Soap Operas and Global Media Culture. Pp. 110–27 in Emile G. McAnany and Kenton T. Wilkenson (eds.), *Mass Media and Free Trade: NAFTA and the Cultural Industries*. Austin: University of Texas Press.

Allen, Robert C. 1997. As the World Tunes In: An International Perspective. Pp. 111–19 in *Worlds without End: The Art and History of the Soap Opera*. The Museum of Television and Radio. New York: Abrams.

Alvarado, Maria Teresa. 2007. "Spreading the Love," http://www.worldscreen.com/print.php?filename=merch0607.htm, June, accessed July 6, 2007.

Anderson, Christopher. 1994. *Hollywood: The Studio System in the Fifties*. Austin: University of Texas Press.

Andreeva, Nellie. 2007. "Networks Pilot Orders Shun Serial Dramas," www.hollywoodreporter.com, January 31.

Andreeva, Nellie and Cynthia Littleton. 2004. Cable Leveling TV's Playing Field. *Hollywood Reporter*, May 28–30: 14.

Ang, Ien. 1985. *Watching Dallas: Soap Opera and the Melodramatic Imagination.* New York: Methuen.

Ang, Ien. 1991. *Desperately Seeking the Audience.* New York: Routledge.

Ang, Ien. 1996. *Living Room Wars: Rethinking Media Audiences for a Postmodern World.* London: Routledge.

Anger, Dorothy. 1998. *Other Worlds: Society Seen through Soap Opera.* Peterborough, Ontario: Broadview Press.

Anthony, Ted. 2004. Chinese Reality Show Goes Home. *The Cincinnati Enquirer,* December 21: E5.

Antola, Livia and Everett M. Rogers. 1984. Television Flows in Latin America. *Communication Research* 11 (2): 183–202.

Auletta, Ken. 1991. *Three Blind Mice.* New York: Random House.

Barker, Chris. 1997. *Global Television: An Introduction.* Oxford, UK: Blackwell.

Barnes, Brooke. 2005. A Good Soap Script Includes Love, Tears, and Frosted Flakes. *Wall Street Journal,* January 17: A1.

Barnouw, Erik. 1975. *Tube of Plenty: The Evolution of American Television.* New York: Oxford University Press.

Barrera, Vivian and Denise Bielby. 2001. Faces, Places, and Other Things: The Cultural Experience of Telenovela Viewing among Latinos in the United States. *Journal of Popular Culture* 34 (4): 1–18.

Bauder, David. 2001. Do Soaps Have More Lives to Live? *The Cincinnati Enquirer,* August 2: E3.

Baumann, Shyon. 2001. Intellectualization and Art World Development: Film in the United States. *American Sociological Review* 66: 404–26.

Bawol, Steven. 1998. Funny Bones. *TBI: Television Business International,* October: 51–56.

Beale, Alison. 2002. Identifying a Policy Hierarchy: Communication Policy, Media Industries, and Globalization. Pp. 78–89 in Diana Crane, Nobuko Kawashima, and Ken'ichi Kawasaki (eds.), *Global Culture: Media, Arts, Policy, and Globalization.* New York: Routledge.

Becker, Anne. 2005. Cable Wins Big in 2004. *Broadcasting & Cable,* January 3: 14.

Becker, Howard. 1982. *Art Worlds.* Berkeley: University of California Press.

Belous, Richard S. 1989. "How Human Resource Systems Adjust to the Shift toward Contingent Workers." *Monthly Labor Review* 112 (3): 7–12.

Bielby, Denise D. and William T. Bielby. 2004. Audience Aesthetics and Popular Culture. Pp. 295–317 in Roger Friedland and John Mohr (eds.), *Matters of Culture: Cultural Sociology in Practice.* Cambridge: Cambridge University Press.

Bielby, Denise D. and C. Lee Harrington. 1992. Public Meanings, Private Screenings: The Formation of Social Bonds through the Televisual Experience. Pp. 155–78 in G. Miller and J. A. Holstein (eds.), *Perspectives on Social Problems,* Volume 3. Greenwich, CT: Jai Press.

Bielby, Denise D. and C. Lee Harrington. 2005. Opening America? The Tele-novela-ization of U.S. Soap Operas. *Television & New Media* 6 (4): 383–99.

Bielby, Denise D., C. Lee Harrington, and William Bielby. 1999. Whose Stories Are They? Fan Engagement with Soap Opera Narratives in Three Sites of Fan Activity. *Journal of Broadcasting and Electronic Media* 43 (1): 35–51.

Bielby, Denise D., Molly Moloney, and Bob Q. Ngo. 2005. Aesthetics of Television Criticism: Mapping Critics' Reviews in an Era of Industry Transformation. Pp. 1–43 in Candace Jones and Patricia Thornton (eds.), *Research in the Sociology of Organizations: Transformations in Cultural Industries*. Greenwich, CT: JAI Press.

Bielby, William T. and Denise D. Bielby. 1994. "All Hits Are Flukes": Institutional-ized Decision-making and the Rhetoric of Network Prime-time Program De-velopment. *American Journal of Sociology* 99 (5): 1287–1313.

Bielby, William T. and Denise D. Bielby. 1999. Organizational Mediation of Proj-ect-Based Labor Markets: Talent Agencies and the Careers of Screenwriters. *American Sociological Review* 64 (1): 64–85.

Bielby, William T. and Denise D. Bielby. 2003. Controlling Primetime: Organiza-tional Concentration and Network Television Programming Strategies. *Journal of Broadcasting and Electronic Media* 47 (4): 573–96.

Biggart, Nicole and Richard P. Castanias. 2001. Collateralized Social Relations: The Social in Economic Calculation. *American Journal of Economics and Soci-ology* 60 (2): 471–500.

Biggart, Nicole and Marco Orru. 1997. Societal Strategic Advantage: Institutional Structure and Path Dependence in the Automotive and Electronics Industries of East Asia. Pp. 201–39 in A. Bugra and B. Usdiken (eds.), *State, Market, and Organizational Forms*. Berlin: de Gruyter.

Biltereyst, Daniel and Philippe Meers. 2000. The International Telenovela Debate and the Contra-flow Argument: A Reappraisal. *Media, Culture & Society* 22: 393–413.

Bird, Elizabeth. 2003. *The Audience in Everyday Life: Living in a Media World*. New York: Routledge.

Blumenthal, Howard J. and Oliver R. Goodenough. 1998. *This Business of Tele-vision*. New York: Billboard Books.

Boddy, William. 1998. The Beginnings of American Television. Pp. 23–37 in An-thony Smith (ed.), *Television: An International History*. Oxford: Oxford Uni-versity Press.

Boliek, Brooks. 2005. "House Panel Wrestles with Analog Cutoff," www.hollywood reporter.com, October 26.

Bonner, Frances. 1997. Television. Pp. 245–66 in Stuart Cunningham and Graeme Turner (eds.), *The Media in Australia* (2nd edition). New South Wales: Allen & Unwin.

Borchers, Hans. 1989. Watching US-Produced Soap Operas in Germany: On Some Implications for Cross-Cultural Understanding. Pp. 268–86 in Peter Funke (ed.), *Understanding the USA: A Cross-Cultural Perspective*. Germany: Gunter Narr Verlag.

Boudreaux, Richard. 1998. Actors May Have the Last Word in Strike by Italian Dubbers. *Los Angeles Times*, September 19: A9.

Bourdieu, Pierre. 1984. *Distinction: A Social Critique of the Judgement of Taste*. London: Routledge and Kegan Paul.

Bowles, Kate. 2000. Soap Opera: "No End of Story, Ever." Pp. 117–29 in Graeme Turner and Stuart Cunningham (eds.), *The Australian TV Book*. New South Wales: Allen & Unwin.

Bratich, Jack Z. 2005. Amassing the Multitude: Revisiting Early Audience Studies. *Communication Theory* 15 (3): 242–65.

Brennan Steve. 1998a. A Room with a World View. *Hollywood Reporter*, January 16: S3–S44.

Brennan, Steve. 1998b. NATPE Is Now a Foreign Affair. *Hollywood Reporter*, January 22: 1, 45.

Brennan, Steve. 1998c. TV Classics Get Foreign Flavor. *Hollywood Reporter*, January 19: 49, 51.

Brennan, Steve. 1998d. At MIPCOM, a Mad Dash for Mobile Formats. *Hollywood Reporter*, October 7: 1, 21.

Brennan, Steve. 1998e. Par TV Int'l about to Act Locally at MIPCOM. *Hollywood Reporter*, October 5: 6, 27.

Brennan, Steve. 2001a. Current Affairs. *Hollywood Reporter*, October 2–8: S1–S44.

Brennan, Steve. 2001b. "ABC's 'Children' Goes Worldwide," www.hollywood reporter.com, August 24.

Brennan, Steve. 2002a. Discovery Acts Locally as It Expands Globally. *Hollywood Reporter*, July 2–8: 12.

Brennan, Steve. 2002b. Sharper Picture. *Hollywood Reporter*, June 5: 38.

Brennan, Steve. 2002c. Globo Romancing Euro Markets. *Hollywood Reporter*, June 25–July 2: 6, 57.

Brennan, Steve. 2003a. Local-language Content Hits the Deutsche Mark. *Hollywood Reporter*, September 30–October 6: 14.

Brennan, Steve. 2003b. "Dr. Phil" Has Right RX for Overseas Markets. *Hollywood Reporter*, September 9–15: 14.

Brennan, Steve. 2003c. All the TV in China. *Hollywood Reporter*, March 18–24: 18–19.

Brennan, Steve. 2004a. "MIPCOM 2004," http://www.hollywoodreporter.com/thr/ television/feature, Sept. 28, accessed January 25, 2005.

Brennan, Steve. 2004b. U.K. Producers Shop TV Wares Stateside. *Hollywood Reporter*, December 14–20: 18.

Brennan, Steve. 2004c. "Buyers Askance at All-Year Bows," www.hollywood reporter.com, May 25.

Brennan, Steve. 2004d. India's in Harmony with "Idol"-Making Program. *Hollywood Reporter*, November 23–29: 14.

Brennan, Steve. 2005a. They Love L.A. Screenings. *Hollywood Reporter*, May 26: 1, 31.

Brennan, Steve. 2005b. MIPCOM Focuses Keen Eye on Fate of U.S. Fare. *Hollywood Reporter*, October 11–17: 1, 73.

Brennan, Steve. 2006a. Sharper Picture. *Hollywood Reporter*, March 1: 18.

Brennan, Steve. 2006b. "Overseas 'Top Model' Is a Beauty by Design," http//www.hollywoodreporter.com, July 25, accessed July 25, 2006.

Brennan, Steve. 2006c. Sharper Picture: NATPE's Feldman Has Passport to Open Doors. *Hollywood Reporter*, January 3–9: 14.

Brennan, Steve and Nyay Bhushan. 2005. Beating the Odds. *Hollywood Reporter*, October 4–10: 17–20.

Brennan, Steve and Mimi Turner. 2005. MIPCOM Light on Deals as Market Wraps. *Hollywood Reporter*, October 20: 1, 31.

Brennan, Steve and Mimi Turner. 2006. Going Mobile. *Hollywood Reporter*, March 28–April 3: S-1, S-19.

Broadcasting & Cable. 2004. *Syndication Media Planning Guide*, March 8: 1A–22A.

Broadcasting and Cable.com. 2007. "NATPE Has a Sordid Past," January 21.

Brooker, Will. 2003. Conclusion: Overflow and Audience. Pp. 322–34 in Will Brooker and Deborah Jermyn (eds.), *The Audience Studies Reader*. London: Routledge.

Brooks, Peter. 1976. *The Melodramatic Imagination: Balzac, Henry James, Melodrama, and the Mode of Excess*. New Haven, CT: Yale University Press.

Brooks, Tim and Earle Marsh. 2003. *The Complete Directory to Prime Time Network and Cable TV Shows 1946–Present*. New York: Ballantine.

Brown, Ivy. 1996. As the World Turns the Dial, It Finds the U.S. Label. *Los Angeles Times*, October 11: F-1.

Bulkley, K. 2004. "Aussie Hit 'Neighbours' in U.S. Deal," www.hollywoodreporter.com, March 24.

Caldwell, John T. 2004a. Industrial Geography Lessons: Socio-Professional Rituals and the Borderlands of Production Culture. Pp. 163–89 in Nick Couldry and Anna McCarthy (eds.), *MediaSpace: Place, Scale, and Culture in a Media Age*. London: Routledge.

Caldwell, John T. 2004b. Convergence Television: Aggregating Form and Repurposing Content in the Culture of Conglomeration. Pp. 41–74 in Lynn Spigel and Jan Olsson (eds.), *Television after TV*. Durham, NC: Duke University Press.

Calvo, D. 2001. Soap Opera Seeks to Speak to Latinos. *Los Angeles Times,* April 19: 52.

Cantor, Muriel. 1971. *The Hollywood TV Producer: His Work and His Audience.* New York: Basic Books.

Cantor, Muriel. 1980. *Prime-time Television: Content and Control.* Beverly Hills, CA: Sage.

Cantor, Muriel G. and Joel M. Cantor. 1986. American Television in the International Marketplace. *Communication Research* 13 (3): 509–20.

Cantor, Muriel and Joel Cantor. 1992. *Prime-Time Television: Content and Control* (2nd edition). Newbury Park, CA: Sage.

Carter, Bill. 2003. Viewer Shift Will Write New Reality for TV, Executives Say. *Austin-American Statesman,* January 25: A1, A20.

Caughie, John. 1984. Television Criticism: A Discourse in Search of an Object. *Screen* 25 (4–5): 109–21.

Caves, Richard. 2000. *Creative Industries: Contracts between Art and Commerce.* Cambridge, MA: Harvard University Press.

Cendrowicz, Leo. 2004. "EU B'cast Ministers Mull Border-Crossing Signals," www.hollywoodreporter.com, March 2.

Cendrowicz, Leo. 2005. "*EU Broadcast Quotas Come under Fire,*" www.hollywoodreporter.com, January 21.

Cendrowicz, Leo. 2006a. "Dutch Flick TV Switch to Digital," www.hollywoodreporter.com, December 12.

Cendrowicz, Leo. 2006b. "EU OKs Looser Rules on TV Product Placement," www.hollywoodreporter.com, November 14.

Champ, Joe. 2007. Horizontal Power, Vertical Weakness: Enhancing the "Circuit of Culture." Paper presented at the Annual Meetings of the International Communication Association, San Francisco, CA, May.

Chang, L. 2000. Cracking China's Huge TV Market. *Wall Street Journal,* August 1: B-1, 4.

Channels. 1990. Primetime's Price Tag. *Channels* 10 (September 10): 50–51.

Chu, Henry. 2002. Where "Thorn Birds" Could Have Kept Flying. *Los Angeles Times,* June 15: A5.

Chung, W-K. and G. Hamilton. 2001. Social Logic as Business Logic: Guanxi, Trustworthiness, and the Embeddedness of Chinese Business Practices. Pp. 325–46 in Richard Appelbaum, William Felstiner, and Volkmar Gessner (eds.), *Rules and Networks: The Legal Culture of Global Business Transactions.* Oxford, UK: Hart.

Cohen, Jonathan. 2002. Television Viewing Preferences: Programs, Schedules, and the Structure of Viewing Choices Made by Israeli Adults. *Journal of Broadcasting & Electronic Media* 46: 204–21.

Colitt, R., A. Fifield, J. Johnson, R. Marcelo, and P. T. Larsen. 2003. The United States of Television. *Financial Times,* July 21.

Collins, Scott. 2005. A Summer of Lost Viewers for TV Networks. *Los Angeles Times*, August 23: E1, E11.

Coons, Joanna. 1996. Does Daytime Need to Look for Alternatives? *Soap Opera Now!* August 12: 5.

Couldry, Nick and Anna McCarthy. 2004. Introductions: Orientations: Mapping MediaSpace. Pp. 1–18 in Nick Couldry and Anna McCarthy (eds.), *MediaSpace: Place, Scale, and Culture in a Media Age*. London: Routledge.

Covington, Richard. 1997. A Bonanza for Export: TV Series Adventure Travels Well, but Sitcoms Rarely Leave Home. *International Herald Tribune*, October 29: 13.

Crane, Diana. 1992. *The Production of Culture: Media and the Urban Arts*. Newbury Park, CA: Sage.

Crane, Diana. 2000. *Fashion and Its Social Agendas*. Chicago: University of Chicago Press.

Crane, Diana. 2002. Culture and Globalization: Theoretical Models and Emerging Trends. Pp. 1–25 in Diana Crane, Nobuko Kawashima, and Ken'ichi Kawasaki (eds.), *Global Culture: Media, Arts, Policy, and Globalization*. New York: Routledge.

Crofts, Stephen. 1995. Global *Neighbours*? Pp. 98–121 in Robert Allen (ed.), *To Be Continued: Soap Operas around the World*. London: Routledge.

Croteau, David and William Hoynes. 2000. *Media/Society: Industries, Images, and Audiences*. Thousand Oaks, CA: Pine Forge Press.

Cunningham, Stuart. 1997. Television. Pp. 90–111 in S. Cunningham and G. Turner (eds.), *The Media in Australia* (2nd edition). New South Wales: Allen & Unwin.

Cunningham, Stuart and Elizabeth Jacka. 1994. Neighbourly Relations? Cross-Cultural Reception Analysis and Australian Soaps in Britain. *Cultural Studies* 8: 509–26.

Cunningham, Stuart and Toby Miller (with David Rowe). 1994. *Contemporary Australian Television*. Sydney, Australia: UNSW Press.

Curtain, Michael. 1996. On Edge: Culture Industries in the Neo-Network Era. Pp. 181–202 in Richard Ohmann (ed.), *Making and Selling Culture*. Hanover, NH: Wesleyan University Press/University Press of New England.

Curtin, Michael. 2004. Media Capitals: Cultural Geographies of Global TV. Pp. 270–302 in Lynn Spigel and Jan Olsson (eds.), *Television after TV*. Durham, NC: Duke University Press.

Curtin, Michael. 2005. Murdoch's Dilemma, Or "What's the Price of TV in China?" *Media, Culture, and Society* 27 (2): 155–75.

D'Acci, Julie. 2004. Cultural Studies, Television Studies, and the Crisis in the Humanities. Pp. 418–45 in Lynn Spigel and Jan Olsson (eds.), *Television after TV*. Durham, NC: Duke University Press.

Dacin, M. Tina, Marc J. Ventresca, and Brent D. Beal. 1999. The Embeddedness of Organizations: Dialogue and Directions. *Journal of Management* 25 (3): 317–56.

Daswani, K. 2000. "Millionaire" Is the Taj Mahal of Indian TV. *Los Angeles Times*, September 30: F12–F13.

Davies, L. 1999. A Question of Culture. *TBI: Television Business International* (NATPE/Monte Carlo Issue), January/February: 36–38.

Davis, Lina Lee. 1997. Prime Time in Ecuador: National, Regional Television Outdraws U.S. Programming. *Journal of American Culture* 20 (1): 9–18.

Davison, V. 1997. Is the Soap Bubble about to Burst? *Soap Opera Weekly*, September 16: 36–38.

Dawn, Randee. 1999. Home & Away. *Soap Opera Digest*, March 16: 34–37.

Dawn, Randee. 2000. 2000: The Future of Soaps. *Soap Opera Digest*, January 4: 34–37.

Dawn, Randee. 2002. Bubble Burst. *Soap Opera Digest*, August 13: 56–58.

DCMS. 1999. *UK Television Exports Inquiry: The Report of the Creative Industries Task Force Inquiry into Television Exports*. London: DCMS.

Dean, Deborah and Campbell Jones. 2003. If Women Actors Were Working. . . . *Media, Culture & Society* 25: 527–41.

De la Garde, Roger. 1993. Dare We Compare? Pp. 25–64 in Roger de la Garde, William Gilsdorf, and Ilja Wechselmann with Jorgen Lerche-Nielsen (eds.), *Small Nations, Big Neighbor: Denmark and Quebec/Canada Compare Notes on American Popular Culture*. London: John Libbey.

Deleuze, Gilles. 1993. *The Fold: Leibniz and the Baroque*. Foreward and translation by Tom Conley. Minneapolis: University of Minnesota Press.

DiMaggio, Paul and Hugh Louch. 1998. Socially Embedded Consumer Transactions: For What Kinds of Purchases Do People Use Networks Most? *American Sociological Review*, October: 619–37.

Djelic, Marie-Laure and Antti Ainamo. 2005. The Telecom Industry as Cultural Industry? The Transposition of Fashion Logics into the Field of Mobile Telephony. Pp. 45–80 in Candace Jones and Patricia Thornton (eds.), *Research in the Sociology of Organizations: Transformations in Cultural Industries*. Greenwich, CT: JAI Press.

Dorsey, Tom. 2007. "Product Placement Is Playing a Bigger Role in Shows," http://www.courier-journal.com/apps/pbcs.dll/article?AID=/20070215/COLUMNISTS 15/702150361, February 15.

Douglas, Mary. 1986. *How Institutions Think*. Syracuse, NY: Syracuse University Press.

Dowd, Timothy J. 2003. Structural Power and the Construction of Markets: The Case of Rhythm and Blues. *Comparative Social Research* 21: 147–201.

Dowd, Timothy J. and Maureen Blyler. 2002. Charting Race: The Success of Black Performers in the Mainstream Recording Market, 1940 to 1990. *Poetics* 30: 87–110.

du Gay, Paul. 1997. Introduction. Pp. 1–10 in P. du Gay (ed.), *Production of Culture/Cultures of Production*. London: Sage.

du Gay, Paul. 2000. Markets and Meanings: Re-Imagining Organizational Life. Pp. 66–74 in M. Schultz, M. J. Haten, and M. H. Larsen (eds.), *The Expressive Organization*. Oxford: Oxford University Press.

du Gay, Paul, Stuart Hall, Linda Janes, Hugh Mackay, and Keith Negus. 1997. *Doing Cultural Studies: The Story of the Sony Walkman*. London: Sage.

Dyer, Richard. 1979. *Stars*. London: BFI.

Dyer, Richard. 1986. *Heavenly Bodies: Film Stars and Society*. London: BFI Macmillan.

Edmunds, Marlene. 2004. Love Dies, but Latin Soaps Go On Forever. *Daily News* 2, October 5: 76–81.

EIDC. 2005. "Television Sustains Los Angeles Entertainment Production as Feature Films Remain Well below 1996 Peak," http://www.eidc.com/EIDC_-_Production_Trends_Release_081905.pdf, August 19, accessed September 2, 2006.

Elasmar, Michael. 2003. An Alternative Paradigm for Conceptualizing and Labeling the Process of Influence of Imported Television Programs. Pp. 157–79 in Michael G. Elasmar, *The Impact of International Television: A Paradigm Shift*. Mahwah, NJ: Erlbaum.

Electronic Media. 2001a. Briefly Noted. October 22: 4.

Electronic Media. 2001b. Briefly Noted. October 23: 4.

Electronic Media. 2001c. Execs Chart Future Strategy. December 17: 1, 18–20.

Ellis, J., 2000. Scheduling: The Last Creative Act in Television? *Media, Culture & Society* 22: 25–38.

El-Magd, N. A. 2002. Cairo's "Millionaire" Unabashedly Takes Palestinian Side in Conflict. *Los Angeles Times*, June 1: F12.

Elmore, Mick. 2002. Gov't, Public Call "Link" Weak Idea for Thailand. *Hollywood Reporter*, March 6: 58.

Faulker, Robert and Wayne Baker. 1991. Role as Resource in the Hollywood Film Industry. *American Journal of Sociology* 97: 279–309.

Feuer, Jane. 1992. Genre Study and Television. Pp. 138–59 in Robert C. Allen (ed.), *Channels of Discourse, Reassembled*. Chapel Hill: University of North Carolina Press.

Fiore, Faye. 2000. Show Biz Icons with Little to Show for It. *Los Angeles Times*, May 17: A1.

Fiske, John. 1987. *Television Culture*. New York: Methuen.

Flint, Joe. 2000. Mergers in the TV Industry Change Tone of NATPE Annual Gathering. *Wall Street Journal*, January 24: B10.

Flores, E. G. 2001. The Real Deal. *Soap Opera Digest*, April 10: 48–51.

Flores, Elaine G. 2004. The Cure. *Soap Opera Digest*, August 31: 46–49.

Ford, Samuel Earl. 2007. *As the World Turns in a Convergence Culture*, unpublished masters thesis, Massachusetts Institute of Technology.

Fowler, Geoffrey A. and Juying Qin. 2006. China's Censors Target Teen Behavior. *Wall Street Journal*, March 23: A4.

Frank, Betsy. 1991. *On Air: Primetime Program Development, 1991–92*. New York: Saatchi and Saatchi Advertising.

Freedman, Des. 2003. Who Wants to Be a Millionaire? The Politics of Television Imports. *Information, Communication & Society* 6 (1): 24–41.

Freeman, Michael. 1995. International Intrigue: Entertainment Companies Look to Sell Long-Term Syndication Deals Overseas. *Mediaweek*, September 18: 14.

Fremantle Corporation. 2003. www.fremantlecorp.com, retrieved February 15.

Friedman, W. 2004. Novellas: Next Wave or Just Plain Ugly? *TV Watch On-Line*, September 29.

Frith, Simon. 1991. Critical Response. Pp. 280–87 in D. Smith (ed.), *Music at the Margins*. Newbury Park, CA: Sage.

Frith, Simon. 1996. *Performing Rites: On the Value of Popular Music*. Oxford: Oxford University Press.

Galetto, Mike. 1997. Bosnia Cries Out for the Return of Its Beloved Kassandra. *Electronic Media*, September 29: 8.

Galperin, Hernan. 1999. Cultural Industries Policy in Regional Trade Agreements: The Cases of NAFTA, the European Union, and MERCOSUR. *Media, Culture & Society* 21: 627–48.

Gans, Herbert. 1974. *Popular Culture and High Culture: An Analysis and Evaluation of Taste*. New York: Basic Books.

Garcia-Canclini, Nestor. 1995. *Hybrid Cultures: Strategies for Entering and Leaving Modernity*. Translated by Christopher L. Chiappari and Silvia L. Lopez. Minneapolis: University of Minnesota Press.

Garnham, Nicholas. 1990. *Capitalism and Communication: Global Culture and the Economics of Information*. Newbury Park, CA: Sage.

Garvin, Glenn. 2007. Prime-Time Soaps Sizzle in Spanish but Fall Flat in English. *Miami Herald*, February 11, online edition.

Geraghty, Christine. 1995. Social Issues and Realist Soaps: A Study of British Soaps in the 1980s/1990s. Pp. 66–80 in Robert C. Allen (ed.), *To Be Continued: Soap Operas around the World*. New York: Routledge.

Gerbner, George, Hamid Mowlana, and Kaarle Nordenstreng. 1993. *The Global Media Debate: Its Rise, Fall, and Renewal*. Norwood, NJ: Ablex.

Giddens, Anthony. 1984. *Constitution of Society: Outline of Theory of Structuration*. Berkeley: University of California Press.

Gitlin, Todd. 1983. *Inside Prime-time*. New York: Pantheon.

Gledhill, Christine. 1992. Speculations on the Relationship between Soap Opera and Melodrama. *Quarterly Review of Film and Video* 14: 103–24.

Gledhill, Christine. 1997. Gender and Genre: The Case of Soap Opera. Pp. 337–86 in Stuart Hall (ed.), *Representation: Cultural Representations and Signifying Practices*. London: Open University Press.

Gledhill, Christine. 2000. Rethinking Genre. Pp. 221–43 in Christine Gledhill and Linda Williams (eds.), *Reinventing Film Studies*. London: Arnold.

Goldsmith, C., E. Nelson, and M. Karnitschnig. 2003. Reality TV: It's No Mean Feat Keeping It Real. *Wall Street Journal Online*, March 7.

Gordon, Bonnie J. 2001. New German TV Comedy Owes Cleese, Letterman. *Hollywood Reporter*, October 3: 14.

Gough, Paul. 2006. Early TV Net DuMont Broke Ground but Failed. *Hollywood Reporter*, January 31–February 6: 14.

Gramsci, Antonio. 1991. *Selections from the Prison Notebooks*. New York: International Publishers.

Granovetter, Mark. 1985. Economic Action and Social Structure. *American Journal of Sociology* 91: 481–510.

Gray, Herman. 1991. Recodings, Possibilities, and Limitations in Commercial Television Representations of African American Culture. *Quarterly Review of Film and* Video 13: 117–30.

Gray, Jonathan. 2003. New Audiences, New Textualities: Anti-Fans and Non-Fans. *International Journal of Cultural Studies* 6: 64–81.

Griswold, Wendy. 1987. A Methodological Framework for the Sociology of Culture. Pp. 1–35 in Clifford Clogg (ed.), *Sociological Methodology*. Washington, DC: American Sociological Association.

Griswold, Wendy. 2000. *Bearing Witness: Readers, Writers, and the Novel in Nigeria*. Princeton, NJ: Princeton University Press.

Griswold, Wendy and Misty Bastian. 1987. Continuities and Reconstructions in Cross-Cultural Literary Transmission: The Case of the Nigerian Romance Novel. *Poetics* 16: 327–51.

Gu, Lin. 2002. Latino Soaps Enthrall Chinese. *Hollywood Reporter*, July 3: 8.

Gulati, Ranjay and Eleonora Di Maria. 2000. Trust in Business-to-Business Relationships: Combining Social and Electronic Networks. Unpublished manuscript, J. L. Kellogg Graduate School of Management, Northwestern University, Chicago, IL.

Gutierrez, Felix and Jorge Reina Schement. 1984. Spanish International Network: The Flow of Television from Mexico to the United States. *Communication Research* 11: 241–58.

Hagedorn, Roger. 1995. Doubtless to Be Continued: A Brief History of Serial Narrative. Pp. 27–48 in R. C. Allen (ed.), *To Be Continued: Soap Operas around the World*. New York: Routledge.

Hall, Stuart. 1980. Encoding/Decoding. Pp 128–39 in Stuart Hall, Dorothy Hobson, Andrew Lowe, and Paul Willis (eds.), *Culture, Media, Language: Working Papers in Cultural Studies*. London: Hutchinson.

Hall, Stuart. 1982. The Rediscovery of Ideology: Return of the Repressed in Media Studies. Pp. 56–90 in Michael Gurevich, Tony Bennett, James Curran, and Jane Woollacott (eds.), *Culture, Society, and the Media*. London: Methuen.

Hall, Stuart. 1992. The Question of Cultural Identity. Pp. 274–316 in Stuart Hall, D. Held, and T. McGrew (eds.), *Modernity and Its Futures*. Cambridge, UK: Polity Press.

Hamilton, Gary and Nicole Biggart. 1988. Market, Culture, and Authority: A Comparative Analysis of Management and Organization in East Asia. *American Journal of Sociology* 94: S52–S94.

Harrington, C. L., and D. D. Bielby. 1995a. Where Did You Hear That? Technology and the Social Organization of Gossip. *Sociological Quarterly* 36: 607–28.

Harrington, C. Lee and Denise D. Bielby. 1995b. *Soap Fans: Pursuing Pleasure and Making Meaning in Everyday Life*. Philadelphia: Temple University Press.

Harrington, C. Lee and Denise D. Bielby. 2001. Constructing the Popular: Cultural Production and Consumption. Pp. 1–15 in C. L. Harrington and D. D. Bielby (eds.), *Popular Culture: Production and Consumption*. Malden, MA: Blackwell.

Harrington, C. Lee and Denise D. Bielby. 2005. Global Television Distribution: Implications of TV "Traveling" for Viewers, Fans, and Texts. *American Behavioral Scientist* 48: 902–19.

Hartley, John. 1992. *Tele-ology: Studies in Television*. London: Routledge.

Havens, Timothy J. 2003a. Exhibiting Global Television: On the Business and Cultural Functions of Global Television Fairs. *Journal of Broadcasting & Electronic Media* 47: 18–35.

Havens, Timothy J. 2003b. African American Television in an Age of Globalization. Pp. 423–38 in Lisa Parks and Shanti Kumar (eds.), *Planet TV: A Global Television Reader*. New York: New York University Press.

Hecht, John. 2005a. Mexican Novelas Go Global. *Hollywood Reporter*, October 14–16: 1, 65.

Hecht, John. 2005b. !Ay Caramba! "Los Simpsons" Strike. *Hollywood Reporter*, February 24: 8–40.

Heilbrun, James and Charles Gray. 1993. *The Economics of Art and Culture*. Cambridge: Cambridge University Press.

Herman, Edward S. and Robert W. McChesney. 1997. *The Global Media: The New Missionaries of Corporate Capitalism*. Herndon, VA: Cassell Academic.

Hielstand, J. 2006. "Actors, Writers Protest Product Placement," www.hollywood reporter.com, February 9.

Hills, Matt. 2001. Virtually Out There: Strategies, Tactics, and Affective Spaces in On-Line Fandom. Pp. 147–60 in Sally Munt (ed.), *Technospaces: Inside the New Media*. London: Continuum.

Hilmes, Michele. 1990. *Hollywood and Broadcasting*. Urbana: University of Illinois Press.

Hirsch, Paul M. 1980. An Organizational Perspective on Television (Aided and Abetted by Models from Economics, Marketing, and the Humanities). Pp. 83–102 in Stephen B. Withey and Ronald P. Abeles (eds.), *Television and Social Behavior: Beyond Violence and Children*. Hillsdale, NJ: Erlbaum.

Hirsch, Paul M. 1991 [1972]. Processing Fads and Fashions: An Organization-Set Analysis of Cultural Industry Systems. Pp. 313–34 in Chandra Mukerji and Michael Schudson (eds.), *Rethinking Popular Culture*. Berkeley: University of California Press.

Hirsch, Paul M. 2000. Cultural Industries Revisited. *Organization Science* 11: 356–61.

Hirschman, Elizabeth C. 1983. Aesthetics, Ideologies, and the Limits of the Marketing Concept. *Journal of Marketing* 47 (Summer): 45–55.

Hockensmith, Steve. 2001. "Gold Rush." *Hollywood Reporter*, September 11–17: 13.

Hollinger, Hy. 1999. The Going Rate. *Hollywood Reporter, MIP-TV Special Issue*, April 6–12: S-6.

Hollinger, Hy. 2003. The Going Rate: Price Ranges from around the World. *Hollywood Reporter*, March 18–24: S6.

Hollinger, Hy. 2005. The Going Rate: Price Ranges for U.S. TV Product in Selected Territories. *Hollywood Reporter*, April 5–11: 24.

Hollywood Reporter. 2005. U.K. Crowned King of Formats. February 15–21: 56.

Hornik, S. 1996. Sunset Is Heating up Overseas. *Soap Opera Now!* December 23 and December 30.

Hornik, S. 1998. The Going Rate: Price Ranges for U.S. Product in Select Territories (in Thousands). *Hollywood Reporter*, September 29–October 5: S-14.

Hoskins, Colin, Stuart McFadyen, and Adam Finn. 1997. *Global Television and Film: An Introduction to the Economics of the Business*. Oxford: Oxford University Press.

Hoskins, Colin and Rolf Mirus. 1988. Reasons for the U.S. Dominance of the International Trade in Television Programmes. *Media, Culture & Society* 10: 499–515.

Howard, T. 2004. Product Placement in TV Shows Moves out of Background. *USA Today*, October 15: 3B.

Hyatt, Wesley. 1997. *The Encyclopedia of Daytime Television*. New York: Billboard Books.

Iwabuchi, Koichi. 2002. From Western Gaze to Global Gaze: Japanese Presence in Asia. Pp. 256–73 in Diana Crane, Nobuko Kawashima, and Ken'ichi Kawasaki (eds.), *Global Cultures: Media, Arts, Policy, and Globalization*. New York: Routledge.

James, Meg. 2006. A Network's Drama. *Los Angeles Times*, August 31: C-1, 3.

Jancovich, Mark and James Lyons. 2003. Introduction. Pp. 1–8 in M. Jancovich and J. Lyons (eds.), *Quality Popular Television: Cult TV, the Industry, and Fans*. London: British Film Institute.

Jenkins, Henry. 2001. Foreword. Pp. xv–xxi in Kurt Lancaster (ed.), *Interacting with Babylon 5: Fan Performances in a Media Universe*. Austin: University of Texas Press.

Jensen, Elizabeth. 2000. The Changing Face of International TV. *Los Angeles Times,* October 27: F-1, 23.

Johnson, Richard. 1986. The Story So Far: And for the Transformations. Pp. 277–313 in D. Punter (ed.), *Introduction to Contemporary Cultural Studies.* London: Longman.

Jones, Candace, N. Anand, and Josè Luis Alvarez. 2005. Manufactured Authenticity and Creative Voice in Cultural Industries. *Journal of Management Studies* 42 (5): 893–99.

Juluri, Vamsee. 2003a. "Ask the West, Will Dinosaurs Come Back?" Indian Audiences/Global Audiences. Pp. 215–33 in Patrick D. Murphy and Marwan M. Kraidy (eds.), *Global Media Studies: Ethnographic Perspectives.* New York: Routledge.

Juluri, Vamsee. 2003b. *Becoming a Global Audience: Longing and Belonging in Indian Music Television.* New York: Peter Lang.

Juneau, Pierre. 1993. Prologue: Overview of Issues in Culture and National Identity. Pp. 15–21 in Roger de la Garde, William Gilsdorf, and Ilja Wechselmannn, with Jorgen Lerche-Nielsen (eds.), *Small Nations, Big Neighbor: Denmark and Quebec/Canada Compare Notes on American Popular Culture.* London: Libbey.

Kang, Jong Guen and Michael Morgan. 1988. Culture Clash: Impact of U.S. Television in Korea. *Journalism Quarterly* 65: 431–38.

Kapner, Suzanne. 2003. TV Shows Losing Potency around World. *New York Times,* January 2: A-1.

Kerbo, Harold R. 2006. *Social Stratification and Inequality.* Boston: McGraw Hill.

Khalil, Ashraf and Jailan Zayan. 2005. How Do You Say "D'oh!" in Arabic? *Los Angeles Times,* December 12, E1: 1, 10.

Kinsey, Travis. 2000. Port Authority. *Soap Opera Weekly,* September 12: 40–42.

Lafayette, Jon. 1998. Consolidation: They May Be Giants. *Electronic Media and Broadcasting,* October 5: 1, 30–35.

Lang, Kurt. 1958. Mass, Class, and the Reviewer. *Social Problems* 6: 11–21.

Lembo, Ron. 2000. *Thinking through Television.* Cambridge: Cambridge University Press.

Levine, Elana. 2001. Toward a Paradigm for Media Production Research: Behind the Scenes at *General Hospital. Critical Studies in Mass Communication* 18 (1): 66–82.

Levy, Steven. 2005. Television Reloaded. *Newsweek,* May 30: 49–55.

Lewes, Jacqueline Lee. 2002. Australian Comedy Situation Is Bleak. *Hollywood Reporter,* June 5: 38.

Liebes, Tamar and Elihu Katz. 1990. *The Export of Meaning: Cross-Cultural Readings of Dallas.* New York: Oxford University Press.

Liebes, Tamar and Sonia Livingstone. 1998. European Soap Operas: The Diversification of a Genre. *European Journal of Communication* 13: 147–80.

Littleton, Cynthia. 2001. NATPE Is Likely Off King World Slate for 2002. *Hollywood Reporter,* August 17–19: 1, 30.

Littlejohn, David. 1972. Thoughts on Television Criticism. Pp. 147–73 in Richard Adler (ed.), *Television as a Cultural Force*. New York: Praeger.

Livingstone, Sonia. 1998. *Making Sense of Television: The Psychology of Audience Interpretation* (2nd edition). Oxford, UK: Pergamon.

Lopez, Ana M. 1991. The Melodrama of Latin America: Films, Telenovelas, and the Currency of a Popular Form. Pp. 596–606 in M. Landy (ed.), *Imitations of Life: A Reader on Film and Television Melodrama*. Detroit, MI: Wayne State University Press.

Lopez, Ana M. 1995. *Our Welcomed Guests: Telenovelas in Latin America*. Pp. 256–75 in Robert C. Allen (ed.), *To Be Continued: Soap Operas around the World*. New York: Routledge.

Lorand, Ruth. 2002. *Television: Aesthetic Reflections*. New York: Peter Lang.

Lowry, Brian. 1997. Hercules and Xena Conquer the World: International Appeal Has Become Key to Survival of New TV Series. *Los Angeles Times*, August 13: F1.

Lowry, Brian. 1998. Change Is on the Air. *Los Angeles Times Calendar*, August 30: 8.

Lowry, Brian. 1999. Leonard Goldenson, ABC Network Pioneer, Dies at 94. *Los Angeles Times*, December 28: A1, A26.

Lowry, Brian. 2000a. The Changing Face of International Television. *Los Angeles Times*, October 27: F1, F23.

Lowry, Brian. 2000b. Court Shows Continuing to Rule Syndication Television. *Los Angeles Times*, January 28: F2, F37.

Lowry, Brian. 2000c. More Shows, Fewer Viewers Fuel Syndicators' Struggle. *Los Angeles Times*, October 21: F1, F20.

Lowry, Brian. 2000d. Where TV Is Just So Much Product. *Los Angeles Times*, February 1: F1.

Lowry, Brian. 2000e. Money Speaks Louder Than Good Ideas. *Los Angeles Times*, March 7: F-1, F11.

Lowry, Brian. 2002. So Not Fun, It's Not Funny. *Los Angeles Times*, January 16: F1, F5.

Lowry, Brian. 2003. Reality Gives Fox a Youthful Jolt during Sweeps. *Austin American-Statesman*, February 28: F6.

Lutgendorf, P. 1995. All in the (Raghu) Family: A Video Epic in Cultural Context. Pp. 321–53 in R. C. Allen (ed.), *To Be Continued: Soap Operas around the World*. London: Routledge.

MacFarquhar, Larissa. 2002. Oakdale Days. *The New Yorker*, April 15: 64–71.

Marc, David. 1997. *Comic Visions* (2nd edition). Malden, MA: Blackwell.

Martin, Joanne, Kathleen Knopoff, and Christine Beckman. 1998. An Alternative to Bureaucratic Impersonality and Emotional Labor: Bounded Emotionality at the Body Shop. *Administrative Science Quarterly* 43: 429–69.

Martin-Barbero, Jesus. 1993. *Communication, Culture, and Hegemony: From the Media to the Mediations*. London: Sage.

Martin-Barbero, Jesus. 1995. Memory and Form in the Latin American Soap Opera. Pp. 276–84 in R. C. Allen (ed.), *To Be Continued: Soap Operas around the World*. London: Routledge.

Masters, Charles. 2004. "Showbiz in Spotlight as EU Expands," www.hollywood reporter.com, April 20.

Matelski, Marilyn J. 1991. *Daytime Television Programming*. Boston: Butterworth-Heinemann.

Matelski, Marilyn J. 1999. *Soap Operas Worldwide: Cultural and Serial Realities*. Jefferson, NC: McFarland.

Mato, Daniel. 2002. Miami in the Transnationalization of the Telenovela Industry: On Territoriality and Globalization. *Journal of Latin American Cultural Studies* 11 (2): 195–212.

Mayberry, Carly. 2007. "CBS Soaps Up for 2nd 'InTurn,'" www.hollywoodreporter.com, April 4.

Mayer, Vicki. 2003. Living Telenovelas/Telenovelizing Life: Mexican American Girls' Identities and Transnational Telenovelas. *Journal of Communication* 53: 479–95.

McAnany, Emile G. and Antonio C. La Pastina. 1994. Telenovela Audiences: A Review and Methodological Critique of Latin American Research. *Communication Research* 21: 828–49.

McCarthy, Anna. 2001. *Ambient Television: Visual Culture and Public Space*. Durham, NC: Duke University Press.

McChesney, Robert W. 1999. *Rich Media, Poor Democracy: Communication Politics in Dubious Times*. Urbana: University of Illinois Press.

McClelland, Steve. 1999. Iger Takes on Global Duties. *Broadcasting & Cable*, March 1: 12.

McClelland, Steve. 2002a. No Big Easy NATPE in '04. *Broadcasting & Cable*, May 20: 31.

McClelland, Steve. 2002b. Slow Recovery for Syndication. *Broadcasting & Cable*, April 15: 24.

McFadyen, Stuart, Colin Hoskins, and Adam Finn. 1998. The Effect of Cultural Differences on the International Co-Production of Television Programs and Feature Films. *Canadian Journal of Communication* 23 (4): 523–38.

McNary, Dave. 2004. Coming to Terms with Reality: Guilds Labor to Organize Workers as Genre Grows. *Variety*, October 4–10: 21, 24.

Mermigas, Diane. 2003a. NBC Taking TV's Future by the Reins with on-Demand Content, Delivery. *Television Week*, September 15.

Mermigas, Diane. 2003b. Television Ad Model under Pressure on Two Fronts. *Television Week*, September 22: 28.

Mermigas, Diane. 2006a. New Media's Effect on the Value of a Viewer. *Hollywood Reporter*, March 14–20: 8.

Mermigas, Diane. 2006b. Social Network Sites Can Be a Tangled Web. *Hollywood Reporter*, March 21–27: 6.

Metallinos, Nikos. 1996. *Television Aesthetics: Perceptual, Cognitive, and Compositional Bases*. Mahwah, NJ: Erlbaum.

Milikowski, Marisea. 2000. Exploring a Model of De-Ethnicization: The Case of Turkish Television in the Netherlands. *European Journal of Communication* 15: 443–68.

Miller, Daniel. 1995. The Consumption of Soap Opera: *The Young and the Restless* and Mass Consumption in Trinidad. Pp. 213–33 in Robert Allen (ed.), *To Be Continued: Soap Operas around the World*. London: Routledge.

Miller, Toby, Nitin Govil, John McMurria, and Richard Maxwell. 2001. *Global Hollywood*. London: British Film Institute.

MIPCOM 2004. Promotional Brochure, *Breakthrough Entertainment*, Toronto, Ontario, Canada.

Mittel, Jason. 2004. A Cultural Approach to Television Genre Theory. Pp. 171–81 in R. C. Allen & A. Hill (eds.), *The Television Studies Reader*. London: Routledge.

Mohammadi, Ali. 1997. *International Communication and Globalization*. London: Sage.

Montgomery, Kathryn C. 1989. *Target Primetime: Advocacy Groups and the Struggle over Entertainment Television*. New York: Oxford University Press.

Moran, Albert. 2004. The Pie and the Crust: Television Program Formats. Pp. 258–66 in Robert C. Allen and Annette Hill (eds.), *The Television Studies Reader*. London: Routledge.

Morley, David. 1980. *The "Nationwide" Audience: Structure and Decoding*. London: British Film Institute.

Morley, D. 1992. Electronic Communities and Domestic Rituals: Cultural Consumption and the Production of European Cultural Identities. Pp. 65–83 in Michael Skovmand and Kim C. Shroder (eds.), *Media Cultures: Reappraising the Transnational Media*. London: Routledge.

Morley, David. 2000. *Home Territories: Media, Mobility, and Identity*. London: Routledge.

Morley, David. 2001. Belongings: Place, Space, and Identity in a Mediated World. *European Journal of Cultural Studies* 4: 425–48.

Mosco, Vincent and Lewis Kaye. 2000. Questioning the Concept of the Audience. Pp. 31–46 in Ingunn Hagen and Janet Wasko (eds), *Consuming Audiences? Production and Reception in Media Research*. Cresskill, NJ: Hampton Press.

Mowlana, Hamid. 1997. *Global Information and World Communication* (2nd edition). London: Sage.

Murphy, Patrick D. and Marwan M. Kraidy. 2003. Towards an Ehnographic Approach to Global Media Studies. Pp. 3–19 in Patrick D. Murphy and Marwan

M. Kraidy (eds.), *Global Media Studies: Ethnographic Perspectives*. New York: Routledge.

Museum of Television & Radio. 1997. *Worlds without End: The Art and History of Soap Opera*. New York: Abrams.

Naficy, Hamid. 1999. The Making of Exile Cultures: Iranian Television in Los Angeles. Pp. 537–63 in Simon During (ed.), *The Cultural Studies Reader*. London: Routledge.

NATPE Brochure. 2000a. "NATPE 2001—It's a Sure Bet." NATPE, Santa Monica, CA.

NATPE Brochure. 2000b. Registration Kit. NATPE, Santa Monica, CA.

NATPE Educational Foundation. 1998a. *Xena: Warrior Princess*: Warrior Princess and Worldwide Phenomenon. Videotaped Proceedings from the 1998 NATPE Conference.

NATPE Educational Foundation. 1998b. Advertising in a Brave New World. Videotaped Proceedings from the 1998 NATPE Conference.

NATPE Educational Foundation. 1998c. International Session: Francly Factual! Videotaped Proceedings from the 1998 NATPE Conference.

NATPE Educational Foundation. 1998d. How to Turn a Homegrown Idea into an International Success. Videotaped Proceedings from the 1998 NATPE Conference.

NATPE Educational Foundation. 1998e. Keynote address at the 1993 NATPE meetings, included in 1998 NATPE Living Curriculum video, *The Future of Television*. Videotaped Proceedings from the 1998 NATPE Conference.

NATPE Educational Foundation. 1998f. Coffee with Dick Wolf. Videotaped Proceedings from the 1998 NATPE Conference.

NATPE Educational Foundation. 1999a. How We Do It: A U.S. Television Market Primer. Videotaped Proceedings from the 1999 NATPE Conference.

NATPE Educational Foundation. 1999b. How to Turn a Homegrown Idea into an International Success. Videotaped Proceedings from the 1999 NATPE Conference.

NATPE Educational Foundation. 2000. From A to Ziv: Legends of TV Syndication. Videotape. NATPE, Santa Monica California.

NATPE Educational Foundation. 2001a. Muy Caliente! The U.S. Latino Market. Videotaped Proceedings from the 2001 NATPE Conference.

NATPE Educational Foundation. 2001b. Doing Business with the U.S.: A Format for Success. Videotaped Proceedings from the 2001 NATPE Conference.

NATPE Educational Foundation. 2001c. The Living Curriculum: Formats: The New Reality. Videotaped Proceedings from the 2001 NATPE Conference.

NATPE Educational Foundation. 2001d. When the Advertiser Turns Producer. Videotaped Proceedings from the 2001 NATPE Conference.

NATPE Educational Foundation. 2002. Beyond the Telenovela: Program Opportunities in the U.S. Latino Market. Videotaped Proceedings from the 2002 NATPE Conference.

NATPE Educational Foundation. 2004. It's the Year 2004: Do You Know Where Your Audience Is? Videotaped Proceedings from the 2004 NATPE Conference.

NATPE Facts. 2000. The Numbers Are in for NATPE 2000! February 28: 1.

NATPE News. 2005. "TV 101," http://www.natpe.org/memberresources/natpenews/articles/story.jsp, July 28–29.

NATPE 2002 Conference and Exhibition Directory. 2002. National Association of Television Program Executives. Los Angeles, California.

Negus, Keith. 1998. Cultural Production and the Corporation: Musical Genres and the Strategic Management of Creativity in the U.S. Recording Industry. *Media, Culture & Society* 20: 359–79.

Newcomb, Horace. 1974. *TV: The Most Popular Art.* Garden City, NY: Doubleday.

Newcomb, Horace and Paul Hirsch. 1983. Television as a Cultural Forum: Implications for Research. *Quarterly Review of Film Studies* 8 (3): 39–55.

New York Times. 2003. "Television Talk," May 13: Z10.

Nixon, Sean. 1997. Circulating Culture. Pp. 177–220 in Paul du Gay (ed.), *Production of Culture/Cultures of Production.* London: Sage.

Nordenstreng, Kaarle and Tapio Varis. 1974. *Television Traffic—A One Way Street? Reports and Papers on Mass Communication No. 70.* Paris: UNESCO.

O'Donnell, Hugh. 1999. *Good Times, Bad Times: Soap Operas and Society in Western Europe.* London: Leicester University Press.

Olson, Scott. 2004. Hollywood Planet: Global Media and the Competitive Advantage of Narrative Transparency. Pp. 111–29 in R. C. Allen and A. Hill (eds.), *The Television Studies Reader.* London: Routledge.

Oltean, Tudor. 1993. Series and Seriality in Media Culture. *European Journal of Communication* 8: 5–31.

Ordonez, Jennifer. 2006. A Turn for Telenovelas. *Newsweek,* September 25: 42.

O'Regan, Tom. 2000. The International Circulation of British Television. Pp. 303–21 in E. Buscombe (ed.), *British Television.* Oxford, UK: Clarendon.

O'Shaugnessy, J. and N. J. O'Shaugnessy. 2000. Treating the Nation as a Brand: Some Neglected Issues. *Journal of Macromarketing* 20: 56–64.

Owen, Bruce M. and Steven S. Wildman. 1992. *Video Economics.* Cambridge, MA: Harvard University Press.

Owens, Devin. 2004. The Power Player: Bradley Bell. *Soap Opera Digest,* August 17: 36–39.

Papandrea, Franco. 1998. Protection of Domestic TV Programming. *Journal of Media Economics* 11: 3–115.

Parkes, Christopher. 2004. Curtain Rises on Brand Casting. *Financial Times,* June 12: 11.

Parks, Lisa and Shanti Kumar (eds.). 2003. *Planet TV: A Global Television Reader*. New York: New York University Press.

Penaloza, L. 2001. Consuming the American West: Animating Cultural Meaning and Memory at a Stock Show and Rodeo. *Journal of Consumer Research* 28: 369–98.

Pescosolido, Bernice, Elizabeth Grauerholz, and Melissa A. Milkie. 1997. Culture and Conflict: The Portrayal of Blacks in U.S. Children's Picture Books through the Mid- and Late-Twentieth Century. *American Sociological Review* 62: 443–64.

Peterson, Richard A. 1982. Five Constraints on the Production of Culture: Law, Technology, Market, Organizational Structure, and Occupational Careers. *Journal of Popular Culture* 16: 143–53.

Peterson, Richard A. 1997. *Creating Country Music: Fabricating Authenticity*. Chicago: University of Chicago Press.

Pham, Alex and Scott Sandell. 2003. In Germany, Video Games Showing Frontal Nudity Are OK, but Blood Is Verboten. *Los Angeles Times*, C1: 1, 5.

Picard, Robert G. 1989. *Media Economics: Concepts and Issues*. Newbury Park, CA: Sage.

Place, Janie. 1978. Women in Film Noir. Pp. 35–55 in E. Ann Kaplan (ed.), *Women in Film Noir*. London: British Film Institute.

Pope, Kyle. 1997. Broadcast TV Lost More Viewers in Latest Season. *Wall Street Journal*, May 22: B7.

Porter, E. 2000. A New Audience Asks: Who Wants to Be un Millonairio? *Wall Street Journal*, December 27: A1, A6.

Powell, Walter W. and Laurel Smith-Doerr. 1994. Networks and Economic Life. Pp. 369–402 in Neil J. Smelser and Richard Swedberg (eds.), *Handbook of Economic Sociology*. Princeton, NJ: Princeton University Press.

Prall, D. W. 1964 [1936]. *Aesthetic Analysis*. New York: Crowell.

Press, Andrea. 1991. *Women Watching Television*. Berkeley: University of California Press.

Project for Excellence in Journalism. 2007. "The State of the News Media 2007." Annual Report on American Journalism. Washington, DC: Pew Research Center.

Pursell, Chris. 2001a. Universal Exits NATPE Floor. *Electronic Media*, September 24: 1, 20.

Pursell, Chris. 2001b. NATPE Pulls Out of '03, '04. *Electronic Media*, November 26: 1, 28.

Pursell, Chris. 2002. Syndicators Go Directly to Ad Buyers. *Electronic Media*, September 23: 1, 22.

Pursell, Chris. 2007a. "Syndicated Stars Hook Viewers, Study Shows," http://www.snta.com/content/presentation/2007_Syndication_Overview-Television_That_Engages_010507.pdf, January 17, accessed January 21, 2007.

Pursell, Chris. 2007b. "NATPE Pushed Later to Avoid Other Events," http://tvweek. com/article.cms?articleId=31424, January 29, accessed January 29, 2007.

Read, William H. 1976. Global TV Flow: Another Look. *Journal of Communication*, Summer: 69–73.

Roberts, Johnnie L. 2005. World Tour. *Newsweek,* June 6: 34–35.

Rofel, L. 1995. The Melodrama of National Identity in Post-Tienanmen China. Pp. 301–20 in R. C. Allen (ed.), *To Be Continued: Soap Operas around the World*. London: Routledge.

Rogers, E. M. and L. Antola. 1985. Telenovelas: A Latin American Success Story. *Journal of Communication* 35: 24–36.

Rolfe, Pamela. 2005. Spaniards in a Lather over Soaps. *Hollywood Reporter*, October 14–16: 1, 63.

Roxborough, Scott. 2002. Austria Ready for Primetime. *Hollywood Reporter*, January 4–6: 75.

Roxborough, Scott and Charles Masters. 2001. MIPCOM Defies Dire Forecast. *Hollywood Reporter,* October 12–14: 4, 120.

Ryan, Maureen. 2005. 6 Ways TV Is Changing—and Changing Your Life. *Chicago Tribune*, May 1, Section 7: 1, 10.

Sandvoss, Cornel. 2003. *A Game of Two Halves: Football, Television, and Globalization*. London: Routledge.

Sandvoss, Cornel. 2005. One-dimensional Fan: Toward an Aesthetic of Fan Texts. *American Behavioral Scientist* 48: 822–39.

Scardaville, Melissa. 2005. Accidental Activists: Fan Activism in the Soap Opera Community. *American Behavioral Scientist* 48: 881–901.

Schaefer, Gary. 2000. Millionaire Quiz Show Flops in Japan. *Santa Barbara News Press*, August 9: B6.

Schement, Jorge, Ibarra Gonzalez, Patricia Lum, and Rosita Valencia. 1984. The International Flow of Television Programs. *Communication Research* 11 (2): 163–82.

Schiller, Gail. 2004. "Golden Rule Hard to Measure," *Hollywood Reporter,* www. hollywoodreporter.com, December 30.

Schiller, Herbert I. 1991. Not Yet the Post-Imperialist Era. *Critical Studies in Mass Communication* 8: 13–28.

Schlesinger, Philip. 1997. From Cultural Defence to Political Culture: Media, Politics, and Collective Identity in the European Union. *Media, Culture & Society* 19: 369–91.

Schlosser, J. 1999a. Davis: Game Show Gamer. *Broadcasting & Cable*, November 1: 24.

Schlosser, J. 1999b. "Millionaire" Times Three. *Broadcasting & Cable*, December 6: 9.

Schudson, Michael. 1989. How Culture Works: Perspectives from Media Studies on the Efficacy of Symbols. *Theory and Society* 18: 153–80.

Scott, Allen J. 2005. *On Hollywood*. Princeton, NJ: Princeton University Press.

Seagrave, Kerry. 1998. *American Television Abroad: Hollywood's Attempt to Dominate World Television*. Jefferson, NC: McFarland.

Seiter, Ellen. 1999. *Television and New Media Audiences*. Oxford: Oxford University Press.

Shamas, Laura. 2000. Love Might Hurt, but We Still Like to Watch. *Los Angeles Times*, August 8: F3.

Sidhva, Shiraz. 2005. French Formats Finally in Favor. *Hollywood Reporter*, October 19: 8–10.

Sinclair, John. 2004. Geolinguistic Region as Global Space: The Case of Latin America. Pp. 130–38 in Robert C. Allen and Annette Hill (eds.), *The Television Studies Reader*. London: Routledge.

Sinclair, John and Stuart Cunningham. 2000. Go with the Flow: Diasporas and the Media. *Television & New Media* 1: 11–31.

Sinclair, John, Elizabeth Jacka, and Stuart Cunningham (eds). 1996a. Peripheral Vision. Pp. 1–32 in John Sinclair, Elizabeth Jacka, and Stuart Cunningham (eds.), *New Patterns in Global Television: Peripheral Vision*. Oxford: Oxford University Press.

Sinclair, John, Elizabeth Jacka, and Stuart Cunningham. 1996b. *New Patterns in Global Television: Peripheral Vision*. Oxford: Oxford University Press.

Skuse, A. 2002. Vagueness, Familiarity, and Social Realism: Making Meaning of Radio Soap Opera in South-East Afghanistan. *Media, Culture & Society* 24: 409–27.

Sloane, Stephanie. 2001. Executive Decisions. *Soap Opera Digest*, May 29: 42–44.

Slocum, Charles. 1997. More Than Ever. *Written By*, September: 34–35.

Smith, Craig S. and Geraldine Fabrikant. 2001. Hungry TV Giants Poised to Win Only a Slice of China's Audience. *International Herald Tribune*, September 11: 11.

Snow, R. P. 1983. *Creating Media Culture*. Beverly Hills, CA: Sage.

Soap Opera Digest. 1999. CBS Woos Hispanic Viewers, April 13: 13.

Soap Opera Digest. 2001a. In Other News, June 26: 14.

Soap Opera Digest. 2001b. Late-Breaking News, December 11: 6.

Soap Opera Digest. 2002. Industry Insider, April 2: 5.

Soap Opera Now! 1995. *The City* Goes Global, November 20: 4.

Soap Opera Now! 1996. Soaps News Overseas, July 22: 4.

Soap Opera Weekly. 2002. Industry Insider, April 2: 5.

Soap Opera Weekly. 2006. The Pretty Story of Ugly Betty, September 12: 12.

Sofley, Kris. 2000. Catering to Changing Tastes. *2000 Review: The Official Review of the 37th Annual NATPE Conference and Exhibition*. Santa Monica, CA: NATPE.

Spano, Susan. 2000. Picturing American Women through the Eyes of the World's "Baywatch" Fans. *Los Angeles Times*, May 7: L7.

Speight, Kimberly. 2005. Stars Brighten NATPE '05: Majors Selling High-Profile Shows. *Hollywood Reporter*, January 21–23: 4, 44.

Speight, Kimberly. 2006. NATPE Eyes Int'l 'Footprint.' *Hollywood Reporter*, January 24–30: 4, 60.

Spigel, Lynn. 2004. Introduction. Pp. 1–34 in Lynn Spigel and Jan Olsson (eds.), *Television after TV*. Durham, NC: Duke University Press.

Spring, Greg. 1998. Syndication Executives as Busy as Ever. *Electronic Media*, October 8: 32–35.

Sreberny-Mohammadi, Annabelle. 1991. The Global and the Local in International Communications. Pp. 118–38 in J. Curran and M. Gurevitch (eds.), *Mass Media and Society*. London: Edward Arnold.

Staneley, T. L. 2000. Soap Operas Look for Ways to Rekindle the Romance. *Los Angeles Times*, November 24: F25.

Stein, Janine. 2006. Many "Factors" to Consider on Asian TV. *Hollywood Reporter*, February 7–13: 1, 75.

Sterne, Jonathan. 1999. Television under Construction: American Television and the Problem of Distribution, 1926–1962. *Media, Culture & Society* 21: 503–30.

Stigel, Jørgen. 2001. Aesthetics of the Moment in Television. Pp. 25–52 in G. Agger and J. F. Jensen (eds.), *The Aesthetics of Television*. Aalborg, Denmark: Aalborg University Press.

Straubhaar, Joseph D. 1991. Beyond Media Imperialism: Asymmetrical Interdependence and Cultural Proximity. *Critical Studies in Mass Communication* 8: 39–59.

Straubhaar, Joseph, Consuelo Campbell, and Kristina Cahoon. 2003. *From National to Regional Cultures: The Five Cultures and Television Markets of NAFTA*, http://www.orbicom.uqam.ca/in_focus/publicaitons/archives/straubhaar.html, accessed June 16, 2003.

Sutel, S., 2000. Networks Cast Their Nets Overseas for New Shows. *Santa Barbara News Press*, September 19: D6.

Sutter, Mary. 1997. Bosnia: Make Suds, Not War. *Daily Variety*, October 6: 19.

Swidler, Ann, Melissa Rapp, and Yasemin Soysal. 1986. Format and Formula in Prime-Time TV. Pp. 324–37 in Sandra J. Ball-Rokeach and Muriel G. Cantor (eds.), *Media, Audience, and Social Structure*. Newbury Park, CA: Sage.

Television Europe. 2002. Volume 5, Issue 1, January. Cahners Business Information, London.

Television Latin America. 2002. Volume 4, Issue 1, January. Cahners Business Information, London.

Thompson, Kenneth. 1997. Introduction. Pp. 1–7 in Kenneth Thompson (ed.), *Media and Cultural Regulation*. London: Sage.

Thornton, Patricia H. 2004. *Markets from Culture: Institutional Logics and Organizational Decisions in Higher Education Publishing*. Stanford, CA: Stanford University Press.

Throsby, David. 2001. *Economics and Culture*. Cambridge: Cambridge University Press.

Tomlinson, John. 1997. Internationalism, Globalization, and Cultural Imperialism. Pp. 117–53 in Kenneth Thompson (ed.), *Media and Cultural Regulation*. London: Sage.

Toogood, A. 1978. A Framework for the Exploration of Video as a Unique Art Form. *Journal of the University Film Association* 30: 15–19.

Turner, Graeme. 2001. The Uses and Limitations of Genre. Pp. 4–5 in Glen Creeber (ed.), *The Television Genre Book*. London: BFI Publishing.

Turner, Mimi. 2005. U.S. Dramas Hot Again. *Hollywood Reporter,* October 18–25: 1, 76.

TV International Sourcebook 1997. 1997. Baskerville Communications Corporation. Torrance, CA.

Uzzi, Brian. 1997. Social Structure and Competition in Interfirm Networks: The Paradox of Embeddedness. *Administrative Science Quarterly* 42 (1): 35–68.

van Elteren, Mel. 1996. Conceptualizing the Impact of U.S. Popular Culture Globally. *Journal of Popular Culture* 30: 47–83.

Van der Weel, Adriaan. 1990. Subtitling and the SBS Audience. *Media Information Australia* (May, no. 56): 22–26.

Variety Market Central. 2005. "Mipcom 2004," http://www.variety.com/mipcom 2004+MIPCOM+2004&hl=e, January 25.

Varis, Tapio. 1974. Global Traffic in Television. *Journal of Communication* 24 (10): 102–9.

Varis, Tapio. 1984. The International Flow of Television Programs. *Journal of Communication* 34 (1): 143–52.

Varis, T. 1986a. Patterns of Television Program Flow in International Relations. Pp. 55–65 in J. Becker, G. Hedebro, and L. Paldan (eds.), *Communication and Domination: Essays in Honor of Herbert I. Schiller*. Norwood, NJ: Ablex Publishing.

Varis, T. 1986b. Trends in International Television Flow. Pp. 95–107 in Cynthia Schneider and Brian Wallis (eds.), *Global Television*. Cambridge, MA: MIT Press.

Video Age International. 2004. Reaching the U.S. Hispanic TV Audience, volume 24, no. 5, October: 46.

Wallenstein, Andrew. 2005. "Fox Sticks to Script for Fall Sked," www.hollywood reporter.com, May 20.

Ware, William and Michel Dupagn. 1995. Effects of U.S. Television Programs on Foreign Audiences: A Meta-Analysis. *Journalism Quarterly* 71: 947–59.

White, Mimi. 2003. Flows and Other Close Encounters with Television. Pp. 94–110 in Lisa Parks and Shanti Kumar (eds.), *Planet TV: A Global Television Reader*. New York: New York University Press.

Whitley, Richard. 2001. The Institutional Structuring of Business Transactions. Pp.

73–99 in Richard Appelbaum, William Felstiner, and Volkmar Gessner (eds.), *Rules and Networks: The Legal Culture of Global Business Transactions*. Oxford, UK: Hart.

Whoriskey, Peter. 2006. Latin American Melodramas That Are Made in the U.S.A. *Washington Post*, July 5: online edition.

Williams, Raymond. 1992 [1974]. *Television: Technology and Cultural Form*. Hanover, NH: Wesleyan University Press.

Williams-Rude, B. 1999. Life before Millionaire. *Broadcasting & Cable*, November 1: 26.

Willis, Andrew. 2003. Martial Law and the Changing Face of Martial Arts on U.S. Television. Pp. 137–48 in Mark Jancovich and James Lyons (eds.), *Quality Popular Television: Cult TV, the Industry, and Fans*. London: British Film Institute.

Woods, Mark. 1999. Global Accent: Oz Shows Suit Taste of Worldwide Buyers. *Variety*, January 25: 65.

Index

About the Authors

Denise Bielby is Professor of Sociology and affiliated faculty in Film and Media Studies at the University of California, Santa Barbara. She is the coauthor (with C. Lee Harrington) of *Soap Fans: Pursuing Pleasure and Making Meaning in Everyday Life* and coeditor (with C. Lee Harrington) of *Popular Culture: Production and Consumption.*

C. Lee Harrington is Professor of Sociology at Miami University in Oxford, Ohio. In addition to her books with Denise Bielby, she is coeditor (with Jonathan Gray and Cornel Sandvoss) of *Fandom: Identities and Communities in a Mediated World* (NYU Press, 2007).